Detecting Forgery

Forensic Investigation
of
Documents

JOE NICKELL

THE UNIVERSITY PRESS OF KENTUCKY

Publication of this volume was made possible in part by a grant from
the National Endowment for the Humanities.

The University Press of Kentucky
Scholarly publisher for the Commonwealth,
serving Bellarmine University, Berea College, Centre
College of Kentucky, Eastern Kentucky University,
The Filson Historical Society, Georgetown College,
Kentucky Historical Society, Kentucky State University,
Morehead State University, Transylvania University,
University of Kentucky, University of Louisville,
and Western Kentucky University.
All rights reserved.

Editorial and Sales Offices: The University Press of Kentucky
663 South Limestone Street, Lexington, Kentucky 40508-4008
www.kentuckypress.com

The Library of Congress has cataloged the hardcover edition as follows:
Nickell, Joe.
Detecting forgery : forensic investigation of documents / Joe Nickell.
p. cm.
ISBN 0-8131-1953-7 (alk. paper)
1. Writing—Identification. 2. Signatures (Writing). 3. Legal documents—
Identification. 4. Evidence, Expert. 5. Forgery. 6. Graphology. I. Title.
HV8074.N53   1996
363.2'563—dc20   95-35048
ISBN-10: 0-8131-9125-4 (pbk: acid-free paper)
ISBN-13: 978-0-8131-9125-6 (pbk.: alk paper)

Manufactured in the United States of America.

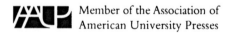

Member of the Association of
American University Presses

Contents

Acknowledgments

———✦———

I am grateful to the many persons who assisted in some way with this book. I am particularly grateful to Charles Hamilton for getting me to begin this project and to Gideon Epstein for urging me to continue it. I also wish to thank John F. Fischer for critiquing the scientific aspects. Others to whom I am grateful for help in various ways include Seth Kaller, Kenneth Rendell, Joseph Rubinfine, and many others. Finally, I want to thank Robert H. van Outer for his professional photographic assistance and my mother, Ella T. Nickell, for typing yet another book manuscript.

Introduction

Forgery is an ancient art. Egyptian law of several millennia ago endeavored to curtail its spread by serious measures: "The punishment was directed more particularly against the offending member; and adulterators of money, falsifiers of weights and measures, forgers of seals or signatures, and scribes who altered any signed document by erasures or additions, without the authority of the parties, were condemned to lose both their hands."[1]

By the third century A.D., Roman jurists had found it necessary to set forth protocols for the detection and proof of forgeries, and during the sixth century the emperor Justinian established additional guidelines.[2] In the fifteenth century, forgeries flourished in European churches: "Clerics comprised the majority of those who could read and write, and a number of them forged and sold papal bulls and dispensations for high prices. On occasion they also supplied themselves with documents that could improve their own power or position; university professors not infrequently engaged in the same practice."[3]

Forgery became increasingly common as literacy advanced, and it became a statutory (rather than common law) offense in England in 1562. At that time, the forger could be fined, pilloried, mutilated (by having his ears cut off or his nostrils slit), or punished by perpetual imprisonment and/or confiscation of land.[4]

Blackstone's common-law definition of forgery, which included any fraudulent tampering with a document, is still useful: specifically, "the fraudulent making or alteration of a writing to the prejudice of another man's right" or "the false making, or making *malo animo*, of any written instrument for the purpose of fraud or deceit."[5] Forgery is also the appropriate designation for spurious printed documents, when the purpose of fraud is established (although the term *counterfeiting* is used when the printed document is dependent "upon pictorial devices or engraved designs for identity or assurance of genuineness," as in paper money or securities[6]). Fake art works, artifacts, and similar items of value are also commonly termed forgeries.

An early forger who achieved notoriety was the teen-age poet Thomas Chatterton (1752–70), who produced a remarkable series of poems allegedly written by a fifteenth-century monk named Rowley. They were penned in pseudo "earlie Englisshe" on parchment. Chatterton supposedly intended to reveal his deception once his verses had been acclaimed by the literati of his day; however, when they were instead denounced as forgeries, the teen-age prodigy committed suicide by drinking arsenic, provoking lamentations from later romantics, including Coleridge and Keats.[7]

Two forgers of Shakespeare have been particularly noteworthy. One was Lewis Theobald (1688–1744), an English man of letters who in 1728 claimed to have discovered a Shakespearean play titled (ironically) *The Double Falsehood*.[8] The other was William Henry Ireland (1777–1835), whose father was an engraver and dealer in rare books. In addition to two imitative plays, Ireland faked legal contracts and various autographed receipts, even a love letter to Anne Hathaway, complete with an enclosed lock of hair. Ireland was exposed by Shakespearean critic Edmund Malone and later confessed.[9]

Other notorious forgers included Robert Spring (1813–76) and Joseph Cosey (b. 1887), who produced numerous faked letters and documents of George Washington, Benjamin Franklin, and other celebrated Americans. Cosey even produced an entire draft of the Declaration of Independence in Thomas Jefferson's handwriting.[10]

More recent forgers have been author Clifford Irving, who launched a grandiose hoax involving an "autobiography" of the reclusive Howard Hughes; German artist Konrad Kujau, who penned the multivolume "Hitler diaries"; document dealer Mark Hofmann, who forged Mormon and other documents, including rare letters from Daniel Boone and Betsy Ross, then turned to bombing-murders in an attempt to prevent exposure; and the inept forger of the "Jack the Ripper diary" (to which crime the "discoverer"—an unemployed scrap dealer named Michael Barrett—confessed, then reportedly retracted his confession).[11]

Among the best known forgers of artworks is Han Van Meegeren, who produced "lost" paintings in the style and with the signature of Jan Vermeer (1632–75). To silence skeptics who doubted a mediocre artist could have produced such works, a jailed van Meegeren produced yet another "Vermeer," *The Young Christ*, before the watchful eyes of his custodians.[12]

Van Meegeren explained that his motive was revenge against the art critics who had rejected his early paintings,[13] but manuscript expert Mary

Benjamin observes that forgers usually operate from a variety of motives, including "financial gain" and "personal ambition" (obvious factors in the Clifford Irving case) as well as "that curious form of arrested maturity which leads adults to perpetrate hoaxes."[14]

Interestingly, as Denis Dutton points out in *Encyclopedia of Hoaxes*, "forgers are often cheered on by a public eager for the embarrassment of the rich elite of the art world" (or the manuscript world, in the case of historic-document forgeries). Explains Dutton: "During his trial in 1949, van Meegeren became a folk hero, not only for having humiliated art snobs, but for having scammed the Nazi leader Hermann Goring, who paid a high price for one of van Meegeren's phony Vermeers. Even van Meegeren's forgeries began to sell for substantial amounts, though nothing near the prices of Vermeers'."[15]

The motives of those who would uncover the forger's work may be no less mixed. Perhaps they have a moral compass that is lacking in their quarry; but they also possess an intellectual attraction to the puzzle that a questioned document or artwork represents and an appreciation for the satisfaction of discovery. There is also a sense of adventure—somewhat comparable, perhaps, to that felt by the forger himself.

This book is intended to provide a clear understanding of forgery detection—both its practical aspects as well as more sophisticated scientific analyses. It should prove helpful not only to document examiners but also to attorneys, archivists, document dealers, autograph and manuscript collectors, investigators, and anyone else with a need to know just how forgers work and the often subtle ways they betray themselves.

In Part 1, Handwriting, I discuss the fundamental basis of forgery and explore such topics as the evolution of handwriting, graphological pseudoscience, forensic comparison, disguised handwriting, and other topics including typewriting comparison and the detection of forged handwriting.

In Part 2, Additional Aspects, I look at such elements of document analysis as provenance, internal evidence, writing materials, and scientific tests. The latter includes chemical analyses; microscopical study; ultraviolet, infrared, and laser examination; document photography; and other sophisticated techniques.

While this book's main focus is on forged documents—both historic and modern—it also provides considerable information that will be of use in uncovering forged prints, paintings, and other works of art. Forgers such as Mark Hofmann develop clever techniques such as the artificial aging of inks and continue to plague individuals and institutions with their bogus productions. This book will serve as a much-needed antidote to their efforts.

PART ONE

Handwriting

1
The Written Word

———❦———

Just as we may speak a common language but each do so in our individual voice, we may all write a common type of script yet render it in our own distinctive hand. And—to continue the analogy—just as a talented impersonator may mimic someone's voice, a skillful forger may produce a convincing imitation of another's handwriting.

To uncover the forger's presence and expose his or her historical fakery, commercial fraud, and other criminal activities, the document detective must have a thorough understanding of all aspects of handwriting. The following discussions of the evolution of handwriting and of graphology versus the forensic approach to handwriting questions provide a necessary prelude to a study of forgery and its detection.

EVOLUTION OF HANDWRITING

This discussion of the history of handwriting comprises the following topics: pre-alphabetic writing, the alphabet, early European developments, the medieval period, the Renaissance, American writing systems, other writing fashions, pencil writing, and the advent of mechanical writing.

Pre-alphabetic writing

The earliest examples of true writing are from a pictographic system used by the ancient Sumerians about 3500 B.C. Some three hundred years later, it was followed by a modified form known as *cuneiform*—from the Latin, meaning "wedge shaped." That designation comes from the shape of the reed used to impress the characters into moist clay tablets. Mistakes were rubbed out with the thumb, corrections were made, and the tablet was baked into a hard, durable form.[1] Tablets bearing private communications might be encased in clay "envelopes" that were crimped shut, then baked.[2]

7

The other major script (or handwritten or hand-printed form) of the ancient Near East, the Egyptian *hieroglyphics* system, also began (about 3000 B.C. with ideographic (symbol) writing. As also happened with cuneiform, it evolved into phonetic writing (wherein symbols represented sounds), then into syllabic writing (in which syllables were combined to make new words).

The alphabet

After syllabic writing came the alphabetical system in which characters represented individual sounds rather than syllables. Apparently it was the Phoenicians, who lived along the Mediterranean's western coast, who inherited earlier, Semitic alphabetic writing and developed it into a vowelless system about 1000 B.C. (The ancestral Semitic alphabet was also the basis of Hebrew, Arabic, Persian, and other scripts. China, however, failed to develop an alphabet, its brush-written writing instead combining ideograms and phonograms.) The Greeks came into contact with the alphabet from Phoenecian traders.

About 700 B.C., while the Greek alphabet was still in development, it was adopted by the Romans, who subjected it to considerable remodeling. Three of today's letters—*J*, *U*, and *W*—were not used by the ancients at all. Both *U* and *W* developed about a thousand years ago from the letter *V*, and *J* developed from *I* about five hundred years later.[3]

Early European developments

The Romans employed several forms of alphabetic characters: a formal type known as "square capitals"; a more freely written form, "rustica"; and an even freer cursive or near-cursive script used for less formal purposes such as correspondence, accounts, and note-taking. (The latter was typically done with a stylus on a wax tablet, the opposite end of the tool being used to rub out errors.)[4] A rounded book hand (as scripts used for manuscript volumes are termed) was the "uncial" (so named because the characters were typically an *uncia*—one Roman inch—in height); uncials were dominant for book use from the fourth to the ninth century A.D. (figure 1.1).

Half-uncials, which had ascender and descender strokes and thus showed a tendency toward *miniscules* (today's "small" or lowercase letters), existed briefly in the third century and were revived in the sixth. About the seventh century word separation and punctuation began to appear; before that words were RUNTOGETHERLIKETHIS and were consequently difficult to read.

The full ascendancy of minuscules alongside capital letters (much as they appear on this page) stemmed from a famous decree by the emperor

Figure 1.1. The evolution of writing, from Roman square capitals through medieval Gothic to modern handwriting systems, is an important aspect of study for the historical document specialist.

Charlemagne (Charles the Great, 742–814). Issued in 789, it ordered that all writings were to be done in a specific, standard hand (one that had evolved from a variety of Roman styles). Now known as the Carolingian or Caroline minuscule (from the medieval Latin *Carolus,* "Charles"), it continued to evolve, reaching its ultimate flowering in the eleventh and twelfth centuries. (See figure 1.1.)

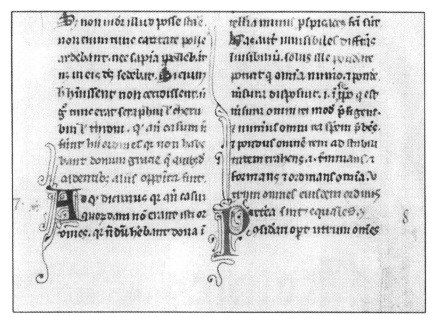

Figure 1.2. Detail from a manuscript book page on vellum produced in the thirteenth century. The bulk of the text is in black ink, and lighter areas (including the ornate *P*) appear in vermilion.

The medieval period

As the Caroline script was widely disseminated and was rendered in different regions by scribes with varying degrees of training, it was inevitable that divergent forms would arise. Among these so-called national hands, or styles, that evolved from the Caroline was "Gothic" or "blackletter" script (sometimes known as "Old English"). It became a distinct style in northern Europe during the twelfth century and predominated there for the next three centuries. It became especially popular in Germany, where it was adopted as a typeface by the early printers and continued in use to modern times. It spread elsewhere in Europe as well, and as a book hand existed in three essential forms: *textura* (an angular version); *rotunda* (a rounded variety), and *bastarda* (various near-cursive forms). (Again, see figure 1.1.)

From the sixth to the twelfth century, scholarship was monopolized by the church, with monasteries typically maintaining libraries and operating scriptoria (rooms where scribes produced manuscript books). In the twelfth century came the rise of universities and the consequent decline in the church's monopoly on book productions. There arose a class of

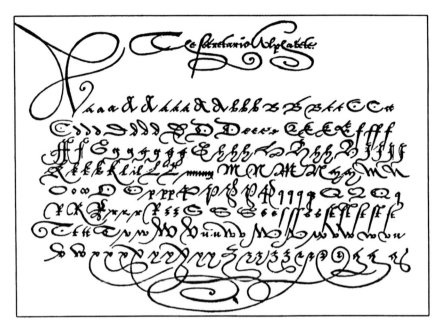

Figure 1.3. The English secretary hand, illustrated here from a penmanship book published in London in 1571, is difficult for the initiate to decipher but can be read with the aid of charts such as this.

secular artisans—including parchmenters, scribes and illuminators, bookbinders, and other craftsmen—who toiled in lay workshops to produce manuscripts commissioned by clients. Now, mere nobles and wealthy merchants could have books as well as princes and ecclesiastics.

The Renaissance

From a cursive form of Gothic bastarda evolved one of the two major hands used during the English Renaissance, the "secretary" hand (figure 1.3). Its more legible rival, the "Italian" hand, evolved from a cursive form of Caroline script. The two hands were used literally side by side: for example, a letter Elizabeth I wrote in 1570 is written in the more everyday secretary hand, but she penned the closing and her signature in italic, or what Shakespeare's Malvolio termed "the sweet Roman hand."[5]

Penmanship up to this time had been produced by the "broad pen"— a reed or quill with the point cut off to make a chisel-edge pen. This produced thick or thin strokes depending on how the pen was held and moved (for example, again see figure 1.1)—the left stroke of the Roman A was thin while the right one was thick. However, "round hand" (a hybrid of secretary and italic) was helped into being by the influence of popular pen-manship copy books.[6] Since these were printed by copperplate engraving in which the engraver's tool produced a different type of thick and thin strokes, "there was," states one authority, "an inclination for the pen to follow the graver, rather than the graver to follow the pen."[7]

As a result, the pen now began to be cut to a pointed shape. Just as the engraving burin produced a hairline when moved lightly on the metal plate but a heavier stroke when pressed to cut more deeply, the pointed pen gave a similar effect: it yielded hairline upstrokes but heavier, "shaded" downstrokes (when pressure caused the two points of the split pen to sepa-rate). Since the pointed pen moved more swiftly than the broad one, it facilitated fluid penmanship characterized by elaborate flourishes.

American writing systems

In colonial America, trends in handwriting followed those of the mother country. From the landing of the Pilgrims at Plymouth Rock in 1620 until the end of the century, the dominant hand was one that has been called "the 'Mayflower Century' Style of American Writing," showing both sec-retary and italic features that blended into round hand by century's end.[8]

This was followed by the American round-hand system, which dominated from about 1700 to 1840 (figure 1.4). It retained the "copper-plate" appearance of its English forebear, and, in addition to flourishes, the writing was characterized by the archaic long s (most often used as the initial letter of an ss combination, and thus somewhat resembling fs or even p). The writing also typically contained superscript abbreviations (e.g., the use of raised letters in such contracted forms as "W$^{\underline{m}}$" for "William" and "Rob$^{\underline{t}}$" for "Robert"). This system was followed by a transitional form called modified round hand (ca. 1840–65). This was basically a round-hand system that incorporated stylish modifications as found in the early edi-tions of the copybooks of Platt Rogers Spencer and of the Payson, Dunton, and Scribner system.

The "Spencerian" system (1865–90) represented the fruits of the two ostensibly competing copybook systems. It was characterized by more an-gular connecting strokes, was relatively devoid of shading on the small let-ters, and had more space between them; it also had a distinctive set of capital letters and a slant set at fifty-two degrees from the horizontal. The result was a new, distinctively American hand that was faster to render than the old round hand, and for a time *Spencerian* became synonymous with penmanship.[9] (Figure 1.5.)

Succeeding Spencerian, the "modern vertical" system (1890–1900) represented a reversion to a slower, more legible hand. The letters were

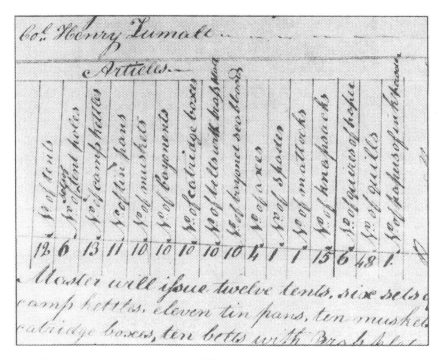

Figure 1.4. Portion of a War of 1812 document penned in American round hand. Note the superscript *1* in "Col." (above chart) and the use of the long *s* in "issue" and "Brass" (below). At the end of the list of items to be provided by the quartermaster (turn chart sideways) are requested 6 quires of paper, 48 quills (to be cut into pens), and 1 paper of ink powder (no doubt an iron-gallotannate variety).

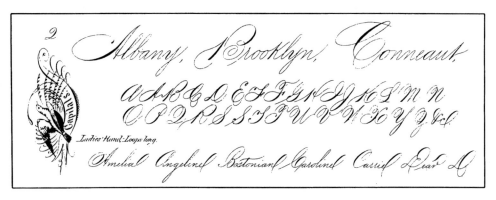

Figure 1.5. Spencerian penmanship (after Platt Rogers Spencer) was dominant in America from about 1865 to 1890.

almost printlike, and there was an absence of both slant and contrast in shading (being rendered with a relatively constant pen pressure). It was entirely too slow to be practical and passed from the American schools after only a decade.

Overlapping modern vertical as successor to Spencerian were a number of "basic popular systems" (1890–1945). Because of their emphasis on a free movement of the arm in penmanship, they were termed "American arm-movement writing" and included the American Book Company, the Palmer, and the Zaner-Bloser methods. Lacking the heavy pressure shading that Spencerian had retained (mostly on the capitals), these systems of handwriting were easy and fast to use and were made popular by the commercial schools.

The period from 1945 to the present is characterized by various mixed forms—all influenced by the ballpoint pen:

Writers were now able to scribble out a check holding it in their hand, or take notes in the field. Desks were not needed. But a physical change also occurred as writers began to write with their fingers and not their wrist or arm. Letters became smaller, cramped, and often found to have groups of two or three letters and then a break in the middle of the word, or letters tapered smaller as the fingers reached without moving the wrist resting on the paper. The old pen and ink system taught arm movement with line after line of practice circles or zig-zag lines [of] neat and even pressure strokes. This was no longer thought important.[10]

A contemporary hand that is sometimes taught is called "joined manuscript." This is a hybrid of what is termed (in the elementary schools) "manuscript" (a neat hand printing with individually formed capitals and small letters) and "cursive" (connected writing). The basic letter forms of joined manuscript are those of ordinary manuscript, but certain letters (*m* and *t*, for example) are given "tails" that link them to the letters that follow. This hand is sometimes used as a teaching transition between manuscript and cursive, but it is also occasionally taught as a distinctive system.[11]

Other writing fashions

In addition to these mainstream American systems, there was also an "angular hand" that was "taught to and written by many women during all of the last century" (i.e., the nineteenth).[12] Back hand (writing done with a backward slant) is basically a variant rather than a distinct hand, but it was taught as such by at least one American writing master, Nathaniel Duren Gould (1781–1864). Gould advertised it as "an easy and fashionable hand for letter writing."[13] It is common to many left-handed writers and has been frequently used as an easy means of disguising handwriting (as we shall see in chapter 2).

Particular affectations in writing are common at different times throughout history. For example, during the seventeenth century a "court hand"—a descendant of Gothic used in deeds, charters, and other legal documents—was in vogue in England. States Mary Benjamin: "This, due both to the unusual method of shaping characters and to the practice of abbreviating extensively, could not even be read by the people as a whole. Scriveners, it was alleged, made something of a racket of it." Indeed, use of the court hand was outlawed in 1735.[14]

Certain occupations have—deliberately or otherwise—seen reflection in people's handwriting. For instance, telegraphers once produced a characteristic five-words-to-a-line writing on telegraph blanks as a result of "the necessity for continuity, speed, and legibility, and the natural inclination to copy the style of those already expert," according to Osborn. He shows an anonymous letter in which the distinctive feature was inadvertently employed.[15] Other occupational traits in handwriting include particular numeral formations or the forms of particular letters that may indicate a draftsman; a primary-school, copybookish style of writing that may suggest an elementary school teacher; and a small, concise hand of a definite style indicative of bookkeepers and accountants.[16]

Of course, indications of one's nationality may also be found in handwriting. An obvious example would be the *fraktur* writing—a derivative of the old Gothic bastarda hand of the Middle Ages (again see figure 1.1)—that was brought to America by German immigrants who became known (erroneously) as "Pennsylvania Dutch" (a corruption of *Deutch*, "German") and was much employed in the late eighteenth and early nineteenth centuries.[17] Various "strange" features in handwriting may also signal a European influence and point specifically to German, French, and other nationalities. These features are often said to give the writing a foreign "accent."[18]

Pencil writing

Replacing the lead stylus used by the ancients for ruling lines on papyrus and parchment, the graphite pencil was made possible with the discovery of a vast graphite deposit in England in 1564. Pencils came into general use about 1785. (Subsequent developments are noted in chapter 4.)

General use does not mean the routine writing of letters or documents, however. Because pencil marks are easily erased, pencils have never been appropriate for legal or other permanent records, and rules of etiquette have generally precluded their use for correspondence.

Thomas Jefferson's account book shows the routine purchase of a pencil, which he may have used to write in his little ivory-page memorandum book (now at the Jefferson museum near Monticello), which was made for such use.[19] Others wrote occasional letters or other writings in pencil—as, for example, Jefferson Davis did shortly before his death in 1889.[20]

Thomas A. Edison loved pencils and, although he signed important letters and documents in ink, he used the pencil for much other writing.[21] (He liked a short pencil, made to fit his vest pocket, and had them made to order in lots of a thousand by the Eagle Pencil Company. Once he had to write to the company that the "last batch was too short." He explained, "They twist and stick in the pocket lining."[22]) Helen Keller, the famous blind author and lecturer, habitually signed her typewritten letters in pencil—no doubt for convenience.[23]

The issue of whether or to what extent a particular writer used pencil is an important one in document study because of the preference for that instrument by the forger. The pencil makes forgery more difficult to detect since it does not readily show retouch strokes, pen lifts, or other subtle features.[24] Also, because a pencil-written document is so easily altered, Osborn notes, one "that for any reason is suspected should be even more thoroughly examined than a pen and ink writing."[25]

Advent of mechanical writing

Wood-block prints and printed books originated in the Orient (an eighth-century printed scroll was discovered in southern Korea). By 1423 wood-block prints were introduced in Europe and block-printed books soon followed. Printing from interchangeable metal type was being used as early as 1454 to produce a papal bull and a year later to publish the famous Latin bible, now known as the Gutenberg or "42-line" Bible. The first printing from a press located in England took place in 1476, in the New World (Mexico City) in the 1530s, and in North America (Cambridge, Mass.) in 1638.[26]

Some other landmarks in the evolution of mechanical writing include the keyboard concept (developed by Samuel F.B. Morse as part of a teletype-like system), before 1845; the first successful commercial "Type-Writer" (developed by Christopher Latham Sholes during 1867–73 and marketed by E. Remington and Sons), in 1874; the Linotype machine (which set and cast type a line at a time and so industrialized printing), in 1886; a shorthand typewriter, the "Stenograph," in 1906; the electric typewriter, after 1920; and the computerized word processor, common in the 1970s.

Mechanical copying of documents began with "letterpress" copies, made by writing with a specially thickened ink, placing upon it a dampened sheet of tissue paper, and pressing the sheets together in a "letter-copying press"; this was patented by James Watt in 1780. The use of carbon paper became common with the introduction of the typewriter, and the sheets were called "carbons" by 1895. Modern duplicating methods began with the hectograph (of which "spirit" duplicating is a type), which was in use by 1880. The mimeograph was patented by Thomas A. Edison in 1876 and improved in 1880. The Photostat process was announced in 1911. Xerography, invented by Chester Carlson in 1938, was not publicly demonstrated until 1948. The "fax" (facsimile) machine, an extension of the old wirephoto system used by newspapers, began to be common in offices in the late 1980s.[27]

GRAPHOLOGY VERSUS SCIENCE

Using the imprecise term "handwriting analysis," the layperson often confuses graphology—the supposed divining of personality from handwriting—with the work of forensic questioned-document examiners. Etymologically, *graphology* (from Greek words for *writing* and *doctrine*) means the study of handwriting, and, at least superficially, it has some similarities with forensic examination (as we shall see presently). However, most forensic experts distance themselves from graphology, as medical doctors do from chiropractic.[28]

The ancient Jews apparently took the first step toward the ultimate development of graphology by recognizing the individuality that is inherent in handwriting. This was accomplished by the time that the Jewish laws were written down in the Mishnah (circa A.D. 70–200): "These when they come of age may be believed when they testify of what they saw while they were yet minors: A man may be believed when he says, 'this is my father's handwriting,' or 'this is my teacher's handwriting,' or 'This is my brother's handwriting.'"[29]

The Romans appear to have been practitioners of a rudimentary form of graphology. Second-century historian Seutonius drew inferences about the character of Augustus from his examination of that emperor's handwriting, and Nero supposedly remarked that he was distrustful of a particular man because "his handwriting showed him treacherous."[30] An even more emphatic endorsement of graphology came from eleventh-century Chinese artist and philosopher Kuo Jo Hsu, who asserted: "Handwriting can infallibly show whether it comes from a person who is noble-minded, or from one who is vulgar."[31]

It remained for a seventeenth-century Italian physician named Camillo Baldi (or Baldo, 1547–1634) to explicate the perceived relationship between handwriting and personality. In 1622 he published his *Trattado come da una lettera missiva si conoscano la natura e qualita dello scriviente (Treatise on a Method to Recognize the Nature and Quality of a Writer from His Letters)*, in which he wrote: "It is obvious that all persons write in their own way. . . . These . . . traits of character can be recognized in any handwriting. . . . Yet it is necessary to observe carefully whether the characteristics of handwriting recur, moreover whether they are in any way artificial." Although Baldi initiated the analysis of handwriting by dividing it into its various elements, his treatise generated little interest. Nevertheless, some itinerant magicians reportedly went "from castle to castle practicing the new art."[32]

The modern interest in graphology is attributed to a particular circle of French Catholic clergymen in the nineteenth century. About 1830 the Archbishop of Cambria, the Bishop of Amiens, and others, including Abbé Louis J.H. Flandrin, began to study and interpret handwriting. According to one commentator, this ecclesiastical impetus "may account for the severity of judgment still to be found in some French graphology."[33] A disciple of this group, Abbé Jean-Hippolyte Michon (1806–81), actually established the term *graphology*, founded the Society of Graphology in Paris (1871), and set forth the results in several treatises.

Michon attempted to give graphology a systematic basis and to associate isolated "signs" or elements (such as flourishes, *i*-dots, and *t*-bars) with particular character traits.[34] His analytical (if pseudoscientific) approach contrasted with the fundamentally intuitive approach of medieval Chinese philosophers and certain eighteenth- and nineteenth-century intellectuals and amateur graphologists, such as Thomas Gainsborough, Edgar Allan Poe (who wrote a brief treatise on the subject), Robert Browning, and Johann von Goethe. Attempting to better understand a writer's personality, these practitioners would often trace over the script, thus supposedly getting a "feel" for the person's character.[35]

Graphology continued to be dominated by the French until the end of the nineteenth century, when the focus shifted to Germany. There Wilhelm Preyer related the physical movements of writing to mental processes, advancing the notion in 1895 that handwriting is essentially "brain writing." Georg Meyer, a German psychiatrist, argued that emotion was expressed not only through handwriting but through all psychomotor functions; he therefore suggested the need for a new science, which he named *characterology*, in addition to graphology. He also advocated a common vocabulary for the two "sciences."[36]

Today, graphology's status continues to reflect its rather checkered

past, and it often seems little removed from the time when it was disseminated by wandering conjurers. Competing theories vie for favor, nowhere
more than in the United States, where some thirty-two different graphological or graphoanalytical societies exist—some of them "using methods
which are not easily combined with other systems."[37]

Belief in graphology is apparently much stronger among university
psychology professors in Europe than it is among their North American
counterparts. Even so, the situation there is not always as favorable to graphology as is sometimes claimed.[38] In any event, acceptance is no substitute for proof. As Martin Gardner observes in his classic work, *Fads and
Fallacies in the Name of Science*:

> One of the major difficulties in all forms of character reading research is that no
> really precise methods have yet been devised for determining whether an analysis
> fits the person or not. Wide margins on a written letter, for example, are supposed
> to indicate "generosity." Is there anyone who would not feel that such a trait ap-
> plied to himself? People are generous in some ways and not in others. It is too
> vague a trait to be tested by empirical method, and even good friends may disagree
> widely on whether it applies to a given individual. The same is true of most of the
> graphological traits. If you are told you have them, you can always look deep enough
> and find them—especially if you are convinced that the graphologist who made
> the analysis is an expert who is seldom wrong.

After describing the need for suitable tests of graphologists' claims,
Gardner concludes: "Until a character analyst can consistently score high
on [such] tests . . . his work will remain on the fringes of orthodox psychology. The fact that millions of people were profoundly impressed by
the accuracy of phrenological readings suggests how easy it is to imagine
that a character analysis fits the person analyzed—provided you know exactly who the person is!"[39]

For a more recent and thorough critique of the claims made about
graphology, one should read *The Write Stuff: Evaluations of Graphology—The
Study of Handwriting Analysis*, edited by Barry L. Beyerstein and Dale F.
Beyerstein. The contributors, who include both practicing graphologists
and their critics from many fields, evaluate graphology in terms of brain
research and other aspects.[40]

In contrast to graphology, the scientific examiner is concerned not
with a writer's "character" but with a panoply or more or less objective
problems, including detecting forged handwritings, uncovering alterations
in documents, and identifying authorship of disputed or anonymous writings. Graphology and questioned document examination do share a basic
concept, however: the belief in the individuality of handwriting. But, sup-

port is spare for graphology's claim that handwriting accurately reflects personality variables.[41] Hilton describes graphology as an "art the scientific basis of which is not clearly established."[42] Osborn, in a chapter entitled "Graphology and the Identification of Handwriting," agrees with those who feel that, regarding graphology, "there is something in it." Nevertheless, he places graphology in the category of pseudoscience, along with phrenology and physiognomy.[43]

British expert Wilson R. Harrison, then director of the Home Office Forensic Science Laboratory, provided a very thoughtful response to graphological claims. In his 1958 text, *Suspect Documents: Their Scientific Examination*, he stated:

There can be no doubt that every handwriting does, to some extent at least, reflect the personality of the writer. A neat and elegant handwriting is more likely to be the work of someone who has at least a modicum of artistic ability, muscular control and careful habits than that of a person who is entirely lacking in these respects. It is when efforts are made to extend general conclusions and a detailed character analysis is attempted from the consideration of small amounts of handwriting—sometimes a single signature seems to be all that is needed—that the graphologist lays himself open to criticism.

Harrison concludes:

It is unlikely that graphology will ever be raised to the status of an experimental science because of the formidable difficulties certain to be encountered in assembling and analyzing numerous specimens of the handwriting of a great many people whose character and capabilities, both realised and latent, are known. This would be an essential preliminary if the principles on which character assessment is to be accomplished are to be sufficiently reliable to allow the conclusions of graphologists to be seriously considered in the courts.[44]

THE FORENSIC APPROACH

Whereas, as Harrison notes, graphological methods "appear to have little or no experimental foundation," the work of the questioned document examiner is established on sound principles. Today's investigative techniques are predicated on a rational basis that can be traced back to ancient times to the first glimmerings of what we now call science. More and more, man began to eschew magical or occult thinking and to seek and to rely on empirical knowledge. *Empirical* (from the Latin *empiricus*, meaning "experienced") refers to that which one learns from direct observation. Underlying the empirical attitude is the belief that there is a real, knowable world, that it operates according to fixed rules, and that effects do not occur without causes.

One of the virtues of science is its self-correcting aspect—a willingness on the part of scientists to change their opinion when faced with new, contrary evidence. As anthropologist Kenneth L. Feder notes, "Though individual scientists may be swayed by personal biases, wishful thinking, or peer pressure, data cannot be explained away for very long." Feder cites an extreme case, the notorious scientific hoax represented by the alleged discovery of man's fossil ancestor, Piltdown Man. With increasing new evidence about evolution, observes Feder, "Piltdown became trivial, even before it was finally proved fraudulent."[45]

Modern science employs a self-policing system to defend against fraud and pseudoscience. This system is comprised of three major aspects: peer review (scrutiny by other experts in the field), refereeing (a peer review process applied to scientific publishing), and replication (the attempt by others to reproduce an experiment or other research endeavor).[46]

The forensic sciences are those applied to answer legal questions; they include fingerprinting, serology, firearms identification, and many other such fields including questioned document examination.[47] The earliest recorded instances of the latter come from the third century. Roman jurists set forth protocols for the detection and proof of forgeries, and additional guidelines were established by the Emperor Justinian in the sixth century. Persons who were especially skilled in writing could give testimony as to whether or not a disputed text was authentic, largely based on the concept of "resemblance or similitude of hands." The Roman approach prevailed in western Europe for the following millennium.[48]

In England (except for ecclesiastical courts, which followed the Roman lead), judicial proceedings invariably required handwriting to be authenticated by testimony of eyewitnesses to the original writing. By the seventeenth century—at least in France, where handwriting experts were known as "master writers"—a more "scientific" (that is, detailed and systematic) approach began to prevail. Two Frenchmen—F. Demelle in 1609 and J. Raveneau in 1666—advocated analysis of such elements as the manner in which the pen was held and moved (as indicated by the nib traces and quality of line), the speed of the writing (as judged by the density of the strokes), and the formation of individual letters.[49]

In America, although colonial practice naturally followed English protocols, after the Revolution most state jurisdictions began to allow the testimony of experts who were permitted to give an opinion in such matters. In the latter part of the nineteenth century, experts in handwriting identification increasingly testified in courts in the eastern United States. In 1894 came the first significant modern text that attempted a thoroughly scientific approach to questioned documents, including chemical tests for detecting alterations—E.E. Hagan's *Disputed Handwriting.* It was followed by Albert S. Osborn's monumental *Questioned Documents* in 1910.[50]

The first forensic science laboratory in the United States, the Scientific Crime Detection Laboratory, began at Chicago in 1929 and was soon affiliated with Northwestern University School of Law. Other law enforcement laboratories followed during the 1930s, all of them equipped to examine questioned documents. According to one historian of the field:

Major progress in questioned document work during this period was the development of a cadre of highly ethical, well-trained private examiners and of improved rules of evidence that allowed thorough, effective testimony in criminal and civil cases. Typewriting identification was expanded. [E.W.] Stein published the first paper on the use of ultraviolet light in questioned document examination. M.E. O'Neill of the Northwestern University Laboratory developed new methods of restoring erased ink writing. Infrared photography was applied to document work, and the determination of the sequence of ink and pencil strokes was tested and improved. Published work of the Bureau of Standards and John F. Tyrrell formed the groundwork for deciphering charred documents. Basically, the principles of handwriting identification and the detection of forgery were standardized. Questioned document examination in the hands of skilled workers was shown to be a scientific procedure.[51]

The status of the expert witness has continued to rise. Despite the well-known legal rule that witnesses should generally testify only to facts and avoid giving their opinions, the expert witness may proffer both. Indeed it has long been recognized that in some cases the expert—generally one who "gives evidence on technical matters not within common knowledge"[52]—may be the only means by which a jury could arrive at a satisfactory conclusion. As one legal text explains:

Because of this, courts have adopted the rule of admitting the opinions of witnesses whenever the subject matter of inquiry is such that inexperienced persons are unlikely to prove capable of forming a correct judgment upon it without such assistance. While it is often difficult to draw the line between legitimate inference and bare conjecture, only such inferences may be drawn as are rational and natural. Mere surmise or conjecture is never regarded as proof of a fact and the jury will not be allowed to base a verdict thereon. No one is permitted to testify what he has never learned, whether it be ordinary or scientific facts. If a witness has not sufficient and adequate means of knowledge, his evidence should not be considered.[53]

This source adds: "The question of the qualification of an expert rests largely on the discretion of the trial court. There can be no arbitrary or fixed test but necessarily only a relative one, dependent somewhat upon the subject and the particular witness."[54]

The document expert may testify as to any of myriad matters—for example, the authenticity of a signature or other writing; the compatibility of paper, ink, and other materials with the purported age of the document; and the presence or absence of alterations. As described in the next chapter, the question of authorship of a writing is answered by examining all of the features, elements, or qualities of that which is questioned and comparing them with known standards.

In court the expert is questioned as to professional qualifications. Irving Goldstein's *Trial Technique* gives example questions and responses for qualifying a handwriting expert:

Q. What is your full name, please?
A. Vernon Faxon.
Q. Where do you reside, Mr. Faxon?
A. Wilmette, Ill.
Q. What is your business or profession?
A. I am an examiner of disputed documents.
Q. Just what does your work consist of?
A. I examine and report matters submitted to me concerning the genuineness of a document and matters of disputed typewriting, interlineations, erasures, matters of paper, pens and inks.
Q. How long has that been your profession?

And so on.[55]

The popular view notwithstanding, the adversarial nature of the American court system does not mean that the expert witness should be an advocate for either the prosecution or defense. Rather, according to C. A. Mitchell's *The Expert Witness*, the evidence he or she provides "should be concerned solely with the truth of certain facts without any reference to how they may affect any person." Mitchell adds: "It is essential that an expert witness should not go beyond the scope of the facts which he is in a position to prove, or of an impartial opinion based upon them. In criminal cases the innocence or guilt of an accused person has nothing to do with him in his capacity as witness, and any bias shown in either direction will weaken the force of his evidence."[56]

In explaining his opinion, the expert document examiner may use photographs as exhibits to illustrate his findings. One set of photos is customarily marked in evidence, with duplicate sets, if desired, being given to each juror. According to an authoritative text:

Photographs may be admitted without objection but it is usually necessary to prove them. This is done not only by the one who made them testifying that he made them and that they are "correct", but they can be proved by any competent witness who can testify that they are correct.

The witness tells what the photograph is made from, whether it is smaller, the same size, or larger, than the original and just how much if any it differs in size. Three or four questions are usually sufficient to prove ordinary photographs. "Is this an accurate photograph?" is the final and essential question.[57]

So-called "juxtaposition photographs," also known as "cut-out exhibits," are frequently used by the document specialist. These are photographic exhibits in which various letters and/or words are cut from both known and questioned documents and arranged side by side so that they can be compared easily.[58] In the case of the Lindbergh kidnapping in 1932, such exhibits were used to demonstrate that the ransom letters were unquestionably in the handwriting of Bruno Hauptmann, who was subsequently executed for murdering the child.[59] Similar exhibits have also been used in scholarly books, where the questioned document case was a historical rather than forensic one.[60]

Although it is not always possible to reach a conclusion in a questioned document case, the knowledgeable, experienced examiner who has access to a sufficient number of known standards for comparison and who has sufficient time for a careful study can usually prevail.

2
Examining Handwriting and Typewriting

I n addition to detecting forgery the document examiner compares a questioned writing with known standards to attempt to make an identification, even in cases in which the writing may be disguised. This chapter discusses the following: class versus individual characteristics, handwriting exemplars and standards, identification factors, handwriting comparison, disguised writing and printing, illegibility and decipherment, and typewriting and other mechanical forms.

CLASS VERSUS INDIVIDUAL CHARACTERISTICS

As noted in the previous chapter, the individuality of handwriting has been recognized since antiquity and is the basis for both the pseudoscience of graphology and the forensic science of handwriting comparison. However, the mere demonstration of similarities between two handwritings is not of itself sufficient to prove common authorship.

Many similarities may exist between two or more examples of writing because their authors learned penmanship from the same writing system. According to a forensic instruction manual:

When a child first begins to learn the art of handwriting, penmanship copy books or blackboard illustrations of the different letters are placed before him and his first step is one of imitation only, by a process of drawing. The form of each letter at first occupies the focus of his attention. As he progresses, the matter of form recedes to the margin of attention, and finally to the subconscious mind. Then the attention is centered on the execution of the various letters—that is, they are actually written instead of drawn. Soon this manual operation likewise is relegated to the subjective mind and the process of writing becomes more or less automatic. Then and not until then, the subject matter to be written occupies the focus of attention.

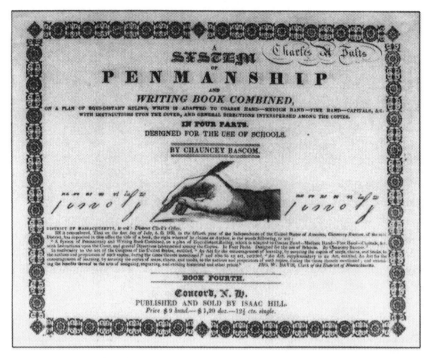

Figure 2.1. Styles of penmanship, such as the round hand taught in this 1826 copybook, represent what are called class characteristics in handwriting. Individual characteristics are those handwriting traits that depart from the copybook norm.

This means that the particular style of system of penmanship learned in early childhood leaves an impress upon the mind which influences greatly the writing of later years. The mature writing is of course modified by other factors, such as education, training, personal taste, artistic ability, musculature, nerve tone, and the like; but once the form of the letters and their manual execution have been crystallized by long usage, the identifying characteristics will undergo but slight if any change as time goes on.[1]

Therefore, it becomes readily apparent that one must not mistake "class characteristics" (those writing features common to a group who has learned to use the same general penmanship style) for "individual characteristics" (those that are highly distinctive or peculiar and not common to any group).[2] (See figure 2.1.) For example, a modern copybook script *a* is closed at the top and the final downstroke retraces the upstroke; those features are class characteristics. An *a* that is markedly open at the top and whose final downstroke combines with the preceding stroke to form a loop would exhibit individual characteristics (figures 2.2 and 2.3).[3]

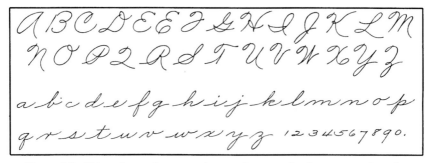

Figure 2.2. Although people are taught to write a copybook system such as the Palmer style penmanship illustrated here, over time they develop their own individualistic traits.

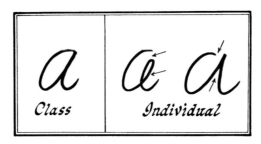

Figure 2.3. The Palmer-style *a* (left), with its closed top and final stroke that retraces the preceding one, represents the copybook norm and therefore exhibits class characteristics. In contrast, the letters at the right depart significantly from the norm, exhibiting individual characteristics that may be used for handwriting comparison.

The prevalence of individual characteristics is the basis of forensic identification of handwriting. According to the great pioneer Albert S. Osborn: "Only a small proportion of the vast variety of forms in writing can be accounted for by tracing them back to a parent system. Thousands of these characteristics are individual inventions and developments." Osborn adds, "This curious and unaccountable variation is of course what gives to handwriting its highly distinctive individuality, and it is undoubtedly true that every developed and mature handwriting shows peculiarities which, in combination of all the various characters and their modifications, cannot be exactly duplicated in the writing of any other person."[4]

To test just such assertions of the uniqueness of handwriting, the United States Postal Laboratory launched a project in which five hundred sets of handwriting of both fraternal and identical twins were studied. The study ranged over several years, as six experienced document examiners carefully examined the sets of handwriting in order to test the theory that twins—who otherwise show many physical and mental similarities—would also exhibit similarities in their handwriting. However, "a complete examination of all of these twin signatures revealed that the differences in handwriting between the 500 sets of twins were as individualistic and as unique as might be expected between any other non-related individuals in the general population."[5]

Failure to distinguish between class and individual characteristics is the mark of the layman or rank amateur. Document examiner Ordway Hilton states that "the most common error of the unqualified examiner is to describe an unusual characteristic as being individual when in fact it merely belongs to a writing system outside the sphere of his experience."[6] Such errors have actually resulted in persons being wrongly convicted of forgery and other crimes, their exoneration coming only after an expert examiner reviewed the evidence.[7]

To avoid such serious problems the examiner must become familiar with all the basic styles of penmanship—including, if he or she is to work with historic documents, antiquated handwriting systems. (For this purpose, I maintain an extensive collection of antique copybooks from as early as the 1830s, as well as reference books with handwriting illustrations dating back to antiquity.[8]) As a rule, the less familiar one is with a handwriting system and/or the more ornate such a system of penmanship is the more likely one is to mistake class characteristics for individual ones.

It might also be noted that the concept of individuality that today may be expressed in a distinctive signature was less valued in the penmanship of an earlier time, when adherence to strict copybook form was regarded as a virtue. As Jonathan Goldberg notes in *Writing Matter: From the Hands of the English Renaissance*, "in fact, what differentiates one italic signature from another is more often a paraph, flourish, than the letter itself."[9] For example, what is really distinctive about Elizabeth I's signature in italic is "the tail of the Z that trails well below her name in loops and zigzags that extend the letter in a series of decorative simulations that are less to be read as Z's and more as the distinctive movement of the royal hand."[10] Indeed, sometimes so distinctive was the eighteenth-century paraph (the elaborate, flourished configuration beneath a signature like that of John Hancock's or Benjamin Franklin's) that it was sometimes used instead of the signature, thus concealing one's identity except to the initiate.[11]

Foreign handwriting presents a similar problem with regard to distinguishing class from individual characteristics. In his admirable article on the handwriting of Dr. Joseph Mengele, the infamous Nazi "Angel of Death," published in the *Journal of Forensic Sciences*, Gideon Epstein states:

Some familiarity with the language that you are working with is necessary. It would be preferable to be able to read and write the language, thereby being familiar with the basics of the language such as the alphabet, accentuation, diacritical marks, punctuation, word order, syllabication, capitalization, compounding, and orthography. This is, of course, the ideal, and we know that the ideal seldom occurs. So what must we do to be prepared for a language that we do not understand or speak? First, we must be willing to take the time to learn something about the language, which usually means that we must be given the time by the person who retains us or asks us to do the examination. With sufficient time, we can research the information in books such as *The Manual of Foreign Languages*, or speak to language teachers, or contact national organizations (of the language we are working with) to obtain information and actually study a random sample of writing in the language we are going to be working in. If you have time, the most ideal would be to contact people who write the language you are going to examine and are about the same age as the person whose handwriting you are going to be working with, and collect samples from them in that language. These would be old writings as well as recent ones.

In the Mengele examinations, the author was fortunate in having a personal familiarity with the German language as well as having sufficient samples of German handwriting by persons born about the same time as Mengele in the files. A study was also made of the various national systems taught at the time Mengele would have been learning to write.

Epstein went on to say:

The Mengele examination was simplified by the fact that the German language uses Latin letter forms as does the English language, but what if we were to be confronted by an examination where the Cyrillic alphabet is used such as the Russian language? The basic rules outlined above would still have to be followed. The time allowed for preparation would have to be extended and known samples of the language would be required. The most important consideration and requirement, however, would be the availability of *exact* known handwriting of the disputed text by the person suspected of having made the writing. These samples would have to be correctly taken and in sufficient repetitions to establish habitual characteristics. Once this has been done, an examiner should have no fear of conducting such an examination even if he does not speak one word of Russian.[12]

EXEMPLARS AND STANDARDS

The basic approach of the forensic sciences is to compare whatever is unknown or questioned with known standards in order to effect an identification. In fingerprinting, a latent print found at the scene of a crime is compared with fingerprints that are on file or that have been recently taken from suspects. Similarly, a bullet removed from the body of a murder vic-

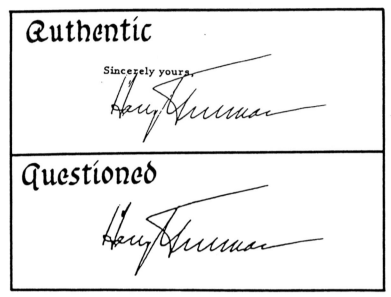

Figure 2.4. Harry Truman signature from an authentic letter matches one on a questioned MJ-12 memo (relating to an alleged flying-saucer crash), although multiple copying has rendered the latter darker and slightly stretched. Since no two individual signatures are identical, the questioned document can be identified as spurious.

tim is matched against a bullet test-fired from a weapon found in posses-sion of a suspect. Again, bloodstains on a suspect's clothing are compared with specimens of the victim's blood left at a murder scene.

And so it is with handwriting. Any questioned writing (for example, an endorsement on a stolen check) is compared with known specimens of a suspect's handwriting (or printing) to determine his or her guilt or in-nocence. But whereas a single fingerprint can be matched to another, in the case of handwriting several known signatures are required for com-parison with the questioned one. This is because—although handwriting is distinctively individual—it is never produced exactly the same twice. (See figure 2.4.)

Any known specimen used for handwriting comparison is called a "standard." (The older term "exemplar" may also be used, but it tends to be more specifically employed to designate "a specimen of standard writ-ing offered in evidence or obtained on request for comparison with the questioned writing."[13])

It is important that standards be as similar as possible to the ques-tioned writing. Therefore, one should compare a questioned signature with other signatures, a scrawl or carefully written specimen with similarly written standards, and a ballpoint writing with other ballpoint writings. In obtaining standards, one should seek out those with words and letter combinations similar to the questioned writing. And since handwriting can change over time, standards should be chosen that are relatively contemporaneous to the questioned writing.

Standards are of two basic types: "request standards" and "collected standards." The former have an advantage in that they may be requested, so to speak, to order. The suspect can be directed to write, or print, such wording as desired, using whatever type of writing instrument was used for the questioned writing. Some police departments have special forms for this purpose—the Chicago Police example being worthy of note. In addition to the subject's name, address, date of birth, and other identifying information, there is a space in which to write each of some eighteen names including, in addition to the person's own signature, Albert Johnson, Charles Quinn, U.X. Zimmerman—the idea being to obtain specimens of all upper- and lowercase letters and various letter combinations that might be employed in a forgery.

On the reverse of the form are certain addresses to be copied, such as "6125 Kilpatrick Rd./Black Woods, New Jersey," followed by various amounts to be written as both figures and numerals. Finally, there is a passage to be copied by handprinting and a space for dictated material. (The latter has been found to produce the most representative standards, since spelling, punctuation, and margins are left to the writer.[14]) Such a form is expected to obtain a wide range of writing and printing samples that should be adequate for virtually any type of criminal case involving questioned writing.[15]

Those examiners without a special form may simply have the subject write or print the following "London Business Letter," which is intended to obtain a complete record of the person's handwriting characteristics: "Our London business is good, but Vienna and Berlin are quiet. Mr. D. Lloyd has gone to Switzerland and I hope for good news. He will be there for a week at Zermott Street and then goes to Turin and Rome and will join Col. Parry and arrive at Athens, Greece, Nov. 27th or Dec. 2nd. Letters there should be addressed: King James Blvd. 3580. We expect Chas. E. Fuller Tuesday. Dr. L. McQuaid and Robt. Unger, Esq., left on the "Y.X." Express tonight." It should be written at least three times, the last time rapidly.[16]

Despite their advantages, request standards also have serious drawbacks. One is that the suspect may deliberately disguise his or her handwriting; another is that requested standards may lack the writer's natural handwriting flow. Both problems can, however, be partially prevented by having the material dictated rather than copied and by having it repeated several times. Never should a suspect be shown a questioned document and asked to copy it, since that would unduly influence the result.[17]

The second category of standards consists of what are termed "nonrequest" or "collected standards."[18] These are specimens of a person's handwriting that are gathered from any of a variety of sources. One examiner has provided the following list[19] of possible sources:

General
1. Letters, personal and business
2. Postcards
3. Manuscripts
4. Memoranda
5. Occupational Writing
6. Checks
7. Endorsements on checks
8. Withdrawal slips (savings accounts)
9. Bank deposit slips
10. Bank signature cards
11. Drafts
12. Deeds
13. Contracts
14. Notes
15. Complaints (legal)
16. Administrators' reports
17. Agreements
18. Wills
19. Mortgages
20. Affidavits
21. Bills of sale
22. Partnership agreements
23. Petitions
24. Leases
25. Transcribed (signed) testimony

Applications for
26. Light
27. Power
28. Water
29. Gas
30. Steam
31. Telephone
32. Credit Accounts
33. Positions
34. Memberships
35. Insurance
36. Gasoline, tires, autos, etc. (government)
37. Passports
38. Surety bonds
39. Bank and trust company loans
40. Marriage licenses
41. Dog licenses
42. Business licenses

Where multiple signatures are required and the subject is either cooperative or subject to subpoena, canceled checks represent an excellent readily available source. (Not long ago I utilized this source on behalf of an attorney whose client denied having cosigned, with her husband, a particular document—one that was leading the couple to financial ruin. The attorney obtained a court order requiring the financial institution to make the document available to me and to provide a place where I could set up a temporary lab. Stereomicroscopic comparison of the signature on the document with several standards in the form of the client's canceled checks proved the signature to be unquestionably authentic.)

Obtaining standards for historical document cases represents quite a different challenge, one that forensic texts do not address. However, there are a number of sources that may prove effective, although they mean that printed facsimiles or photocopies must be used for standards rather than originals.

First, regarding the autographs of famous personages, there are a number of books that contain facsimiles, notably Charles Hamilton's *The Book of Autographs* (1978), *The Signature of America* (1979), and (in two volumes) *American Autographs* (1983). Other valuable sourcebooks include Ray Rawlins's *Four Hundred Years of British Autographs* (1970) and his *The Guinness Book of World Autographs* (1977), Kenneth Rendell's three-volume *The American Frontier, from the Atlantic to the Pacific* (1980), and many others listed in the list of recommended works, including such specific selections as Cahoon, Lange, and Ryskamp's *American Literary Autographs from Washington Irving to Henry James* (1977) and John M. Taylor's *From the White House Inkwell: American Presidential Autographs* (1968).

In the case of signed art prints and signatures on paintings where the artist's signature is not represented in the foregoing compendiums, one can consult such reference works as Radway Jackson's *The Visual Index of Artists' Signatures and Monograms* (1991) and Kenneth Rendell's *Autograph Letters, Manuscripts, Drawings—French Artists and Authors* (1977).

Most large university and public libraries will have some of these, possibly in their department of special collections, where one may also find many original letters and other papers written by famous historical figures. (At the University of Kentucky, for example, I have been able to use for authentication purposes several Charles Dickens letters, a survey document by Daniel Boone, and a long letter by Mary Todd Lincoln.)

To find which libraries, historical societies, and other archival sources have the papers of a given historical personage, one should consult the *National Union Catalog of Manuscript Collections*. Then, to obtain the library's address, one can consult the most current edition of the two-volume *American Library Directory*.[20] The *Directory of Archives and Manuscript Repositories in the United States* is another guide to locating sources of archival materials.[21] Where the targeted figure is more obscure, one may consult the *Biography and Genealogy Master Index*[22] and use the biographies thus located for clues as to where to search for wills and other possible handwriting sources.

The quantity of known standards needed in a case must necessarily be left to the judgment of the expert, based on the situation at hand. As mentioned earlier, handwriting is never produced the same way twice: no two signatures and no two combinations of words are ever identical. Therefore, since writing varies to a greater or lesser degree from specimen to specimen, it is necessary to obtain several examples in order to determine the range of variation. And that range is different with each individual. Osborn's advice in this regard is still sound:

Several signatures should always be obtained, if possible, before any final decision is rendered, five signatures always constituting a more satisfactory basis for an opinion than one and ten being better than five. It is not often helpful to use more than twenty-five to seventy-five except in unusual cases and it is not usually desirable to use those of widely different dates if sufficient contemporary writings of the right class can be obtained. In many cases a few contemporary signatures furnish an adequate basis for a positive opinion and with certain distinctive and skilful writers one good standard signature is sometimes sufficient on which to base a preliminary opinion.

He continues:

Notwithstanding the common practice of bankers in this regard, it is dangerous to base a positive and final conclusion that a suspected signature is *genuine* on a comparison of it with only one genuine signature unless it is a highly individualized and skilful signature. For comparison with a disputed letter one good complete standard letter may be sufficient, but even in an inquiry of this kind more writing should always be obtained if possible. Many errors in the examination of questioned writing are due to the fact that an adequate amount of standard writing is not obtained before a final decision is given.

Osborn does add that "a suspected signature, however, may contain so many inherent qualities indicating that it is not genuine that one good standard signature may be sufficient on which to base a positive opinion that it is not genuine."[23]

It should go without saying that standards must be authenticated in order to have evidentiary value. In one case, endorsements on some paychecks were belatedly discovered not to have been signed by the payee; rather, they were apparently proxy signatures made by the man's wife, who cashed the checks when she went shopping.[24] Another case involved the notorious "Hitler Diaries," several volumes of fake writing by the forger Konrad Kujau. In 1983 three examiners declared the diaries genuine.

Unfortunately they had allowed the *Stern* magazine, who commissioned them, to supply the alleged standards; it turned out that some of those were also Kujau forgeries.[25] Ironically, one of these experts was Ordway Hilton, who wrote the excellent textbook, *Scientific Examination of Questioned Documents* (revised edition 1982), in which he stated: "Standards are the cornerstone of the examination of disputed writings, and no identification can be more accurate than the standards that support it."[26]

Both types of standards—request and collected—can be used together in a case. Request standards can be used to supplement collected ones when they are of insufficient quantity, and collected standards can be compared with request exemplars to insure against disguised writing.

IDENTIFICATION FACTORS

Two main categories of handwriting questions face the document examiner. The first is whether a given writing is a forgery; the second is that of the identity of the person who produced a writing, whether the writing is in a natural hand or disguised.[27] Identification of handwriting—in which the questioned writing is compared with known standards—is based on a number of factors, which I have grouped into three main categories: form, line quality, and arrangement.[28]

Form

The factor called "form" refers to a number of characteristics related to the shape of the elements in the handwriting (or printing). One of these is the *formation of letters*, the factor relied upon almost exclusively by the layperson. Form relates to the shape of the individual upper- and lower-case letters and numbers. The examiner looks for distinct formations that vary from the copybook models; in contrast to a normally proportioned loop in the *b* for example, the questioned handwriting might consistently exhibit a very tall and thin loop, or a notably broad one, or one with a flattened top or a closed loop with the downstroke essentially retraces the upstroke, or even a missing loop with the letter lacking an upstroke. Again, the *i* may lack an upstroke or be open at the top, and/or have one or two "eyelets" (small loops)[29] where the pen changes direction.

The letter formations may point to a particular *writing system* having been practiced in childhood. This may obviously help differentiate one writing from another—either when each comes from a different system or differs in distinctive ways from the copybook standard.

The letter formation may also to some extent be a function of the

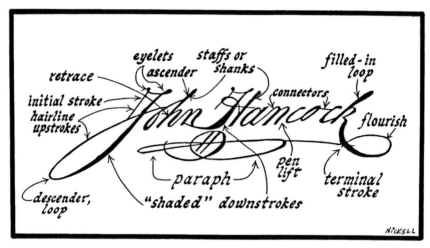

Figure 2.5. Parts of a signature are illustrated on the world's most famous
signature, that of John Hancock, signer of the Declaration of Independence.

movement of the writing. Some writers employ only the fingers, producing
writing lacking smooth lines and having broad curves, possibly with irregular connecting strokes between letters. In contrast, hand movement,
in which the fingers play a lesser role, produces a somewhat freer writing.
And forearm movement allows the ultimate in freedom and may be typified by smoothness in the long strokes.

This type of writing requires practice and may show considerable
manual dexterity. Such dexterity and other features such as legibility and
symmetry represent the "pictorial aspect" or skill that may be exhibited in
writing. Ornate embellishments in the form of flourishes and other su-
perfluous strokes are especially found in signatures and are often quite
individualistic. (See figure 2.5.)

Another important aspect of form is *proportion*—the relative height
of letters. While modern forensic document examination rejects measuring exact heights, spacings, or other precise measurements in writing, because of the variations that can naturally occur, nevertheless certain ratios
are studied. An example would be the relation of the above-the-line height
of *g* to the height of the entire letter, a measurement that tends to remain
constant for a given writer regardless of the size of the writing. It should
be remembered, however, that each system of penmanship establishes
certain proportions, and it is the deviation from these proffered norms that
has significance.

Still another feature is the *slant* of the writing, which can range from
about 35 degrees to the right, to vertical, to more than 50 degrees to the

Figure 2.6. Connections, or connector strokes, may exhibit normal curvature and thus represent class characteristics (left), or they may be distinctive in some way, such as being notably angular or even absent, exhibiting individual characteristics.

left. The slant is measured by using a transparent protractor and making sure it is parallel to the writing base line. The slant of a tall letter such as *f* is more accurately measured than that of a short one such as *o* or *e*. (Like proportion, slant becomes an important feature only when it differs from the copybook norm, especially when "the axes of certain letters deviate from the general slant of the writing, and that this peculiarity is quite stable."[30]

Still another form characteristic is known as *retrace*. In the various handwriting systems, the staffs of certain letters such as the *t* (and the *d* in the Zaner-Bloser system) are retraced rather than looped. The amount of the retrace may be limited or entirely absent in a writing, or it may be excessive; whenever it is noteworthy in some way and consistent, it represents an important factor in handwriting identification. (Again see figure 2.5.)

Similarly, *angles, straight lines, and curves* may constitute distinctive writing features whenever they are seen to depart from the norm. For example, the final downstroke of the *a* may form an angle with the preceding stroke rather than retrace it; there may be curved crossbars on the *t*'s where straight ones are expected; or where curves should be, as on the capital *K*, there may be straight lines. Again, *connections*, the strokes that link one letter with another, may be distinctive by being notably angular rather than uniformly curved or by being absent where they should be present or vice versa. (See figure 2.6.)

Still other form characteristics include unusual features that differ from copybook standards or that are not common to any writing system per se. These are termed *trademarks*. For example:

Many unusual trademarks are found in pen written checks. . . . A double horizontal line under the amount in cents is sometimes used, or a single line with "xx" underneath. After the written amount, the words "and no/100" are expressed in a

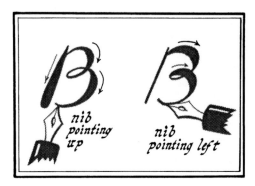

Figure 2.7. Shading, the accenting of pen stroke by use of pressure, is affected
by the position of the pen as shown here (arrows indicate where pressure
is normally applied).

variety of ways. A simple plus sign may take the place of "and," and dashes or "xx"
or "oo" used in place of "no." In the usual check form, the word "Dollars" is printed
in, but some writers have a habit of also writing the word in after the "no/100."
The space between the written amount and the printed word "Dollars" is filled in
by various devices, such as a line of dashes, a sinuous or wavy line, a double straight
or curved line, or even a series of dots. Such devices may also be used on the payee
line between the name and the amount in figures.[31]

Line quality

In addition to those characteristics relating to form, other distinctive features in writing are those having to do with the quality of the line. The
type of *writing instrument* itself will produce a characteristic line that can be
identified by stereomicroscopic inspection (as discussed in chapter 5). The
nib pen—the quill, the steel pen, and the semiflexible-point fountain
pen—produce lines that are the most expressive and revealing of a writer's
habits; the ballpoint pen and the pencil less so. With the pointed nib pen,
hairlines are produced on upstrokes, but because the points of the nib separate with pressure accented lines occur on the downstrokes. This is termed
shading (figures 2.5 and 2.7). A pen held nearly vertical can produce little
shading; one held low relative to the plane of the paper yields it abundantly.
As well, strokes that are more heavily shaded when they run horizontally
indicate a pen held so as to point to the right, whereas downwardly accented strokes show a pen held so that it points to the top of the page.
Thus, a careful analysis of the shading reveals the writer's habitual *pen
position* as well as the amount of *pressure* exerted in writing (figure 2.7).[32]

The skilled penman produces a flowing script that is in contrast to
the more labored efforts of the beginning or unaccustomed writer. The

latter writing may be characterized by a uniform pressure throughout and may exhibit the shakiness or *tremor* that is indicative of slowly drawn lettering. In contrast, a deftly wielded pen yields a smooth line that is accented accordingly—having light upstrokes (visible even with ballpoints) and strong downstrokes. The *speed and rhythm* of the writing are evident in these characteristics.

Speed is also indicated by the quality of the *beginning and ending strokes*. These are usually tapered or feathered in the case of rapid writing, because the pen is typically in motion before it is pressed to the paper and is still in motion when it is lifted. Blunt beginning and ending strokes result from the pen being placed on the paper before writing commences and being lifted only after the word is completed. The latter writing is common to illiterate writers and amateur forgers but is also performed by some more skilled writers. (Abraham Lincoln, for example, habitually paused at the end of his signature—though not his other writing—and there is usually a blunt ending or even a slight "tick" mark where the pen is lifted directly off of the paper.)

When writing is done in a smooth, uninterrupted fashion, it exhibits *continuity*, and there are usually connecting strokes between letters (as discussed under form). Some writers, however, habitually eliminate the connection before certain letters, notably the letters containing ovals, such as *a*, *d*, and *g*, (and possibly other small letters within words). The clear absence of a connector means the pen was lifted from the paper as it made the transition from one letter to another. (Such "pen lifts" are common to some writers and may be distinguished from the unnatural pen lifts that are typical of forgeries—as discussed in the following chapter.)

Arrangement

The third and final category of handwriting identification factors consists of several characteristics relating to placement. The first of these is *spacing* between letters, words, and lines. The spacing between connected letters depends naturally on the length of the connecting strokes. Short connectors produce a more compact, even crowded, writing, while long connecting strokes result in an extended or spread-out style. Both speed and movement affect spacing, with forearm writing generally having greater spacing than does writing done only with the fingers.

Spacing between words—even between lines, if the writing is on unlined paper—also varies from writer to writer. The spacing there does not necessarily correlate with the spacing of letters; that is, the writing may be compact within words that are widely spaced or vice versa.

Another characteristic relating to placement is *alignment*, the relation

Figure 2.8. Authentic signature of Abraham Lincoln typically exhibits a
stair-stepped baseline, a feature that forgers often miss. (Note also Lincoln's
characteristic pen lift between the *n* and the *c*.)

of letters in a word or words in a line to the "base line," an actual or imagi-
nary line on which the handwriting rests). On unruled paper, laying a
straightedge along the bottom of the writing can reveal deviations from a
straight, uniform base line. The writing may thus be seen as a concave or
convex curve, or a straight line that tends in an upward or downward direction, or as a sinuous line. According to one text: "With the wrist acting
as a center of motion, the arc will be shorter than those produced by the
forearm movement. In the finger movement particularly, individual words
or even letters may be out of their horizontal alignment. This may take
the form of steps, with each succeeding word a little higher or lower than
the preceding." The source adds, "Occasionally, the fault affects only certain
individual letters, or letters in certain combinations, which produce an
uneven baseline." Again, Abraham Lincoln's signature is a good example
of this. Lincoln wrote it so that the base line extended from left to right
like two or three upward stairsteps: "A. Linco/ln," or even "A./Linco/ln"
(see figure 2.8).[33]

The width of *margins* and their vertical alignment, or lack of same,
are characteristics that may have evidentiary value. So are other aspects of
formatting, which refers to the layout or arrangement of elements, such as
the parts of a letter, on a page. For example, there is the case of the notorious MJ-12 documents, sensational papers that supposedly proved a government cover-up regarding crashed UFOs and their recovered alien bodies.
Concerning one paper, a memorandum from President Truman to the
secretary of defense, I noted, among other problems, a glaring format error: the "memorandum" contained a salutation or greeting—an element
reserved for letters. A search through countless Truman letters and memoranda failed to turn up another instance of such a hybrid memo/letter.[34]

Related to formatting, but a somewhat more subtle point, is signature *placement*—the "positioning of a signature with respect to the body of

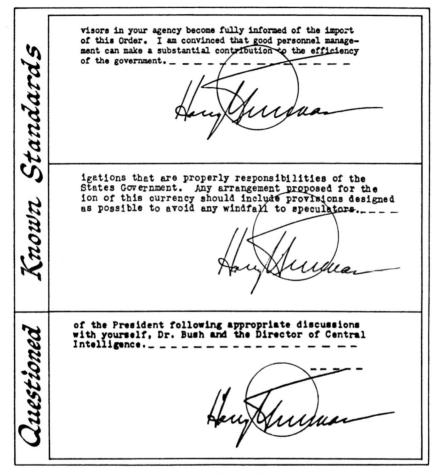

Figure 2.9. President Truman invariably placed his signature close to the text, as shown in the top two examples. With the T as a radius, an inscribed circle cuts well into the typewriting. The questioned MJ-12 example (below) fails this test.

the writing."[35] As we see in figure 2.9, the inept forger of the MJ-12 papers erred in just this way.

Related to spacing and serving a similar purpose is *punctuation*. Because it has evolved over time and can vary with certain writers, it can both betray a forger and have value in identifying handwriting. According to one text:

Despite its simplicity, the period may be made in a variety of forms. When the pen is applied to the paper without pressure, the period may be the merest dot, circular or slightly elongated. The spreading of the two nibs when pressure is applied may result in a heart-shaped or triangular shaped mark, with point up or down, or it may assume the form of a comma, with tail up or down. In the matter of placement, it may be too far away from the letter it follows, or too close. With relation to the base line, it may be too high or too low.

. . . The comma may be triangular shaped with the point in any direction, or it may be in the form of a simple short dash, with any degree of obliquity. The normal form consisting of a round body and curved tail may be varied with a reversed tail or one that is disproportionately too long or too short.

In addition:

The colon and semicolon may exhibit any of the peculiarities or abnormalities of the period and comma just described, and their placement may be similarly faulty. The exclamation point may be in the form of a straight vertical line with a period at the bottom. The staff may be curved slightly in either direction, shaded at top or bottom, and the period omitted.

The normal dash is in the form of a short, straight, horizontal line. It may be abnormally long or short, curved or wavy, or inclined upward or downward. Some writers habitually use the dash in place of other punctuation marks.[36]

Then there is the matter of insertions and other *corrections*. These can occur in many forms.[37] While insertions may be of a fraudulent nature,[38] they may also be innocently done—as in revisions of a literary manuscript. There, they may accompany a penned cancellation: Walt Whitman often canceled short words with one or more slash marks, whereas William Makepeace Thackeray struck through them with a single line; Dickens commonly employed a series of loops, while Max Beerbohm sometimes obliterated words and whole phrases with solidly inked oblong shapes that resemble ink blots.[39]

The foregoing is not exhaustive. O'Hara lists spelling as one of the identification traits, for example,[40] while I have considered it not as a handwriting factor but as a form of "internal evidence" (see chapter 4). Of course it can be both. If a factor is distinctive and habitual, it can have significance as an identification characteristic. How such characteristics are assessed is taken up in the next section.

HANDWRITING COMPARISON

A major function of the document examiner is to determine the identity of the writer of a document. Whether it is received from a client or a police investigator or other party, the expert's first step is to ensure that the document is preserved throughout the examination. It is handled by wooden or plastic tongs, kept unfolded in a transparent Mylar folder, envelope, or stiff paper folder, and protected by being stored flat, away from excessive light, heat, and moisture.[41] The old tendency to place identifying marks on the back (case number, date, and investigator's initials) is fortunately being replaced by the making of accurate notes and/or a photocopy by which the document can later be positively identified.[42]

Known standards are used for comparison with the questioned writing, using the identification factors previously discussed, in an attempt to reach an opinion about authorship. As noted document expert Gideon Epstein explained in the war-crimes trial of former Nazi death-camp guard, John Demjanjuk: "In the comparison and identification of handwriting, the first thing that must be done is that the disputed writing or the disputed signatures . . . must be examined to determine that [they]are naturally executed, freely executed, executed with what we consider careless abandon or unconscious effort, and that the habits that are there are in fact unconscious, habitual movements. . . . And that they were not drawn or traced or in some manner forged."[43] The questioned writings are examined first without reference to the standards, so as not to be "influenced by the pictorial resemblance which often exists between two handwritings." Thus, the examiner's judgment will be unbiased.[44]

The second step in handwriting comparison is to carefully examine the known or standard writings to determine what the genuine handwriting habits of the individual are. These consist of the characteristics previously detailed as aspects of form, line quality, and arrangement. (Hand printing relies on different characteristics, but the basic procedure is the same. The forms of the letters and often the choice of capital or small letters or their intermixture will yield characteristics for comparison.)

Finally, the examiner compares the questioned or disputed writing with the standards. O'Hara explains: "In comparing two specimens of handwriting the expert searches for characteristics which are common to both the questioned and standard writing. If the characteristics are sufficient in kind and number and there are no significant unexplainable differences, he may conclude that the writings were made by the same person."[45]

Although a forger may assume that only letter formations provide identity, we have seen that there are numerous additional types of characteristics, some applicable to multiple letters. Indeed, it has been estimated that a handwriting specimen might have between five hundred and one thousand individual characteristics—justification for one police-science text to state: "The theory upon which the document expert proceeds is that every time a person writes he automatically and subconsciously stamps his individuality in his writing," and therefore "through a careful analysis and interpretation of the individual and class characteristics, it is usually possible to determine whether the questioned document and the standards were written by the same person."[46]

One instructional text attempts to tabulate the individual characteristics for each of the two writings, using a form for the purpose and assigning to each capital and small letter that deviated significantly from the norm a value of 1 to 3. (Zeros were assigned to ordinary forms.) Values for twenty-three writing characteristics were also factored in, the two columns were summed, and the total values for the questioned and standard writings were compared.[47]

While there is indeed an implied mathematical probability at the base of a handwriting identification, the modern tendency is to avoid attempting precise calculations except in special cases. Instead, the expert uses his knowledge and experience to insure that, as Epstein states, "the same distinctive, personal writing characteristics are found in both the known and unknown writing in sufficient number that the likelihood of accidental coincidence is eliminated—and that there are no basic or fundamental differences between the two sets of writing." Epstein continues:

The document examiner is occasionally asked how many points of identification are necessary to establish that two writings are by the same person. Such criteria have not been established, and probably could not be, because of the nature of handwriting identification. It involves not only factors of form that are subject to relatively easy count, but also the qualities of execution, freedom, movement, skill, emphasis, spacing, and the like that influence the entire writing and are not susceptible to tabulation. As a consequence, the combination of a unique set of similarities coupled with the lack of significant basic writing differences must be used as the true basis for a positive identification.[48]

Obviously some characteristics will be so distinctive that they may be given considerable weight in forming an opinion. Such occurred with the identification of Bruno Hauptmann as the author of ransom notes and other writings in the Lindbergh kidnaping case. One of the experts, Clark Sellers of Los Angeles, based his conclusion on a very large number of characteristics, some of which were exceedingly unusual. For example, the anonymous letters contained two forms of the word *the* that were unique, both of which lacked a crossbar: one, in which the *t* combined with an *h* that lacked a hump to create a form that looked like "Ue"; the other, in which the first two letters were transposed so that the result appeared to be "hle." The known Hauptmann writing also had the two distinctive forms, underscoring the conclusive nature of the identification. (All the eight ex-

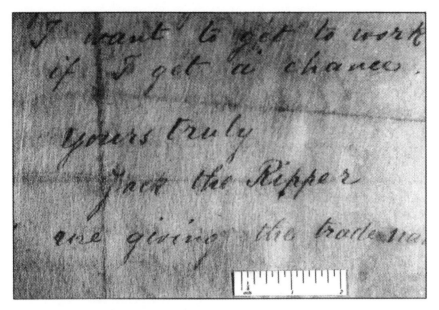

Figure 2.10. Photographic exemplar of handwriting from the 1888 "Dear Boss . . . Jack the Ripper" letter (Owen's "K-1") fails to match the penmanship in the alleged Ripper diary.

pert document examiners in the case were unanimous in concluding that Hauptmann was the anonymous author of the fifteen ransom letters.)[49]

Evidence of nonidentity in the writing of a historic document is well illustrated by the notorious Jack the Ripper's diary, which showed up under suspicious circumstances in 1991 in the possession of an unemployed scrap dealer named Michael Barrett. The diary, actually a recycled scrapbook with its used pages excised and the remaining ones used for writing, purported to be the confession of one James Maybrick, a Liverpool cotton merchant who died of poison in 1889.

A book on the "find" was to be published in 1993 by Warner Books, but at the eleventh hour Warner executives sought to obtain their own opinion about the diary, which had purportedly been authenticated by the British publisher, Smith Gryphon. Warner commissioned manuscript authority Kenneth Rendell, who had investigated the "Hitler Diaries" for *Newsweek* magazine, to determine whether or not the diary was authentic.

Consulted in the matter, I recommended that the handwriting portion of the questioned document work be assigned to noted handwriting expert Maureen Casey Owens, for twenty-five years the Chicago Police Department's forensic document expert, now in private practice. The diary

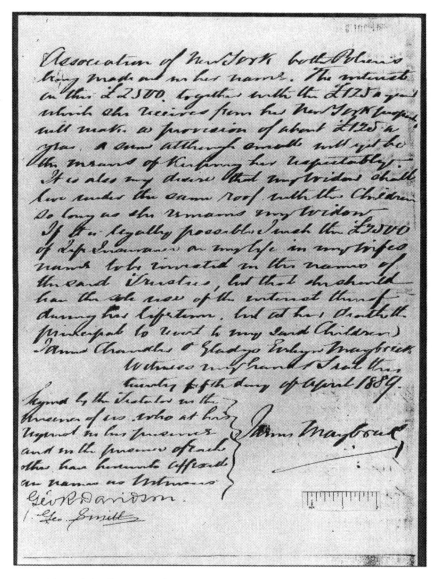

Figure 2.11. Writing in the will of James Maybrick fails to match that of
the handwriting—supposedly by Maybrick—in the alleged diary of
Jack the Ripper.

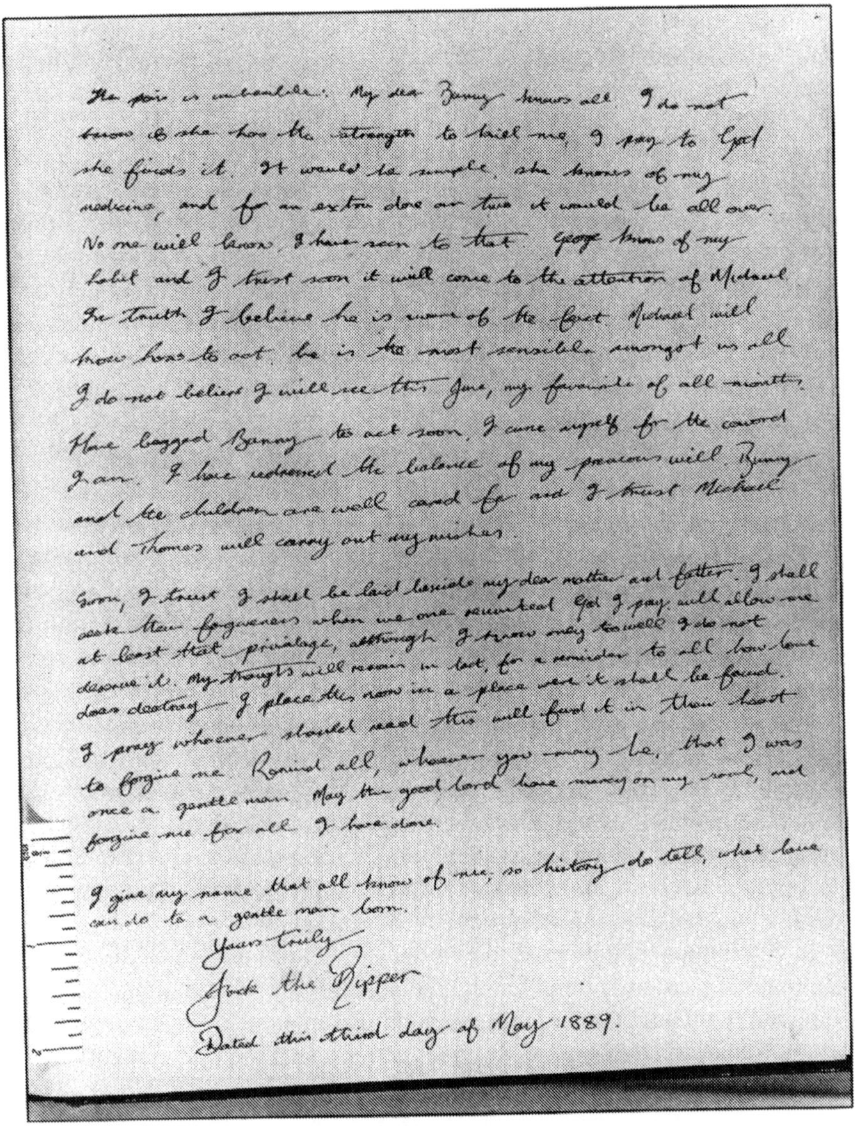
The pain is unbearable. My dear Bunny knows all. I do not know if she has the strength to kill me. I pray to God she finds it. It would be simple, she knows of my medicine, and for an extra dose or two it would be all over. No one will know, I have seen to that. George knows of my habit and I trust soon it will come to the attention of Michael. In truth I believe he is aware of the fact. Michael will know how to act, he is the most sensible amongst us all. I do not believe I will see this June, my favourite of all months. Have begged Bunny to act soon. I curse myself for the coward I am. I have redeemed the balance of my precious will. Bunny and the children are well cared for and I trust Michael and Thomas will carry out my wishes.

Soon, I trust I shall be laid beside my dear mother and father. I shall seek their forgiveness when we are reunited. God I pray will allow me at least that privilege, although I know only too well I do not deserve it. My thoughts will remain in tact, for a reminder to all how love does destroy. I place this now in a place where it shall be found. I pray whoever should read this will find it in their heart to forgive me. Remind all, whoever you may be, that I was once a gentle man. May the good lord have mercy on my soul, and forgive me for all I have done.

I give my name that all know of me, so history do tell, what love can do to a gentle man born.

Yours truly

Jack the Ripper

Dated this third day of May 1889.

Figure 2.12. Final page of the alleged Jack the Ripper diary, supposedly written by James Maybrick, fails to match known standards of Maybrick's handwriting, including that from his holographic will.

was made available for a day, during which we studied the handwriting with a stereomicroscope and Owens photographed each page for further study.[50]

She was provided with some interesting "standards." The first was a photograph of an 1888 letter, addressed "Dear Boss" and signed "Jack the Ripper," supposedly from the Whitechapel serial killer himself (but apparently a hoax). Because the "diary" adopted specific phrases from this letter, it purported to be written by the same crazed author. Two other standards, whose very existence must have surprised the diary's forger, were photos of James Maybrick's 1881 marriage license, bearing his signature, and his 1889 holographic (i.e., entirely in his handwriting) will. Owens designated the "known" documents as "K-1" (the "Ripper" letter) and "K-2" (the Maybrick papers) and the alleged diary as "Q-1." (See figures 2.10-2.12.)

Owens, in her subsequent report, concluded: "It is the opinion of the examiner that neither of the writers of Exhibits K-1 or K-2 executed the writing on Exhibit Q-1." As she explained: "The characteristics of the Dear Boss letter follow closely upon the Round Hand writing style of the time and exhibit a good writing skill. The Will shows a fine hand and exhibits significant shading in the writing. Both of these items contain a writing skill superior to that of the diary." She continued: "The Diary contains many varieties in letter forms. Some letter forms resemble elements in the Round Hand style and other forms are significantly different in design and movement. Shading seems to be incidental to the writing as opposed to by design and lacks uniformity."[51] In 1994 Mike Barrett confessed he had forged the diary, conducting research at his local library, obtaining an old photo album at a house clearance sale, and purchasing "Victorian" ink from an art shop.[52] Later, Barrett reportedly repudiated his confession, squandering what little credibility he had left.

Such important cases as the Lindbergh ransom notes and the alleged Ripper diary not only demonstrate the accuracy of handwriting comparison, where proper standards are available and where the work can be conducted by competent experts, but they also underscore the scientific basis of this forensic approach.

DISGUISED WRITING AND PRINTING

Disguised writing represents a special problem for the document expert. Authors of "poison pen" or character-assassination letters, ransom notes, and other anonymous missives frequently attempt to disguise their handwriting as a protection against being identified.

The letter writer may adopt any of the following techniques of disguise:[53]

Slant. The most common disguising ploy is to change the direction of slant, thus instantly imparting a new look to an entire page. Commonly, the writer simply shifts from the usual forehand slant to a backhand one. (Of course it should not be assumed that backhand writing is disguised writing, since many people affect that style as their normal writing.)

Change of hand. The writer may simply switch from the right to the left hand (possibly thereby also shifting to backhand) or vice versa.

Size. A change may be effected in the size of the script, resulting in a handwriting that is much larger or much smaller than the person's natural hand. However, it should be noted that merely changing the size of the handwriting does not affect the proportions involved.

Speed. By producing a slow, belabored writing or a hastily scribbled one, an anonymous author hopes to disguise his or her identifying characteristics.

Printing. The writer may simply substitute hand printing for cursive writing.

Inversion. The handwriting may be produced upside down—a feat more easily accomplished if handprinting is used.

Alteration of letter forms. Some writers attempt to change the obvious letter features, usually by altering some of the forms of the capital letters, sometimes in grotesque fashion.

Irregularities. Another common mode of disguise is simply to write with a deliberate carelessness or sloppiness which, some writers believe, will make the writing difficult to identify.

Illiteracy. As with the previous method, the writer adopts the guise of illiteracy, producing writing that is misspelled and uncouth in grammar but which may fail to camouflage the paragraphing and other aspects of arrangement as well as punctuation and other factors.

Imitation. The disguise may be a consequence of the writer's attempt to forge the writing of another (discussed more fully in the following chapter).

Despite such techniques, writing patterns tend to be so habitual that they are difficult to suppress or alter. The attempt to disguise is apt to be more successful in a short writing than in a large one. Indeed, if subtle inconspicuous factors are consistently repeated over a considerably lengthy text, the writing is unlikely to be disguised, because of the difficulty of sustaining the unnatural mode.[54] Hilton observes that "the task of maintaining an effective disguise grows more difficult with each additional word."[55]

Because of its difficulty, disguised writing often displays evidence of conflict, thus generally being less skillfully produced than the writer's usual penmanship. It may have a slowly drawn appearance and exhibit hesitation; it may also be characterized by irregularities and inconsistencies, including variations in slant and odd or even grotesque letter formations. It is usually the most obvious features—capital letters and slant—that are subjected to the greatest alteration, while the less prominent ones, possibly totally unapparent to the penman, retain their normal identifying characteristics.[56] Thus the experienced examiner may look beyond the tricks and grotesqueries of the disguise and be able to effect a positive identification.

A few years ago I was asked to examine some handwritten "poison pen" letters that had been sent anonymously to a newspaper regarding a political candidate. As often happens in such cases, the newspaper editor had a suspect and sent along a specimen of her handwriting. Except for the change in slant adopted for the disguise, the writer's own individual characteristics were readily apparent, including some distinctive aspects of the formatting and even the choice of felt-tip pen. (See figure 2.13.)

Unintentional "disguise" of handwriting may also occur. Such factors as age and illness, even unusual writing conditions, can significantly alter a handwriting.[57] The fact of such changes, however, may be learned from investigation or deduced from careful study. Again, the individual's subtle characteristics are likely to remain and serve as a basis for identification.

ILLEGIBILITY AND DECIPHERMENT

Writing may require decipherment for several reasons. It may be faded, erased, obliterated, or otherwise rendered illegible because of factors other than the quality of handwriting. Techniques for dealing with these are discussed in part 2 of this book.

Here we are concerned with factors that affect the handwriting quality, that render it "illegible" because of the extreme effects of age or illness, haste, deliberate disguise, illiteracy, or mere lack of writing skill. In addition, the reader's unfamiliarity with the handwriting system employed may cause a clearly written script to seem unintelligible.

In the latter case, the text and illustrations in chapter 1 should help, but there is no substitute for experience. As one reads more and more writing of a given period, whether it is eighteenth-century round hand or even the earlier and much more difficult secretary hand, one finds that ease of reading comes with familiarity.

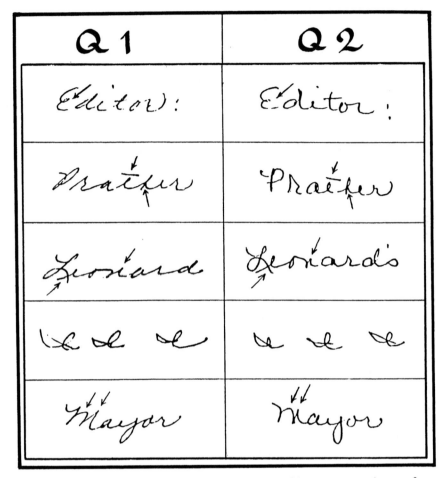

Figure 2.13. Chart comparing "Q-1" and "Q-2," in this case two specimans of anonymous writings. Despite an attempt to disguise the writing by changing the slant, it is obvious that these "poison pen" letters were written by the same individual.

Archaic forms are particularly difficult. One Old English letter, "þ"— called thorn—survived into the sixteenth century even though it had become obsolete. The thorn originally resembled a *y*, with which it became confused, leading to phrases like "ye olde inn."[58] The long *s* of secretary and round hand also causes difficulty to those doing genealogical research who are unfamiliar with that form. Resembling *f*, it was used especially as the first letter in *ss*, sometimes causing that combination to resemble *p*.

Round hand's other lookalike letters, notably common forms of capi-

tal letters *L* and *S*, *I* and *J*, also cause confusion: "Lawyer" for "Sawyer,"
for instance. Cursive lowercase letters, especially those comprised of min-
ims, or short downstrokes (*i*, *m*, *n*, *u*,and *w*), are another source of difficulty and can easily result in mistaken interpretations. The problem is often
magnified by the archaic, or even "creative," spelling of the period.

To decipher old writing, begin with the letters and words that are
easily recognized, then compare them with the unfamiliar ones. Do not
guess whether a letter is an *L* or an *S*, but rather learn how that writer
made each, seeking known instances of them from elsewhere in the text.
In her *How to Decipher and Study Old Documents*, E.E. Thoyts cautions:
"Beware of too imaginative guesses. Although this fault is easily remedied,
still, it is better to spell a word out letter by letter, however unintelligible
and depressing the result at first may be. It is so easy to take a name for
granted, and an idea once seized upon is not quickly eradicated, and may
bring about absurd results and deductions." She adds:

Do not ponder too long over a word which puzzles you, but go on, leaving gaps in
your copy with a stroke underneath corresponding with or leaving sufficient space
for the missing word. These spaces can then be filled in afterwards, when the general sense of the document has been mastered, and the aspect of the particular style
of writing has become familiar. Then it will be found that words hitherto seemingly unintelligible resolve themselves into readable form, and although apparently
impossible to decipher at the first reading, later on they present no difficulty. A
little practice and patience soon overcome the difficulties of the first start, and after that the progress is rapid.[59]

A similar approach is followed with difficult-to-read modern writing. One begins with known elements and uses those as keys to unlock
further meaning. One thus begins to assemble a specimen alphabet for a
given handwriting that can be applied to difficult words. Sometimes one
finds an illegible word repeated additional times, and one of these may be
recognizable where the others are not. Perseverance in studying a text usually pays dividends. After one peruses a given handwriting for a time, one
becomes acclimatized to it. Then that which is difficult may be read with
relative ease, and the impossible may become only difficult.

Illegible signatures are especially difficult to decipher, particularly
when one differs markedly from the individual's other handwriting and/
or when the signature is the sole example of that person's writing on a
document. If the signer appears to be a historic personage of note, one may
search signature specimen books, such as those listed in the bibliography,
for hopes of a match. It is, of course, much easier to verify such an identification than to make one initially.

Reactions to illegible writing range from annoyance to humor. Osborn huffs that "many wholly illegible scrawls, like mumbling speech, also show a disregard for the comfort and convenience of others that in other connections would be construed as ill manners."[60] On the other hand, Mark Twain saw much humor in Horace Greeley's scrawl, notorious for its illegibility. He penned a hilarious caricature of it with writing that leapt wildly about the page. Then there was Twain's yarn about a minister who wrote to Greeley, then repeatedly attempted to decipher the reply. His first attempt read: "Polygamy dissembles majesty; extracts redeem polarity; causes hitherto exist. Ovations pursue wisdom, or warts inherit and condemn. Boston, botany, cakes, felony undertakes, but who shall allay? We fear not." Later he reconsidered and revised his translation: "Poultices do sometimes choke swine; tulips reduce posterity, causes leather to resist. Our notions empower wisdom, her let's afford while we can. Butter but any cakes, fill any undertaker, we'll wean him from his filly. We feel hot." And so on.[61]

Illegibility does have one dubious virtue, as Osborne explains: "Abbreviated, distorted and illegible forms, which are sufficiently free and rapid, often actually indicate genuineness rather than forgery even though they are very unusual and not exactly like those in the standard writing. Those who write with difficulty or hesitation through some physical infirmity may sometimes produce broken and unfinished signatures and these results, which in themselves are distinctly divergent as compared with signatures produced under conditions of strength and health, may forcefully indicate genuineness."[62] Forgers, as we shall see in the next chapter, frequently produce writing that is more legible than that which they are imitating.

TYPEWRITING AND OTHER MECHANICAL FORMS

Since the first commercial model was introduced in 1873, typewriters began increasingly to be used to replace handwriting, first in the field of business, then in other areas. Mark Twain became, in 1883, the first author to submit a typewritten manuscript, *Life on the Mississippi*, to a publisher.[63] It was "inevitable," as one text notes, "that typewriting should become a frequent messenger of crime, and that the identification of typewritten material should assume a role almost equal in importance to that of handwriting."[64]

The most common objectives in comparing typewritten materials are: identifying the manufacturer and model of the machine that produced

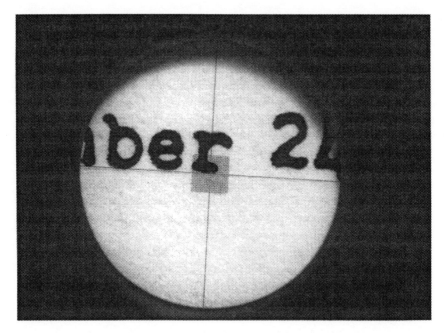

Figure 2.14. Detail from one of the MJ-12 documents reveals that the date numerals are out of alignment with the other characters, indicating that the numbers were typed at a different time.

a text, identifying a specific machine, proving that alterations in a typewritten document were made with a machine other than that with which the document was typed originally, and establishing a date before which a certain document could not have been typed based on the year of manufacture of the typewriter.[65] (See figure 2.14.)

As with handwriting, typewriting has both class and individual characteristics. Class characteristics are those of a particular make and model of machine, identifiable by the specialist examiner from the typeface by comparing it with a reference collection that may consist of thousands of type specimens.

Certain points of comparison are useful in determining whether two specimens of typewriting were produced by the same model of typewriter: the overall size of letters; the lengths of serifs, or the horizontal bars at the terminals of strokes; the relative curvature of endings (in f, g, m, t, and y); and the size and design of figures (for example, the relative areas and shapes of the ovals in the 8).[66]

The individual characteristics are those that develop through use and abuse, such as wear and faulty alignment. With the common old shift-key typewriter, which had the letters on the ends of type bars, specific factors contributed to the individuality of a given machine: the alignment of characters, both horizontally and vertically, relative to each other; the vertical alignment of the characters in relation to the horizontal base line of the typewriting; variations in individual type impressions from top to bottom caused by faulty adjustment of the typeface's plane with regard to that of the paper; wear or other defects or damage to the typeface; and the strength of the impression of a character relative to that of others.[67]

In 1961, IBM introduced the "Selectric" typewriter, which replaced type bars with a ball-shaped "type head." In contrast to the earlier typewriters, the carriage remained stationary while the type head revolved to strike the ribbon and make the impression. This machine also develops individual characteristics that permit identification of a specific machine. These characteristics are vertical and horizontal misalignment caused by faulty tilt and centering mechanisms, respectively, uneven impressions because of a misalignment of type head or roller, and improper line spacing. A complicating feature of the Selectric is that type heads may be interchanged from machine to machine.[68]

With the word processor, the printer's type wheel is the most likely source of identification characteristics. The typefaces can become worn and slight alignment and printing defects can also occur.[69] Because of the complexity of modern typewriters and word processors, some document examiners have become specialists in this narrow field.[70]

As with handwriting and handprinting, comparisons of typewriting begin with the acquisition of suitable exemplars or standards. These should be as similar as possible to the questioned writing in terms of paper and cleanliness of typeface; also, a carbon copy should be compared with another carbon impression. According to Hilton, "the person preparing standards has a simple task, for he merely has to make several exact copies of the questioned document on each suspected typewriter."[71] If much time has elapsed, however, one should select standards typed as near the date of the questioned typewriting as possible, preferably with some just before and some just after.[72]

The importance of typewriter comparison was demonstrated in the Alger Hiss espionage case. Expert examination proved that copies of classified government papers were typed on Hiss's personal Woodstock typewriter, there being numerous distinctive points of similarity, including damage to the lower serif of the *d*, and the *O* consistently printing heavier on the right side.[73]

Kenneth Rendell shows how knowledge of typewriters can expose blatant forgeries. In *Forging History* he states:

I once ordered what was described as *Typewritten Quotation Signed* of Douglas McArthur, "Old soldiers never die, they just fade away," together with a quotation signed by Albert Einstein, "E=mc²." When I received the two pieces I realized that while the two signatures were certainly genuine the quotations were done on a typewriter of the same make. In returning the pieces to the dealer I added a note saying that while I had great respect for Einstein, I had no idea that he had invented the IBM Selectric eight years before IBM had! The dealer telephoned to ask what I was referring to, and I pointed out that both pieces were typed on an IBM Selectric, using in fact the same typeface that the dealer used to type his invoice.[74]

In addition to typewriting, the examiner may be consulted about questioned printing, especially in regard to historic documents. Typographic forgeries now abound, successors to the printed fakes of the notorious Thomas J. Wise (1859–1937), who, together with Harry Buxton Forman (1842–1917), produced fake first editions of Elizabeth Barrett Browning's *Sonnets* and forty-six other bogus books.

Wise took advantage of the 1880s trend of literary societies to publish imitative reprints of their favorite author's works, either ordinary reprints, obvious as such, or "type facsimiles," editions that reproduced the exact layout and other details down to defects caused by worn type. After Wise was put in charge of the Shelley Society's reprints, he duped an honest printer and had extra copies printed on special sheets of what looked like old paper.

The fraud was discovered by two booksellers, John Carter and Graham Pollard, who were suspicious of the proliferation of apparently rare publications. Subjecting the *Sonnets* to numerous tests, they discovered type that dated from 1876 rather than 1847 (for example, they found "buttonhook" *f*'s and *j*'s, that is, ones lacking the "kern" or curled head, at the top of the former and the tail of the latter). They also discovered that the paper contained esparto grass, which was not used in England until 1861, and chemical wood, produced by a process introduced in 1874. (See part 2.)[75]

In more recent times, in 1972, Sotherby's sold a collection of limited-edition pamphlets—the works of Thomas Mann, T.S. Eliot, and others—produced by Frederick Prokosch. The Eliot pamphlets ended up at Harvard, where suspicions about their appearance were soon raised. The science of type analysis was applied, and in one "1940" pamphlet the Aster typeface was recognized. *The Encyclopedia of Type Faces* revealed that it was produced by an Italian typefoundry in 1958.[76] There are many other examples of type-printed forgeries. *The Oath of a Freeman*, forged by Mark Hofmann, and a spurious broadside printing of the Texas Declaration of Independence are discussed in part 2.

Figure 2.15. Facsimilies, such as the Confederate currency, handwritten document, and wanted poster shown here, are increasingly the bane of amateur collectors.

One problem for laypersons that often turns up at the document examiner's door is that of printed facsimiles of both handwritten documents, such as Lincoln's Gettysburg Address, and early printed ones, such as a wanted poster of Jesse James (figure 2.15). Many of these fakes can be spotted at a distance because of the imitation, antique "parchment" paper upon which they are printed (see chapter 5). Others, such as a clerical copy of "General Order No. 9," relating to the surrender of the Confederacy and bearing General Lee's signature, may be detected by the use of a magnifier, which reveals the tiny screenlike pattern of dots from the modern halftone printing process.[77] Still others are detected by stereomicroscopic examination, which readily reveals the ink buildup, nib tracks, and other indications of genuine writing versus the printing-plate evenness of the ink surface in printed reproductions of handwriting. More difficult cases may require more detailed inspection, such as chemical and microscopical analysis of the paper and ink.

3
Forged Writing

A part from handwriting comparison, in which the document examiner attempts to make an identification as to authorship of a writing by comparing it with known standards, forgery detection represents the major portion of the work of both the forensic examiner and the historical document specialist. In this chapter we examine the forger's techniques, the warning signs that point to forgery, and the detection of nonforgery fakes.

THE FORGER'S TECHNIQUES

In attempting to fraudulently reproduce a particular handwriting, such as a given person's signature, the forger resorts to one of a few methods: tracing, freehand copying, or mechanical placement.

Tracing
The most amateurish means of forging a signature or (usually brief) text is by tracing it. Typically one of two means is employed: the trace-over method or the light-box technique.

In the trace-over method, the faint outline of a genuine signature is transferred onto a sheet of paper placed underneath it by means of heavy pressure or the use of transfer paper. This outline, either an indented or a graphite- or carbon-paper copy, is then traced over in ink with an appropriate pen.

The obvious drawback of such an approach is that it tends to leave evidence. It is difficult to follow the outline exactly, so traces of the indentations or the carbon or graphite outline may show in the final pen work. And although the graphite traces may be erased, the erasure itself may be detected. (Such detection methods are discussed in part 2.) Moreover, as with any type of traced or otherwise slowly drawn writing, the result will lack the qualities of freely penned writing. That is, it may have uncharacteristically blunt beginning and ending strokes together with an unnaturally even pen pressure and other qualities (discussed more fully in the following section of this chapter).

With the second method of tracing, using a light box or window, similar problems obtain. In this method the original signature is placed under the sheet being used for the forgery and backlighting is employed to render the writing visible through the overlying paper. The tracing may thus be accomplished without leaving telltale traces on the forged document. However, the result will usually have a belabored appearance or at least lack the smooth quality of natural penmanship. As well, even with very thin paper and strong lighting, some of the fine detail of the writing will inevitably be lost.

Traced forgeries may also be detected when the suspected model for the writing is available. As Ordway Hilton notes: "In more than one instance, a forger has created two or more signatures by tracing the outline of a single model. The forgeries can be detected in part by the near coincidence and constant returning to the same outline of the two forgeries." He continues: "For one important case, no model signature was located nor was there any outline around either signature, but the near identity of the signatures indicated clearly how the two forgeries had been prepared."[1] (To see the variation in genuine signatures and the ease with which a traced signature can be identified, have someone provide, say, a dozen exemplars of his or her signature with an additional one that has been traced from one of the others. Use a light box to superimpose each in turn over the others. The results will be most instructive.)

A famous case involving four signatures, each on a different page of a will, was that of the W.M. Rice will, the June 30, 1900, document designed to defraud the more than six-million-dollar estate. Whereas genuine signatures of Rice made on the same day showed the natural range of variations, one from another, the signatures on the will were unnaturally similar, almost as if they had been produced by a rubber stamp. (They lacked other features of genuine writing as well—notably the natural shading of pen strokes, as discussed in the previous chapter).[2]

Signatures on wills, checks, and other documents are the prime targets of such amateurish techniques. Traced forgeries are perhaps more likely to be encountered by the forensic examiner than by the historical specialist,[3] but there are exceptions. Hamilton states, for example, that the famous forger Robert Spring, unlike most forgers, "used two methods: tracing and freehand."[4] When imitating Washington and Jefferson, he was well practiced and wrote freehand, but when he was able to obtain genuine letters of certain other celebrities "he traced them on a sheet of paper removed from the front or back of an old book, then stained his product with coffee grounds to make it look ancient."[5]

An interesting type of tracing is described by Kenneth Rendell, who terms it "the most unusual and well executed tracing I have encountered."[6] A photograph of Prime Minister Winston Churchill is signed, apparently, in a bold manner. In fact, however, as revealed by a light table, the "signature" is simply a heavy ink tracing over a printed signature (of the type common to many celebrity photographs).

Freehand copying

Far superior to tracing is the freehand technique of producing forgeries— at least in theory; a good tracing may still be better than an ineptly drawn one.

The most inept of freehand forgeries is what Ordway Hilton terms a "spurious signature." This technique, common to forged endorsements on stolen checks, is often resorted to when the bad-check passer has no specimen of the payee's signature for copying. He or she simply writes the name in a signaturelike fashion, utilizing his or her own handwriting or perhaps a disguised hand, and attempts to pass the check before its obvious fakery is detected.[7]

Somewhat more successful, the slowly copied forgery is produced in a manner similar to the tracing and therefore often has similarly poor qualities—for example, an unnaturally even pen pressure and tremulous strokes—that betray the fact it was drawn rather than written. Close inspection may also reveal suspicious pen lifts that are absent from a subject's genuine signature; these are typical of a forgery in which the forger frequently pauses to check his work in progress.[8]

Much more successful is the practiced freehand forgery. A talented artist or calligrapher, who has taken the time to practice a given signature, may eventually learn to sign a name or, with considerable more difficulty, imitate a handwriting that is remarkably similar to the targeted writing and that is comparatively smoothly and freely written. Consider, for example, the matter of Howard Hughes's "autobiography." Although the reclusive billionaire emphatically disavowed it, McGraw-Hill publishers consulted famed handwriting firm Osborn, Osborn, and Osborn, providing them with specimens of Hughes's handwriting for comparison with that in letters and in marginal notes in the typewritten manuscript. The resulting report stated:

Both the specimen and questioned documents reveal great speed and fluency of writing. Yet the questioned documents accurately reflect in every detail the genuine forms and habit variations therefore which make up the basic handwriting identity of the author of the specimen documents. Moreover, in spite of the prodigious quantity of writing contained in the questioned documents, careful study has failed to reveal any features which raise the slightest question as to the common identity of all the specimens and questioned signatures and continuous writing. These basic factors . . . make it impossible . . . that anyone other than the writer of the specimens could have written the questioned signatures and continuous writing.[9]

In fairness to the document experts, they were pressured into rendering a speedy opinion because of an accelerated publishing schedule. As well, Charles Hamilton has this to say: "In the light of subsequent developments, it is easy to criticize the Osborns for their mistake; but as a handwriting expert I must concede that Irving's forgeries of Howard Hughes were masterfully executed. Irving's artistic talents did not fail him when he picked up his felt-tipped pen, for he captured the eccentricities of Hughes's script as adroitly as he caught the oddities of his personality in the 'autobiography.'"[10]

The Irving forgeries do illustrate how a talented freehand forger can produce a credible handwriting that may withstand a considerable amount of scrutiny. Other talented freehand forgers include Joseph Cosey, who learned to pen his fakes with such confidence and speed that they lacked the usual signs of forged writing (see figure 3.1),[11] and Robert Spring (mentioned earlier), who "spent so many hours practicing the handwriting of our first president," says Hamilton, "that he was familiar with every curve and flourish and could write Washington's script almost as swiftly as his own."[12]

Similarly, there were the renderings of Thomas McNamara, who during the 1970s forged entire manuscript poems and letters of various poets, including Langston Hughes and Edna St. Vincent Millay. These were rather poorly done, but his Robert Frosts were "superb imitations," as Hamilton notes, adding: "They lacked the customary personalized inscriptions which Frost invariably put at the bottom of the poems he copied out for admirers, but in all other respects they were masterfully executed."[13] In May 1993, one of McNamara's excellent Frost forgeries made its reappearance in a somewhat amusing manner. Undetected, it found its way as the cover illustration for a major autograph company's auction catalog—a special edition prepared for the annual melting of the prestigious Manuscript Society. The forgery was spotted as such by an observant member, and embarrassed company officials withdrew it from the auction and donated it to the society.

An even more talented freehand forger than McNamara and simi-

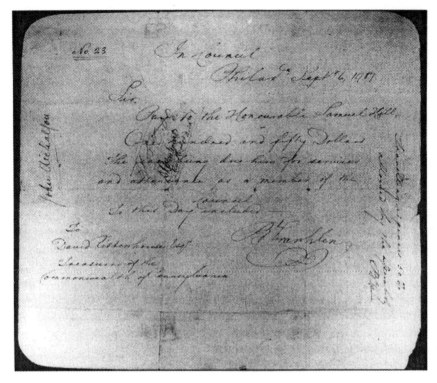

Figure 3.1. Joseph Cosey forgery of a Revolutionary War pay warrant signed by Benjamin Franklin. The rounded corners were a gratuitous Cosey touch.

larly featured in Hamilton's classic book, *Great Forgers and Famous Fakes: The Manuscript Forgers of America and How They Duped the Experts*, was Arthur Sutton. Sutton, an unemployed grocer's clerk in Rumford, Maine, had attended a Catholic parochial school, where his talent for pen and ink artwork—copying portraits and signatures of celebrities—emerged. He made his debut as a forger in 1976. A truly versatile penman, Sutton could, Hamilton observes, "sign any name." From "Sitting Bull" to "Picasso" bogus autographs poured from Sutton's facile pen. His "Adolph Hitler" and "Lyndon Johnson" were masterful and, according to Hamilton, Sutton "honed his chirographic skills to the point where not even Richard Nixon could tell his own signature from Sutton's imitation. No wonder philographers eagerly bought up every pen sketch that came out of Rumford."[14]

Convicted at the instigation of Hamilton, who subsequently persuaded the judge to give him a suspended sentence, Sutton wrote letters to those he had bilked. To Hamilton he said (in part): "I cannot tell you how badly I truly feel and which I have felt since this whole mess started. I am *glad* I have been *caught* and can promise not only to you, but to all the other dealers and collectors that I will never forge any autographs ever again, and that all previous forgeries in my possession have been destroyed." Hamilton closes his discussion of the case by saying: "But now I am going to let Arthur Sutton in on a little secret: *It is the forgeries and fakes that give piquancy and excitement to the chase. Without them philography would be a pretty dull pursuit.*"[15]

Mechanical placement

In addition to tracing and freehand copying, there are also methods of mechanically placing a signature onto a check: projections, stampings, and signature splitting.

Projections involve using an optical system to reproduce a given signature onto a check or other document. Xerography represents one means of accomplishing this, and computer-generated signatures, whereby a signature is scanned into a computer, then placed where desired, represent another means. There are also devices that are not publicly available and "have been utilized in security agencies for the production of clandestine documents in documentation mills. For security reasons, no further discussion of this technique is practical."[16]

Stampings involve the simple forging of rubber-stamped or imprinted facsimile signatures, which are increasingly being utilized on corporate checks. According to one authority: "Unfortunately, rubber stamp signatures are relatively easy to procure and to forge. Sometimes, as was the case in one . . . check theft, the signature stamp or equipment used to produce the facsimile signature was stolen along with the checks. Before the checks could be recalled or payment stopped, there was wide distribution of the checks. Facsimile signatures produced with metal dies and multicolored impression ribbons are safer than rubber stamps, but are not foolproof."[17]

Split signatures, while easy to spot, are still occasionally employed. According to E. Patrick McGuire's *The Forgers*:

Many professional forgers have come to realize that the signature materials themselves, that is, the ink or graphite impressions, are capable of being split. The technique here is to obtain a sample of the original signature, preferably while still new, and to apply a pressure sensitive facing to the signature. The facing is carefully removed, usually from a dense paper stock, and the signature is in effect "split." The signature is then transferred to a forged document where it is placed in the signature portion with the pressure sensitive sheet attached. Sometimes it is made to appear that the check has been torn at this point and that the pressure sensitive tape is merely serving as a repair strip.[18]

McGuire adds: "Interestingly enough some bank tellers and businessmen have been deluded into believing that the application of the tape was a security device to prevent tampering with the signature. This is one more evidence of the con man aspect of the successful forger."[19]

While most forgers are criminals, one of quite a different stripe was a Polish art student who discovered his talent for producing forged documents during World War II. Using only photographs, a typewriter, various pens and inks, and a newspaper for blotting, nineteen-year-old Marian Pretzel forged food and accommodation vouchers, ration cards, currency forms, and travel passes for himself and others. By meticulously simulating with a mapping pen and stamp ink the requisite rubber stamps, he created the forged documents and passes that enabled him to return again and again behind Nazi lines to effect daring rescues, including one of a young woman from the ghetto at Budapest. (Pretzel tells his story in his book, *Portraits of a Young Forger*, which features illustrations of some of his simple but effective fake documents. He had a postwar career as a graphic designer and artist and is active in Holocaust memorial activities.)[20]

WARNING SIGNS OF FORGERY

Among the numerous indicators that a writing may be spurious, several of them, such as lack of provenance and incorrect writing materials, are discussed in part 2. Here we look at those warning signs that derive purely from the handwriting.

Incorrect writing characteristics for time period indicated

The style and form of a writing (see chapter 1) should be consistent with the time and place it was allegedly produced (figures 3.2 and 3.3). As Osborn states: "To be entirely safe and successful the forger in America in many instances must have some historical knowledge of American handwriting; fortunately he seldom uses it."[21] For example, I once dismissed a Daniel Boone letter as a forgery merely by looking at a photocopy of it. Instead of the English round hand that Boone actually wrote in, the letter was penned in Palmer-method script!

In addition to the handwriting system, the same rule applies to individual handwriting features. Handwriting and signatures evolve over time. For example, in his old age Benjamin Franklin's writing became more tremulous, he had some difficulty in forming the capital *F*, and there was a lack of roundness in his *n*'s; yet Cosey's elderly "Franklin" was the same as his youthful one—"timeless," says Hamilton, "an eternal youth whose

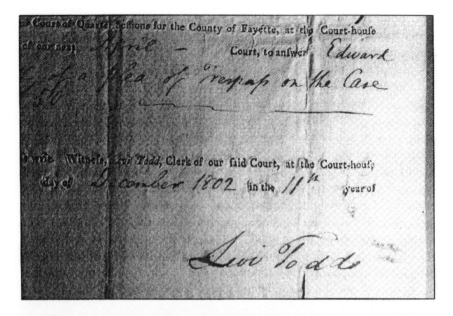

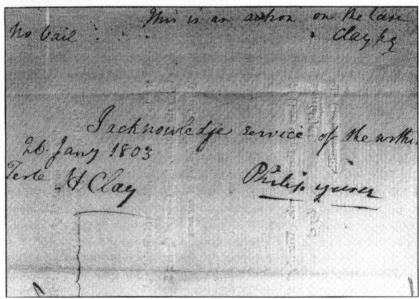

Figures 3.2 and 3.3. Genuine, freely written signatures of Levi Todd (grandfather of Mary Todd Lincoln) and Henry Clay (American statesman) penned, respectively on the recto and verso of an 1802 Kentucky document. Not only is the writing correctly rendered with a quill, but the paper, printing, and ink are correct for the period.

Figure 3.4. Forged Benjamin Franklin signature by Joseph Cosey (a detail of
figure 3.1), smoothly penned and lacking the obvious signs of forgery, it is
nevertheless betrayed by being too youthful a hand for the date,
three years before Franklin's death.

hand never trembled and whose handsome script remained firm and bold
to the very end."[22] (See figure 3.4.)

Evidence of tracing or prior drawing

As indicated earlier, traced signatures may retain evidence of their method
of production, such as carbon or graphite traces or out-of-line indentations. Attempts to erase carbon-paper or graphite marks may yet leave traces
of those substances; if not, evidence of the erasure itself may be detected
by various means discussed in part 2. As well, the act of erasing may damage or dull the signature or other traced writing, and this may be observed
by microscopic observation. Infrared photography will penetrate many
overlying inks and thus reveal the carbon tracing (carbon being opaque to
infrared). Oblique lighting may enhance the indentations and demonstrate
that they do not exactly correspond with the inked line of writing.[23] Finally, if a suspected model of the signature or other writing is available,
transmitted light examination is used to superimpose it with the questioned writing to see if the latter is unnaturally similar. (In the case of paper or parchment too thick for this, photographic transparencies made to
the identical scale can be employed.)[24] All of these scientific techniques
are discussed at length in part 2.

Figure 3.5. Forged signature of Robert E. Lee is characterized by incorrect
shading and by unmistakable evidence of forger's tremor.

In addition to specific evidence of tracing or prior drawing, forgeries produced in this manner typically have a drawn appearance and other
features that are common to writing that is not spontaneously produced.
Each of these features is discussed in turn.

Forger's tremor

While tremor may naturally occur in handwriting as the result of old age,
illness, or lack of skill in writing, it is also symptomatic of forgery, either
the traced or the slowly drawn variety. Determining that shaky handwriting is the result of forger's tremor is accomplished in either or both of
two major ways. The first is by elimination. For example, in the case of a
genuine carte de visite photograph of Robert E. Lee that bore a questioned,
tremulous signature, Lee's writing skill was a given, and research showed
that his handwriting remained vigorous until his death. Obviously, the
inscription on the photo was written by someone other than "R E Lee
Genl," after his death. (See figure 3.5.)

Besides the elimination process, forger's tremor may be deduced
from internal factors within the writing. For instance, if the overall form
of the writing was that typical of swiftly and freely done writing but the

line quality was otherwise, the obvious conclusion would be that the writing was forged.[25] As well, tremor combined with other suspicious features, such as inconsistent shading because of irregular pen pressure, which was also present in the "Lee" signature, would be indicative of forgery.

Evenness in pen pressure

Normal handwriting is freely and rapidly executed and thus usually characterized, especially when a nib pen is used, by light or hairline upstrokes and shaded or heavy downstrokes. Although ballpoint and felt-tip pens tend to minimize this contrast between strokes, it is still a significant factor in writing. Conversely, writing that is traced or copied is typified by an appearance that betrays the belabored manner in which it was produced. Lacking the natural pen emphasis, it thus exhibits an unnatural, overall evenness in pen pressure, manifested by uniformly heavy strokes.[26]

Unnatural hesitations

A hesitant quality to a writing will be in contrast to the typical writer's habitual speed of execution.[27] As Osborn notes, "in genuine writing there are certain natural places for the pen to hesitate, or even stop, but in forged or fraudulent writing, which is usually produced by a drawing movement, the movement may show hesitation at any place—on upward or downward strokes, or even in the middle of what are naturally continuous strokes."[28]

Uncertainty of movement

A lack of certainty in the direction a stroke should go may result in abrupt shifts in the movement of the line, thus giving a kinked appearance to a line that should instead be smoothly curved.[29]

Blunt beginnings and endings

Another effect of slowly copying or tracing a signature or other writing is a loss of the "feathered" beginning and ending strokes that are characteristic of most genuine writing. Such tapered strokes result from speedy writing in which the pen is in motion before it touches the paper and continues in motion as it is lifted away. In contrast, a slowly drawn or traced writing will tend to have blunt starts and stops, as the pen is carefully placed in position and then carefully comes to a halt before the pen is lifted off the page.[30]

Unnatural pen lifts

Typically, writing is produced in a more or less connected fashion and exhibits only an occasional pen lift. In marked contrast is the work of the

Figure 3.6. Enlarged letter *A* from a forged autograph, "Mrs. A. Lincoln,"
exhibits many of the characteristics of a poorly executed forgery, including the
tremulous drawn appearance, patching (at top and bottom of left side), and
pencil marks (at bottom left of the right side and below the period) that
show it was first written in pencil, then traced over.

unskilled forger, either the drawer or the tracer, who cannot resist the
temptation to pause frequently and check his or her work as it progresses.
As a result, such writing is characterized by an over abundance of pen lifts
and/or by pen lifts at incorrect places. (Some writers have distinctive habits of lifting the pen prior to or subsequent to making certain letters, and
such habits may be unnoticed by the imitator.)[31]

Patching

Occasional touch-up of a faulty stroke or writing feature can be expected
in normal, genuine handwriting. In fact, the habitual retouching of certain letters can represent a point of identification. However, such repair
work is typically done in a bold, even slapdash manner. In contrast, repeated, careful "patching"—going back over a poorly made writing feature—is a characteristic that is common in forged writing.[32] (See figure
3.6.) In copying heavily shaded writing, some forgers even first omit the
shading so they can give full attention to the overall form, then carefully
patch in the heavier strokes. All such evidence of patching will usually

be obvious under the stereomicroscope.[33] (See chapter 5.) Kenneth Rendell cautions that "rewriting or retouching is unusual in genuine writing and is done only to make it more legible. Great care is not normally taken by the writer. If a pen runs out of ink, or otherwise fails, a writer will begin again where the quality of the writing was affected. Rewriting or retouching which shows an intention of continuing a smooth form, in the absence of ink depletion, should always be a signal of possible forgery."[34]

In addition to the above features, which may be detected by inspection of a signature or other writing, there are other indications of forgery that become apparent only after the questioned writing is compared with known standards. These include the following.

Uncommon forms

The investigator should be suspicious of any writing form, particularly of a signature, that differs from a given writer's usual one. For example, amateur forgers have frequently used the wrong form of Abraham Lincoln's signature. Lincoln customarily reserved "Abraham Lincoln" for official documents, avoiding that form, with three or four exceptions, for letters. For those, he employed "A. Lincoln" or, rarely, in letters to intimates, "A.L." or "Lincoln." He never used "Abe." Similarly, Patrick Henry avoided using his full name, other than in the text of a document, and instead signed "P. Henry." George Washington signed "G. Washington" in his youth but "Go: Washington" in his mature years.[35]

As well, unusual forms may appear in writing other than signatures. For example, Konrad Kujau, who forged the Hitler diaries, had a paucity of genuine Hitler handwriting to use as a model. As a result, he consistently wrote the capital *H* in the highly stylized form the Fuhrer reserved for his signature, using an ordinary *H* elsewhere in his handwriting.[36]

Off-scale writing

Quite often a forger unconsciously shrinks the writing of his subject. Charles Hamilton suggests this is "probably because of a psychological desire to conceal his fraud by making it less easy to read."[37] Robert Spring's "Go: Washington," for example, was typically only one-half to two-thirds the size of the first president's actual signature[38] (figure 3.7). Again, forgeries of Richard Nixon's signature, a sprawling rendering up to four inches long, are often smaller and more cramped by comparison.[39]

Conversely, a forger may inadvertently enlarge a diminutive handwriting by copying from a facsimile that is not to scale, as from a book. It should be cautioned, however, that a particular writing situation can change the size of a signature or other handwriting. For instance, a small signa-

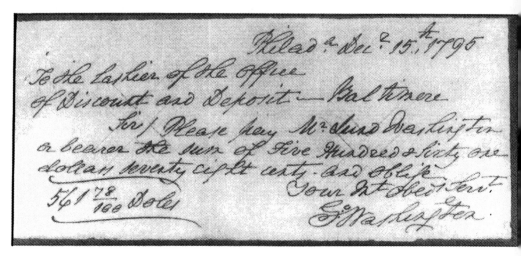

Figure 3.7. Forged check of George Washington by Robert Spring, shown actual size. The cramped writing and signature are approximately a third smaller than those of the first president.

ture box on a printed form might cause a signature to be rendered smaller than normal for a particular individual.[40]

Excessive attention to detail

Because of the care taken in producing them, forgeries will often have signatures and other writing that is more legible than the targeted writing.[41] For example, Joseph Cosey's forgeries of Lincoln's handwritten letters are invariably more easily read than are those penned in the president's rugged script; so are Charles Weisberg's forgeries of Walt Whitman, and Robert Spring's of Benjamin Franklin.[42]

The same intense concentration on individual letters can produce other tell-tale signs of forgery, including lines of handwriting having a tendency to undulate. This characteristic is seen in Cosey's otherwise excellent forgeries of Edgar A. Poe letters and in "Lord Byron" letters penned by the forger De Gibler, alias "Major George Byron."[43] By turning such a forgery sideways and holding it up to the eye so that one can sight down the lines (as one would look down plowed rows of corn), one can easily see the wavy lines of the forgeries and the contrastingly straight ones of the genuine authors.

Similarity of scripts

To the person unfamiliar with a given writing system, such as round hand, different scripts may seem essentially similar until familiarity with individual features reveals otherwise. But in the case of forged documents, supposedly different handwritings may indeed resemble each other, because each was done by the same hand. For instance, the forger John Laflin (1893–1970), who changed his name to John Laffite, forged letters by the pirate Jean Laffite (whom he claimed as his great-grandfather) and by Abraham Lincoln with many features in common. Again, his forged scripts of Andrew Jackson and David Crockett bear strong resemblance to his own "fastidious" handwriting.[44] Similarly, Robert Spring's forgeries of Benjamin Franklin and John Paul Jones have a remarkably similar handwriting, evident in a comparison of such common words as *and, me, the,* and *will*.[45]

The reason for such similarity is not hard to determine. It is difficult to sustain an imitation of an individualistic handwriting line after line; invariably, one's own traits creep in to a greater or lesser degree. Some forgers thus limit themselves to executing forged signatures only, or at least keep the forged handwriting to a minimum.

Context of signature

One trick that solves many problems for the historical document forger (including the difficult one of obtaining suitable paper) is to add the forged signature of a famous historical figure as a witness or co-signer to a genuine, but otherwise relatively worthless, old document. One forger penned "Daniel Boone" beneath the signee's name on one document dated 1799. Another added an exceedingly rare signature of Button Gwinnett (signer of the Declaration of Independence from Georgia) to a leaf from a 1760 edition of the Book of Common Prayer, while still another forger placed a Gwinnett signature in an old account book (circa 1770).[46]

One thing to look for in a document bearing a valuable autograph of a supposed witness or co-signer is a crowded appearance. The last-mentioned Gwinnett entry, for example, occupied a more narrow vertical space than any of the other nine entries on the page. Again, a forgery by Henry Woodhouse (b. 1884) of an autograph by "Thos. Stone" (another signer of the Declaration), placed on an eighteenth-century document, has a distinctly crowded appearance between the text and a witness's signature, having been shifted to the right in order to avoid the large capital *D* of the latter.[47]

Such "extra" signatures are also discredited when they, alone, have a fuzzy or feathered appearance on the page, the result of old paper that has lost its sizing over time and consequently become porous. Equally suspicious is the appearance of a celebrity signature on a document that there was no need for him or her to sign. Such was the case with a forged "S.L. Clemens (Mark Twain)" signature gratuitously placed on an 1876 shipping document.[48]

A similar forger's trick is to add a desirable autograph to a genuinely old, but relatively inexpensive, book of the correct period. If the book is one written by a luminary, then he can be made to pen a posthumous inscription in it. Or the book may merely bear a celebrated person's signature on the inside front cover or flyleaf. I once exposed as a forgery a "Go: Washington" penned at the top of the title page of an eighteenth-century volume and intended to show that it came from his library. Not only did the book lack Washington's characteristic bookplate,[49] but the alleged signature contained anomalous features and exhibited forger's tremor.[50] Other examples include the numerous "Stonewall" Jackson–autographed pocket Bibles forged by Thomas Chancellor in the early 1890s.[51]

In addition to documents and books, forgers have learned that bogus autographs can be affixed to an imaginative variety of genuine artifacts. Among these are photographs, such as the carte de visite of Robert E. Lee (figure 3.5),[52] as well as photos of Lincoln and other historical figures and movie stills of Greta Garbo, Clark Gable, and others. Additional items include newspapers (such as the unlikely autograph of John Adams in the upper margin of the December 29, 1803, *Boston Gazette*), printed invitations (such as one for a Union Railroad celebration bearing the signatures of poet Eugene Field and author Bret Harte, forged by Field's son, the notorious Eugene Field II), other printed documents and even blank forms (including genuine printed ones from the Office of Discount and Deposit at Baltimore, which Robert Spring filled out as payment orders and completed with George Washington's signature), commemorative envelopes (such as airmail "covers" with spurious autographs of Charles A. Lindbergh), and many other items.[53]

Suspicious check elements

Of course the check forger plies his trade upon bank checks, either by forging them outright, by forging an endorsement on a stolen check, or by "raising" a check.

The notorious check forger William Hamilton Harkins (b. 1870) developed shrewd but bold techniques. (Harkins, a college-educated schoolteacher, turned to a life of crime after the failure of a bank in which he and his bride had entrusted their entire savings of twenty-thousand dollars. Harkins insisted the bank had swindled him, and he vowed to get even, although his dishonest talk caused his wife to leave him in 1898.) As Harkins explained one of his ploys:

I would pretend to be a grief-stricken son or husband, seeking a suitable memorial for my mother or wife or even brother or sister. While I was in the office of the memorial-maker, I would pretend to be so stricken with grief, that I would fake a faint. The memorial maker would have to go out of the office for some smelling salts. While he was gone, I would open his desk drawer and steal out blank as well as cancelled checks.

You would be surprised how many people keep these in the top drawers of their desks. It's almost a sure thing. When the memorial-maker returned with salts or water, I would be recovered and would thank him, saying that I was too shaken and would come back at a future date.[54]

With both blank and model checks in hand, Harkins could fill in the former by copying the latter. After cashing checks for thousands of dollars, he would flee the area before bank officials had time to discover his ruse.

A little rule I made was not to use the same city too often. If I cashed checks in New York, I would then go to California. Or else, I would do it in Maine, and then go to Texas. I would go across the country this way, and it would give the impression that there were many forgers, instead of just one.

Oh, I wouldn't cash checks all the time. I would give myself . . . and the banks . . . a little respite, during which time I would have a good time at the horse races, with some women, good hotels, good restaurants.

After all, what's money for, if not enjoyment?[55]

To facilitate cashing his forged checks, Harkins had another ploy. He would buy some cashier's checks and so obtain the signature or initials of a bank official. He would copy the initials or signature onto his phony checks, then present them to a teller. The latter, seeing the checks having apparently been approved, would happily count out cash to the elegantly dressed "businessman."[56]

As to forged endorsements on genuine checks, these range from the spurious signature (mentioned in the first section of this chapter, whereby, lacking a specimen of the payee's signature for copying, the forger simply writes the name in a signaturelike fashion) to more skillfully forged endorsements. In one interesting case that transpired in New York in the 1960s, an employee defrauded his company out of more than $130,000 within a single year by creating a string of fictitious payees, then forging their equally fictitious endorsements on the backs of the checks.[57]

So-called raised checks are those in which the amount has been increased by some method of falsification. One way is to remove the original amount by erasure or with ink eradicator, then carefully pen in the desired wording and numerals. Another is to carefully alter the existing letters and figures so as to increase the value. For example, where wide-spaced writing permits, the *o* of "two" can be altered to an *e* and "nty"

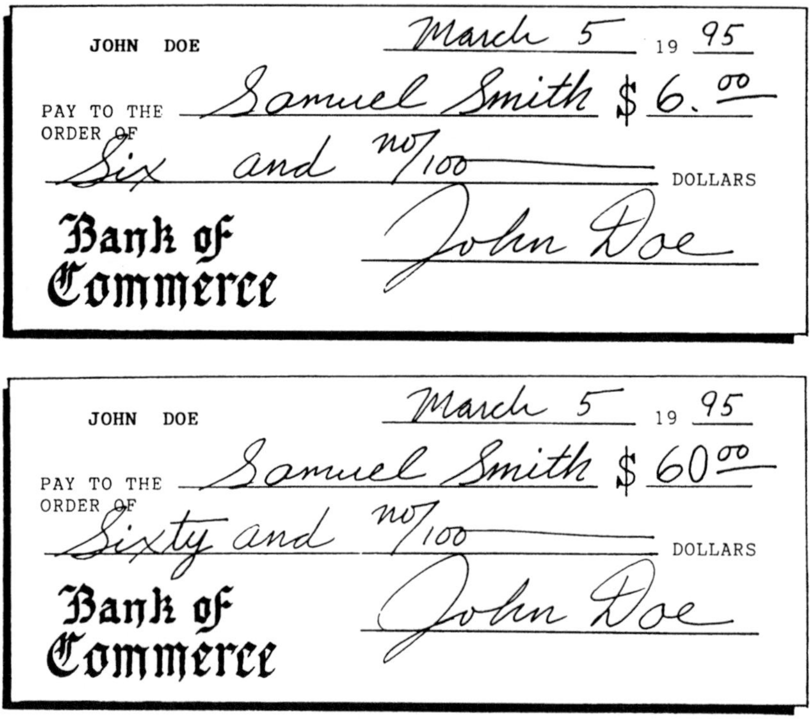

Figure 3.8. Original check (above) is raised to a larger figure (below) by the addition of a few pen strokes. The process is made even easier if the dishonest payee supplies his own pen to the check writer.

added—along with a numeral 0 following the 2. Or perhaps a "six/6" can be transformed to "sixty/60," and so on, in each case the forger taking advantage of the check writing's own configurations as they present themselves. (See figure 3.8.)

Some check-raisers work a particularly vicious racket against the ill and the elderly. This type of technique is often discovered in retirement communities and in cities such as Fort Lauderdale, Florida. In this particular technique the salesman, selling a relatively simple item or perhaps a magazine subscription, gives the customer a particularly good "buy." He then "helps" the victim fill out a check, specifying that payment must be made in check. In helping his victim fill out the check he is careful to space the volume portion of the check form to provide for subsequent "raising" of the check. The forger—con man—also will utilize numerical amounts, in payment for the goods he alleges to sell, which lend themselves to ready "raising." The victim is defrauded two ways. His check is fraudulently raised and subsequently cashed and the goods or services that he purchases [are] rarely provided.[58]

Figure 3.9. Devices to protect against forgery include the antique check
protector (left), which, when pounded with the fist, embossed a pattern into
the paper over the amount, and the antique check writer (right), which
impressed the check amount into the paper.

To prevent the raising of checks, mechanical check protectors (such
as the antique ones shown in figure 3.9) and check writers, as well as
"safety" paper (which protects against erasures) were invented.

It must be kept in mind that many of the forgery indicators we have
discussed—tremulous writing, pen lifts, and patching—may be found in
genuine writing. It is the particular way in which the feature appears, or a
combination of features, that may point to forgery. Whenever possible, the
questioned writing should be compared with known standards of approximately the same time period. If it is discovered, say, that the subject frequently retouched his or her handwriting, then similar retouchings in the
questioned writing would not be suspicious.

DETECTING NONFORGERY FAKES

Not all fake writings are deliberate forgeries. Indeed, facsimile documents, autopen signatures, and various types of what I call "genuine fakes" deserve discussions.

Facsimile documents

Exact, printed copies of historical documents—known as facsimiles—are frequently encountered. They may appear on paper of varying degrees of resemblance to the original and may be printed by any of several methods including lithography and halftone process.

Facsimiles of type-printed documents are distinguished from typographic forgeries (discussed in the previous chapter) by the question of *intent*, whenever it is known or can be inferred. Facsimiles are not usually intended to appear as more than they are—indeed they may be clearly labeled as reproductions—but they can be considered forgeries when they are deliberately altered and sold as genuine. Alterations can include trimming off any identifying printing, tracing over printed handwriting with pen and ink, and adding signs of apparent age.

Trimming off tell-tale wording, such as those that identify it as a reproduction, from a facsimile of a printed document can be deceptive, as indicated by a copy of the *Vicksburg Daily Citizen* of July 4. That printing office was captured by Union troops, who discovered the July 2 issue intact and containing an anti-Yankee sentiment. The soldiers inserted a humorous response and ran off extra copies. Like the July 2 edition, the Yankee one of two days later was printed in a one-page edition on the backs of sheets of wallpaper, sometimes used by Confederate printers because of wartime paper shortages. Various facsimiles of the July 4 *Citizen* were printed, many as advertising give-aways.[59] While most of these are set in different type and/or have various typographical errors or changes, one, notes manuscript expert Mary Benjamin, "is identical with the authentic original save that an underlined running head proclaims that it was 'Printed on the original form for Daniel E. Jones, Vicksburg, Miss.'" She adds, "This line, the bottom of which is only one-quarter inch above the top of the paper's printed outline form, if cut off, would make distinction from the original virtually impossible."[60] (Another example is shown in figure 3.10.)

Tracing over the printed handwriting of a facsimile letter or manuscript represents another method of converting it to an apparent original. It can be surprisingly effective, as we saw in the case of the "signed" Churchill photo mentioned earlier in this chapter. Mary Benjamin tells a story about a more elaborate example:

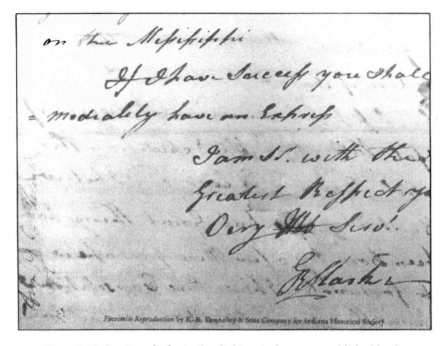

Figure 3.10. Portion of a facsimile of a historic document published by the Indiana Historical Society. Laypersons would be easily deceived by such a document if the line beginning "Facsimile Reproduction" were removed. In that case, magnification would still reveal the mechanical pattern of dots produced by the halftone process.

Some who have autographs to sell frequently wish to do so by showing photographs. They are obliged to handle the transaction by mail, since they live nowhere near dealers and are not willing to entrust their possessions to the postman. Were the dealer to evaluate and buy under such circumstances, he would run many risks. A typical example is that of a photostat which arrived in a dealer's office, sent by an owner who believed an offer would be immediately forthcoming, According to the photostat, the original was a most important Lincoln item—an A.L.S. [Autograph Letter Signed] in which the President quoted from and discussed his Emancipation Proclamation. The dealer, keenly interested, but prudently alert, insisted on seeing the original. When it arrived, many factors not shown above in the photostat soon became evident and justified his caution.

Benjamin continues:

The paper of the original was not that customarily used by Lincoln, although it could have passed as proper to his period. The ink corresponded with that of the date, and the writing seemingly was his. Yet it was tremulous, and never before had this characteristic appeared in the hundreds of Lincoln letters and documents which the dealer had examined. Suspicion aroused, an eradicator was applied to the ink in a small inconspicuous portion of the letter. The result was surprising and illuminating—the visible ink disappeared, and into view came printer's ink which naturally resisted the testing solution. It was then proved that someone had secured a good photostat of a fine original Lincoln A.L.S. and traced the entire writing over in ink. The owner stated that he had bought it from a book dealer in the West at a price which was overly respectable. Its only rather dubious value was as curious testimony to the ingenuity of the dishonest.[61]

Among common facsimiles are those of colonial American and Confederate currency, often printed on imitation parchment (parchmentized paper—see chapter 4), that is usually of the "antiqued," or browned, variety. Since such currency was never printed on parchment, these fakes are simply ridiculous, although they fool enough people to cause considerable trouble annually. Similarly untenable parchment fakes are reproduction wanted posters of Jesse James, Billy the Kid, and the Sundance Kid; the will of Ulysses S. Grant; and Lincoln's Gettysburg Address.

Facsimiles of the U.S. Constitution and Declaration of Independence are likewise often printed on parchment paper, which makes sense because the originals are on parchment. Actually, that is not true of the earliest manuscript copies of the Declaration but applies to the formal version, which Congress ordered be "fairly engrossed" (that is, rendered in fine penmanship) and which was signed by members of Congress—not on July 4, 1776, the date of the original manuscript document, but on August 2, with some absentees signing still later. An official printed edition followed, originals of which are currently quite valuable, and in 1823 Congress authorized issuance of the first facsimiles, a lot of two hundred copies, engraved by W.T. Stone of Washington, D.C. This was identical to the original, with the exception of the ink and the material upon which it was printed—paper rather than parchment.[62] Five years earlier, in 1818, the first *reproductions* (i.e., not exact facsimiles) had appeared, printed by Benjamin O. Tyler. States Mary Benjamin: "In the same year John Binns issued another and at the time criticized Tyler's work in comparison with his own. Neither, however, could be classed as true facsimiles. These and other subsequent reproductions, including some with decorative borders in color or with patriotic scenes, generally carry either the mark of the printer or other notation which shows clearly the commemorative or advertising purpose that was being served."[63]

Another, much more realistic fake document is a copy of the famous General Order No. 9, relating to the surrender of the Confederacy and signed by General Robert E. Lee. It is on a sheet of blue paper common to the Civil War era,[64] and the clerical handwriting and Lee's signature both appear genuine, as do stains and a watermark visible on the verso of the document. All of this was accomplished by color halftone printing of both sides of the paper.[65]

Among famous letters that have been reproduced as facsimiles is one by Thomas Jefferson to Craven Peyton and dated November 27, 1803, at Washington.[66] Another is Lord Byron's letter to the editor of *Galignani's Messenger*, 18 Rue Vivienne, Paris, dated April 27, 1819, a copy of which once sold at auction as authentic.[67] Still another is Abraham Lincoln's letter "To Mrs. [Lydia] Bixby, Boston, Mass.," dated November 21, 1864. Once branded a forgery, the letter is now known to have been written and sent by Lincoln, although the original is lost and the facsimiles are reproductions of a forgery. This forged "original" was once owned by Charles Hamilton, who described it as "the most famous—and profitable—forgery ever perpetrated, and it was easily the worst." He adds: "Retraced, labored, erased and thoroughly unconvincing. . . . In it, the forger had stumbled badly. The paper was not of the variety used by Lincoln, the ink was modern, the folds were not correct to accommodate envelopes of Lincoln's era, and the letter itself had first been drawn in pencil and then retraced in ink. Yet this forged missive has been published in facsimile in scores of history books and hung in the parlors of half a million homes"[68] (See figure 3.11.) Facsimiles of the forged Bixby letter exist on both fake parchment and ordinary paper; one version I was asked to examine was gratuitously emblazoned with an engraved portrait of Lincoln, something the sixteenth president's stationery never bore.

Still another facsimile of a historical letter is that written by Benjamin Franklin to his longtime friend William Strahan, the English printer who published Samuel Johnson's historic *Dictionary*. Written on July 5, 1775, after Franklin received word Strahan had been elected to the British Parliament, the letter was actually never sent. It read: "You are a member of Parliament, and one of that majority which has doomed my Country to Destruction. You have begun to burn our towns and murder our People. Look upon your Hands! They are stained with the Blood of your Relations. You and I were long Friends. You are now my Enemy, and I am Yours, B. Franklin." (There are also forged copies of this dramatic letter.)[69]

As early as 1890, there appeared facsimiles of John Brown's last letter, dated December 2, 1859, written at Charlestown, Virginia, and handed to his prison guard just hours before he was hanged for murder and treason. The abolitionist had written: "I John Brown am now quite *certain* that the crimes of this *guilty land will* never be purged *away*, but with Blood. I had *as I now think vainly* flattered myself that without *very much* bloodshed

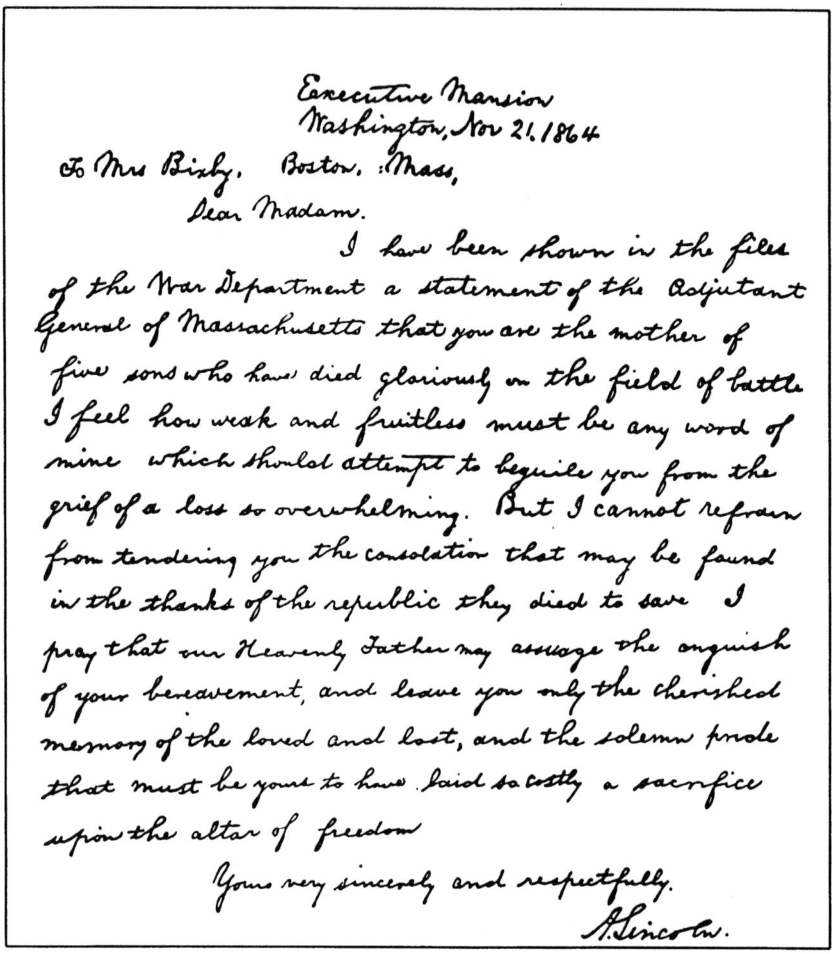

Figure 3.11. Abraham Lincoln's moving letter to Mrs. Lydia Bixby on the death of her sons exists only in the above facsimile of a forgery. Historical evidence, however, proves such a letter was sent from the Lincoln White House, and linguistic analysis confirms the text as Lincoln's own.

it might be done." (The original six-line note is now owned by the Chicago Historical Society.)[70]

Many, many more facsimile letters could be listed. Mary Benjamin informs, for example, that "Chancellor Bismarck's letters, acknowledging birthday greetings, which he received by the hundreds, are almost invariably facsimile. The famous German statesman could hardly have been expected, in his advanced years, to have written out these notes in longhand. Facsimiles of Schiller, Walter Scott, Admiral Nelson, Robert Burns and others have all been sources of trouble in this manner. Washingtons are also common and repeatedly come on the market, especially pages, running into many folio sheets, from his expense account with the United States Government."[71] More modern facsimile holograph letters include those of Harry S. Truman and Sir Winston Churchill.[72] Kenneth Rendell cautions: "Some facsimiles are, especially if lithographed, very deceptive. Among the most difficult to detect and the most frequently offered as genuine are military documents bearing Adolf Hitler's lithographed signature and letters thanking his unnamed correspondent for birthday or Christmas greetings."[73] He adds:

Many facsimiles are also of a nature that should make an examiner suspicious. Purported handwritten letters without a specific salutation sending thanks for birthday or Christmas greetings, or written just after an important event, such as an election or award (when the writer would receive a large number of letters), automatically should be suspect. It should seem unlikely to all but the most gullible that George V could have sent a personal message to every soldier who served in the First World War, or that Churchill could have personally written to all those who commiserated with him over the loss of the election in 1945 or those who wrote each year congratulating him on his birthday.[74]

Detecting facsimiles is not difficult, if the following procedures[75] are conducted:

• Learn to recognize parchment paper. Genuine documents were written on parchment or paper, not imitation material.

• Use a magnifier to look for a dot-screen pattern that is indicative of halftone printing, or the tell-tale appearance of color copiers, or other evidence of mechanical reproduction.

• Employ the stereomicroscope (see chapter 5) to look for nib tracks, indentation from pen pressure, and the irregular deposit of ink that are characteristics of genuine writings. In contrast, facsimiles will lack these features. If printed in black ink, a facsimile will be uniformly black from beginning to end, without shadings of gray. Keep in mind that most old, once-black writing ink was iron-based and will have turned a rusty brown with age, unlike printer's ink, which is carbon-based and will remain eternally black.

• Search the inked areas for tiny white dots—ink voids—that are caused by bubbles in the printing ink and that are thus characteristic of facsimiles and other printed documents. (Be careful not to mistake for these the tiny areas in genuine ink writing that can result from the pen skipping over spots of depressed paper fibers.)

• If necessary, test the ink by using *fresh* ink eradicator applied in an out-of-the-way place using a toothpick. (Immediately afterward, remove the eradicator fluid with a blotter.) Writing inks (except india ink) will immediately fade out, because of the strong bleaching quality of the eradicator (which is essentially chlorine bleach).

• Be alert to anomalies, such as paper of the wrong size, apparent watermarks that are not translucent, and similar warning features. For example, in the case of the 1803 Jefferson to Payton letter, it was accompanied by an envelope, but envelopes did not come into use in the United States until 1832 or later and were not common until the 1840s.

Autopen signatures

Many busy persons—political figures, movie stars, astronauts and other celebrities—supply the large demand for their autographs with a mechanical device called an Autopen. Actually the robot signing device may be a different make such as Signa-Signer or other brand, some machines being more sophisticated than the original, but autograph dealers and collectors now use "autopen" as a generic name,[76] and I will follow that trend here.

President Kennedy began the use of the autopen in the White House in 1960, and his lead has been followed by his successors (see figures 3.12 and 3.13). Prior to their presidencies Gerald Ford and Jimmy Carter eschewed the use of the machine but finally succumbed because of the great volume of mail that faced them.[77] Knowing that presidents usually employ the autopen, collectors often specifically request a genuine autograph. However, the following reply to one collector from the Clinton White House's director of presidential correspondence, Jeff Riley, is typical:

[I respond] to your letter requesting President Clinton's personal signature on an inaugural poem booklet. Although I appreciate your desire to receive the President's original signature for your collection, I regret that the President will not be able to fulfill your request at this time. As you may know, the President receives an overwhelming number of requests for his original signature. Therefore, we follow longstanding White House policy of generally denying them. As we have learned from former Presidents, the opportunity for original signatures is much greater after the President has left office. I respectfully suggest that you consider trying again then."[78]

As Kenneth Rendell observes: "It should always be assumed that any letter, signed photograph, or other piece not of a truly personal or important business nature could have been signed by a machine if it is from a well-known person who receives many routine letters requiring an answer."[79]

Figures 3.12 and 3.13. Photograph of the first family (above) bears autopen signatures of President and Mrs. Kennedy. Detail shows the blunt endings and (right of center) the machine-produced waverings that are typical of such robot signatures.

Figure 3.14. Like other presidents since John F. Kennedy, Bill Clinton makes use of the autopen for many nonofficial purposes. The uniformity of the stroke thickness and blunt ending strokes are among the identifying characteristics.

In general, it is said that autopen signatures match exactly, and that the most certain method of detection is by superimposing a questioned specimen over a known autopen (using a window or light table to provide sufficient illumination). But, according to *Autograph Times*: "Unfortunately, autopen signatures don't always match precisely. One frequent mistake is to assume that unless every single letter matches, the signature isn't an autopen. The use of different pens, and the way the pens are attached to the machine can make signatures look different. There are even examples where inscriptions, or other sentiments, are added to an autopen to make it appear authentic. In these cases, you'll have to examine the questionable signature more carefully." The *Times* adds: "Often, the most obvious give-aways in two almost-identical signatures are the dots over the 'i's and strokes across the 't's. Loops of letters, especially 'o's, are also a good checkpoint. Look to see if the letters in the two signatures are evenly spaced, or if they touch at similar points. One important warning is that different pen thicknesses can often make it seem like two signatures are signed differently. If two examples are signed with different pens, concentrate more on the form of the letters than on their position."[80] As well, the subject may even use several different signature patterns over the years, because the autopen matrix eventually wears out with use. The White House is even said to have a number of the robot devices, all with President Clinton's autograph pattern.[81] (See figure 3.14.)

There are other means of detecting autopen signatures, even when known examples are not available. Sometimes the signature begins as a sequence of overlapping dots that lead into the initial stroke. Mysterious dots occasionally appear at the pattern's end as well, typically about an eighth of an inch from the final stroke. Then there is tremor—strange jagged areas in the signature, usually in long strokes, although they can occur anywhere. These are not part of the actual autopen pattern but are caused by an ill-fitting pen that drags or pushes on the paper and will vary from signature to signature. Finally, there are the characteristics that give a drawn appearance to the signature: usually uniformly heavy strokes plus blunt stroke endings.[82]

"Genuine fakes"

In my book *Pen, Ink and Evidence*, I apply this term to autographs that are neither quite genuine nor yet forgeries. In addition to the facsimile and autopen signatures, I include several other mechanical varieties. One is the reproduction signature, which exists in at least three subtypes: an artist's "signed-on-the-plate" signature reproduced on an original lithograph or other art print; a printed signature (i.e., printed with the rest of the document, as is done, say, on form letters [see figure 3.15]); and the hand-stamped signature.[83] Edwin M. Stanton, Lincoln's secretary of war, often used a stamped signature during the Civil War (figure 3.16).[84] Also, Lincoln's successor, President Andrew Johnson, who had a crippled right arm that prohibited his signing countless commissions and other documents, authorized his secretary to employ such a device.[85] And movie star Robert Redford is an example of a modern celebrity who, according to *Autograph Times*, "does not like to be bothered by autograph seekers and is known to employ both a secretary for mail requests as well as a replicating stamp."[86]

Identifying these mechanically produced fakes as such is relatively easy (although distinguishing one printing process from another may not be). Essentially, detection follows the same methods as used for facsimiles, except that the eradicator test might falsely indicate that a rubber-stamp impression—which is not generally made with printer's ink—is a genuine signature. Ordway Hilton informs: "Distinguishing qualities of the stamp impression are the unevenness of the line edges and the line thickness and the difficulties exhibited in the tapering of ending and beginning strokes. These qualities can distinguish the imprint from a duplicate or copy of the stamp. In addition, stamp pad ink has a different quality or appearance from writing inks when examined under magnification, which is an additional means of recognizing a hand stamp signature. Stray ink marks from dirt on the stamp or areas around the signature can also be encountered from time to time."[87]

Apart from such mechanical fakes, there are what might be termed official renderings. This category is represented by the *clerk's copy* (a file or other copy in which the entire document, including the signature, is in

Figure 3.15. Engraved portraits such as this one of Abraham Lincoln are often accompanied by engraved copies of the subject's signature, which are sometimes mistaken for authentic autographs.

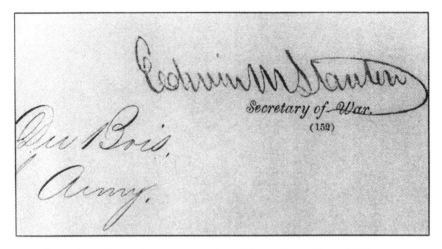

Figure 3.16. Stamped signatures such as this one from Edwin M. Stanton, Lincoln's secretary of war, are sometimes encountered, but can be distinguished easily and often without magnification.

the hand of a clerk) and the *notarized copy* (such as a U.S. Grant letter that I rescued from the accusation of forgery—which actually bore the notary's seal and signature on the verso). Also in this category is the *proxy signature* (one that is legally signed for the subject by a secretary or other person authorized to do so). Proxy signatures include the "Martin Van Buren" appended to many land grants and similar documents (followed by "By" and the secretary's own signature).[88]

Distinguished from the proxy signature, which is usually identified as such, is the related *secretarial signature*, whereby the autograph is, essentially, forged deliberately by someone hired to do so. Such signatures have been used by many presidents including Theodore Roosevelt, William Howard Taft, Warren G. Harding, and Calvin Coolidge (all of whom, however, personally signed all of their White House letters). Franklin D. Roosevelt had various secretaries. So did Dwight D. Eisenhower, but only during his presidency of Columbia University and the first presidential campaign in 1952 and again late in life (but then without his middle initial). Harry S. Truman used a secretarial signature only on White House cards (intended for autographs) and then had his secretary place a period after the *S.* John F. Kennedy (figure 3.17), Lyndon Johnson, and others have employed secretaries (Kennedy more than a dozen) to sign their names for them.[89]

Most of the presidential secretaries learned to imitate their employer's signatures so well and penned them with such rapidity that they

Figure 3.17. John F. Kennedy frequently employed secretaries to sign autographs for him, as in this example from the author's case files.

not only lack the obvious signs of forgery but are often deceptively similar to the autographs they simulate.

Many movie stars also employ secretaries and others to sign for them. Our only actor/president, Ronald Reagan, when he was in the movies, had his fan mail and other correspondence answered by his brother, who was employed for that purpose by Warner Brothers.[90] Paul Newman reportedly detests being asked for his autograph and apparently uses a secretary to grant some requests. *Autograph Times* attempted to circumvent this problem by purchasing one of his personal checks only to learn that there too, the actor was entrusting the signing to various persons to whom he had assigned power of attorney (including his actress wife, Joanne Woodward). The signature on the check was not authentic.[91]

Detecting such signatures begins by being forewarned. That is followed by research on whatever president allegedly penned a given signature. Careful study of known standards of both genuine and secretarial signatures from compendiums of such signatures[92] should enable one to distinguish the former from the latter.

Finally there are cases of what Joseph E. Fields terms, in the title of an article on them, "Confused Identities."[93] In a chapter of the very same title in her *Autographs*, Mary Benjamin lists an impressive number of such cases, those of people with the same name, whereby one may be confused for another—in autograph collecting, usually the little known one for the celebrity.

For instance, Abraham Lincoln had a cousin of the same name who was a justice of the peace—a fact that has caused some to conclude that the martyred president held that office. Similarly, Thomas Lynch Jr. (1749–79), signer of the Declaration of Independence, obviously had a father of that name, Thomas senior, and there was a New York City merchant of the same appellation. To make matters still more confusing, the merchant's handwriting shares some similarities (class characteristics) with the signer. The matter of identity here is very important, since Lynch's autographic material is the rarest of the signers—even more so than Button Gwinnett; both men died soon after their momentous signing. (Lynch was lost at sea some three years later, and Gwinnett, only one year after the signing, died from a dueling wound.)[94]

The autograph of American patriot Nathan Hale (1756–76), who was captured as a spy in his disguise of a Dutch schoolteacher and who was hanged the following day, is also rare. Less so is that of the other Nathan Hale (1742–1813), who served fifteen sessions in the Connecticut legislature. Other famous figures who have intended or unintended namesakes include U.S. statesman Samuel Adams (1722–1803), there being an unknown person of that name who worked as a carpenter and cooper; President George Washington (1732–99), with other contemporaries having had his name, including George S. Washington, who was apparently in the livery business; Admiral George Clinton (b. ca. 1686), whose younger, unrelated, and more notable namesake (1739–1812) also served as governor of New York but whose autograph is much less scarce and valuable; and many, many others.[95]

Joseph E. Fields—who advises collectors to avoid buying the wrong autograph by purchasing only from honest dealers, knowing the biography of the person whose autograph is desired, and becoming familiar with that person's autograph—offers a further word of advice: "Do not belittle dealers' listing of items such as 'Hancock, John, Signer of the Declaration of Independence.' The listing is not done to sneer at the reader's lack of elementary knowledge of history and biography. Dealers are trying to tell readers not that Hancock signed the Declaration, but that this specimen is the Signer's, and not that of some other John Hancock (there were at least four in America before 1800). *Read dealers' lists carefully!*[96]

Document examiners often must go beyond handwriting to look at such additional elements as provenance, internal evidence, writing materials, and scientific tests—all part of a "multi-evidential approach" to document analysis, which will be discussed in the following section.

PART TWO

Additional Aspects

4

A Multi-Evidential Approach

Although handwriting evidence is a major component of the document examiner's work and may often be decisive in establishing forgery, other evidence can also be brought to bear on questions of authenticity, as has long been recognized. In the Roman era, for example, Quintilian (ca. A.D. 88) observed: "It is therefore necessary to examine all the writings relating to a case. . . . We may often too, find a thread broken, or wax disturbed, or signatures without attestation; all of which points, unless we settle them at home, will embarrass us unexpectedly in the Forum."[1] More recently, in his *Scientific Examination of Questioned Documents*, Ordway Hilton emphasized: "A comprehensive approach to any document problem is essential. Many times the question of a document's authenticity, or its fraudulent nature is answered only by a careful consideration and correlation of all or a number of the various attributes that make up the document."[2]

The wisdom of taking a "holistic" or multi-evidential approach is illustrated by the case of the "Oath of a Free Man." Although the oath is known to historians as the first example of printing in America, no actual specimen of its printed text had ever come to light. Then in the mid-1980s first one, then another, copy surfaced, both allegedly discovered by the document dealer Mark William Hofmann. The young Hofmann's talent for discovering rare historical documents—including sensational Mormon papers and letters from such figures as Daniel Boone and Betsy Ross—was at its zenith.

Despite the suspicions naturally raised by this document-world equivalent of lightning striking twice and despite other warning signs including anomalies in the typography, one scientist concluded that the ink's bonding to the paper was consistent with an age of some three hundred years—supposedly proof that the document was indeed authentic.

As it happened, however, Hofmann had used an artificial aging technique to reproduce the bonding effect of old printing ink. Nevertheless, the typographical anomalies were fatal, enabling scholars to demonstrate the document's spuriousness despite scientific pronouncements to the contrary. For example, printing experts observed that there was an overlapping of descenders (the tails of letters like *j*) with ascenders (letters like *b* and *d*) in the following lines. Such overlapping could never happen with authentic hand-set type, wherein each line is self-contained.[3]

A somewhat similar case was that of the purported discovery of a manuscript copy, actually the second page of what was ostensibly a two-page draft, of Lincoln's immortal Gettysburg Address. As with the "Oath of a Free Man," the folded paper was allegedly discovered in an old book. If that raised suspicions, so did the fact that the dealer who sold the document to Lincoln collector Lloyd Ostendorf wished to remain anonymous. Nevertheless, Ostendorf and some fellow collectors proclaimed the document authentic on the basis of a scientific test of the ink; this measured the ion migration of the ink into the paper, such migration reportedly being consistent with authorship in Lincoln's lifetime.

It was noted that the "Lincoln blue" paper on which the document was penned exhibited strong fluorescence under ultraviolet light, unlike genuine specimens of such paper. This raised at least the possibility that the paper had been subjected to some artificial aging technique and prompted the ink expert to rue the fact he had not himself conducted an ultraviolet-light inspection of the document and been able to at least consider the results.[4]

Additional evidence against the authenticity of the purported draft manuscript included historical considerations, notably that Judge Wills, to whom the manuscript was ostensibly presented by Lincoln (the inscription and signature appearing on the verso), apparently never owned the copy.[5] Then there was the handwriting evidence provided by the present author as well as Charles Hamilton and others, including an antiquarian expert for the Library of Congress and distinguished experts formerly employed by the Chicago police and the U.S. Secret Service. The writing contained a number of adventitious strokes, exhibited noticeable "forger's tremor," and appeared to have been traced from an earlier draft of the address known as the "Hay copy."[6]

To take still another example, consider the case of the notorious "MJ-12" documents—papers purporting to reveal a government cover-up in the case of a crashed flying saucer (complete with little humanoid occupants) supposedly recovered in New Mexico in 1947. Curiously, the documents had been sent to a little-known UFO buff in the form of a roll of unprocessed 35mm film. Among the documents on the film was a "MEMORANDUM FOR THE SECRETARY OF DEFENSE" dated September 24, 1947, and ostensibly signed by President Harry S. Truman. It bore an official-looking stamp, "TOP SECRET/EYES ONLY." To some, the documents seemed entirely credible, and one UFO proponent, Stanton T. Friedman, called attention to several elements he believed pointed to authenticity, including the observation that "the signature matches that on an October 1947 letter from Truman."[7]

Unfortunately for Friedman, the document's anomalies outweighed its perceived congruities. For example, the format of the "memorandum" was actually a hybrid: In addition to its typed designation as a memo, it also bore a salutation or greeting, an element reserved exclusively for letters. A search through countless Truman letters and memoranda at the Truman presidential library at Independence, Missouri, and at the National Archives in Washington, D.C., failed to turn up a single example of such a hybrid piece of correspondence produced by President Truman.

Other problems with the Truman document included the fact that it purported to serve as an executive order, although no orders were issued on the date given; as well, its content was incompatible with the legal requirements for an executive order. In addition, the numerical portion of the date had anomalous features—it was both horizontally and vertically out of alignment—that pointed to alteration at some time or other. (Again see figure 2.13.)

As to the signature, not only was its placement wrong (it was located significantly farther below the text than was Truman's demonstrable habit), but there was a much more serious problem: The signature was identical to one on an authentic Truman letter of October 1, 1947, even as to a distinctive, anomalous pen stroke at the top of the *H*, proving that the document was produced by pasting a copy of a genuine Truman signature onto a bogus memorandum, then recopying the whole on a photocopier. In short, the case was one of a signature "transplant"—an authentic signature utilized in a photocopy forgery. (Again see figures 2.2 and 2.5.)

In such cases it is well to remember that it is not what is correct about a document that is important but what is incorrect. For instance, that a purported letter by Thomas Jefferson was penned on late-eighteenth century paper would count less than that the handwriting was rendered by the Palmer method; the modern penmanship would betray the forgery. Less obvious errors might not be individually revealing, but a number of such anomalies could constitute a pattern that represented strong evidence against authenticity.

According to Albert S. Osborn, the great pioneer of modern questioned document examination: "Documents are shown not to be genuine for many reasons, and those who first suspect a document may have an

Figure 4.1. Robert Smith, British publisher of a book on the reputed Jack the
Ripper diary, examines the missing pages that were excised from the
volume—one of many suspicious elements.

entirely incorrect idea as to its shortcomings, but nevertheless it finally
may be shown to be fraudulent in numerous ways, and, if for any good
reason a document is suspected, *everything about it* should be promptly and
thoroughly examined"[8] [emphasis added]. (See figure 4.1.)

The various factors that may be considered in a multi-evidential approach to document examination include provenance, linguistics and other
internal evidence, evidence from writing materials, and the results of scientific analyses.

PROVENANCE

The term *provenance* (or *provenience*) refers to the origin or derivation of an artifact. It is commonly employed by experts in the fields of rare manuscripts and valuable objets d'art to refer to a work's being traceable to some particular source or quarter. In short, the provenance of a valuable piece is the evidence that establishes its historical origin and hence, potentially, its authenticity. A bookplate in a rare volume, evidence of repair or restoration of a document or painting, or a bill of sale are pieces of evidence that may collectively help establish provenance. (See figures 4.2 and 4.3.)

It is naturally desirable to learn the provenance of any work, and the loss of provenance (as by the removal of a page from a scrap book, sentiment album, or other volume that might have a traceable provenance) is unfortunate.[9] Nevertheless, according to one expert, a professional art dealer: "Failure to record does not necessarily indicate any deception; rather, one might consider it like a missing piece of a complicated puzzle. When a painting is known to have been in a designated collection from 1875 to 1910 and in another from 1910 to 1925, but cannot be traced from 1925 to 1955, and then appears in another collection from 1955 to 1979, it may be determined that the unrecorded years were either a result of unrelinquished or lost information." He adds:

Occasionally by very concentrated research some of these gaps can be filled, but the validity of the findings depends on the reliability of the sources and on the present status of the names listed in the provenance. If many years have passed, you can expect that certain names will have become untraceable because of death and the absence of heirs or relocation of the owner with no forwarding address. It is also possible that one or more names in a given provenance are invalid—that is to say, names are listed that never had any affiliation with the painting. The names could have been simply invented and the same for corresponding dates, or the names could be those of collectors who did in fact exist but who never had a connection with the item.[10]

Of course, provenance will be more significant in the case of a sensational work, and the refusal of an owner to explain how he or she obtained an item is, prima facie, suspicious—suggestive of possible fakery or, alternatively, theft. As the noted manuscript dealer Mary Benjamin comments in her *Autographs*, "Where there is secrecy on matters which cannot be substantiated by records, suspicion is inevitable.[11] A few, brief, case studies will prove the point.

Take, for example, the case of the Beale treasure papers. They describe an early American bonanza, a fabulous treasure whose present loca-

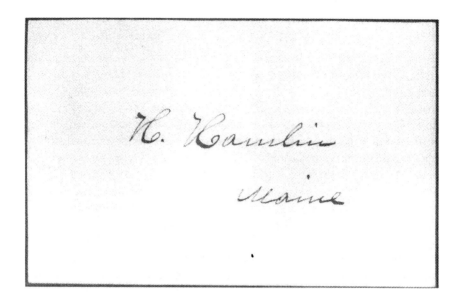

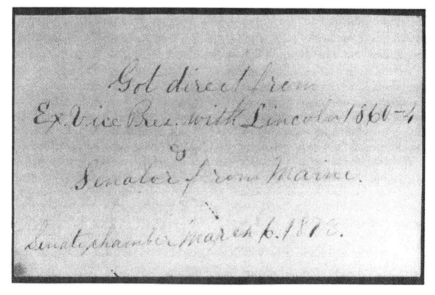

Figures 4.2 and 4.3. Typical of nineteenth-century autographs is this signature
on a card by Hannibal Hamlin, vice-president during Lincoln's first term
(above). On the back (below) is the collector's notation that he obtained
the autograph in 1873 when Hamlin was U.S. Senator from Maine.

tion is protected by unsolved ciphers. Although allegedly penned in the 1820s, the documents first came to public notice in a pamphlet published in 1885, at which time it was claimed that a fire at the printing plant destroyed the original documents. As it happens, however, the treasure tale is not only riddled with implausibilities, but the document's text is replete with errors and anachronisms that reveal it was produced at a more recent date than alleged.[12]

Or consider the "Lincoln conspiracy" documents of the 1970s. They purported to prove the existence of high-level government involvement in the assassination of President Lincoln in 1865. However, the originals were supposedly unavailable for examination, being in the possession of certain "Stanton descendents" who wished to remain anonymous; therefore only transcripts were available. In fact (as will be discussed later) Civil War historians exposed the papers as bogus based on internal evidence.[13]

Then there is the example of the notorious Hitler diaries. After they surfaced in 1983, it was alleged they had been rescued from a burning Nazi plane that had crashed while fleeing Berlin only days before Hitler's suicide. Supposedly, the rescued cargo had remained undiscovered in a tiny East German village during the interim. In fact, such a plane had indeed crashed and burned at the village in April 1945 and served as a basis for the elaborate tale that was supposed to provide the diaries' provenance. Soon, however, scientific tests and handwriting evidence conclusively proved the fraud, and the forger, Konrad Kujau, who had given conflicting stories about his acquisition of the diaries, eventually confessed.[14]

Other examples of missing and dubious provenances come readily to mind. There was the case of the Vinland Map, which was purportedly drawn by a fifteenth-century monk and which indicated that Leif Ericson had visited America some five centuries before Columbus. Unfortunately, it completely lacked any provenance—the dealer who acquired it refused to reveal his source—and scientific tests soon revealed the presence of a twentieth-century pigment.[15] And we have already discussed the case of the MJ-12 documents: That they were available only on film, which effectively prevented examination of the paper and ink, raised suspicions— justifiable suspicions, as subsequent study proved.

In addition to missing provenances and those based on contrived tales, provenances are sometimes forged in much the same manner as the works they are supposed to authenticate. Dealer markings are sometimes added to a document, as are penciled notations and other markings that are supposed to indicate previous ownership. Fake repairs and other restorative efforts may be added to give the impression that the work is sufficiently old to require such conservation measures. Even evidence of prior mounting or framing may be faked to give the impression that the piece has previously been considered genuine by a putative earlier owner.[16] As well, bills of sale, dealers' certificates of authenticity, written statements purporting to come from previous owners—all can easily be fabricated by the determined forger. Indeed, even published descriptions of a document from old sales catalogs mean little, since many of the autograph dealers of the past sold their wares "as is." Quite often, fakes pass through the hands of various dealers before they are eventually exposed as such.[17]

Because of such possibilities, Roy L. Davids states: "Provenance can be important, but it can never be unimpeachable—externals must always be inferior to a thorough examination of the manuscript itself."[18] Nevertheless, contradictory stories with regard to provenance or evidence that a provenance may have been faked should prompt the most thorough investigation and examination of the document in question.

INTERNAL EVIDENCE

Many a skilled penman—careful in his selection of paper and ink and well practiced in the handwriting he seeks to imitate—has been tripped up by inattention to content. Such elements as format, grammar and spelling, the various historical details that are alluded to, and similar "internal" evidence often can betray inauthenticity.

In the case of the MJ-12 crashed-UFO documents, for example, there was the hybrid memo/letter, supposedly emanating from the Truman White House, mentioned earlier.[20] As well, another of the spurious documents, an alleged briefing document for President-elect Dwight D. Eisenhower, bore an erroneous date format: "07 July, 1947." This is a pseudomilitary style, containing both an anomalous zero and comma.[20] (It should actually have been written either in military fashion as "7 july 1947" or in civilian government style as "July 7, 1947.") No one has yet demonstrated the existence of both anomalous features in any genuine U.S. government document of the period.[21]

Similarly, letters supposedly written by such Revolutionary-era notables as Patrick Henry, Richard Henry Lee, and George Washington but actually forged by the notorious Joseph Cosey have anachronistic complimentary closes. The respective "Yours very sincerely," "Cordially Yours," and "as ever—" were rarely used during the period, and, while not conclusive in themselves, portended the results of an examination of the handwriting.[22]

What scholars term orthography—spelling—was instrumental in exposing several false Daniel Boone inscriptions. Despite numerous carv-

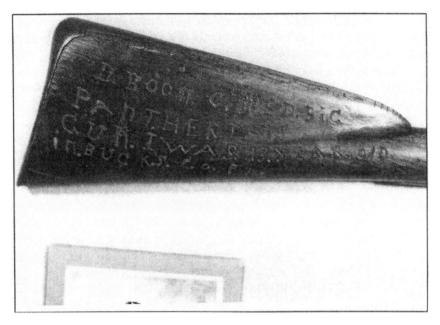

Figure 4.4. Simple spelling (orthography) can sometimes expose as forgeries inscriptions such as the one on this alleged Daniel Boone musket. Boone's spelling, although phonetic, was remarkably consistent, and he never used the spellings "Boon" or "Cilled." The gun also lacks any provenance before 1979 and has other phony elements (such as a series of notches on the stock— visible on the curve at upper right in the photo—presumably for Indians killed, although that is a custom from the much later "Buffalo Bill era").

ings that render his name as "Boon," the frontiersman did know how to spell his own name properly: with the final *e* in all authentic instances.[23] Forgers often represent Boone's spelling in what may be dubbed a "li'l Abner" fashion, crudely rendered to suggest illiteracy. Actually, Boone's spelling was remarkably consistent and invariably represents a sensible phonetic rendering of his Southern Appalachian speech: "sarvent" for "servent," for example; "clark" for "clerk"; and "rad" for "red."[24] Purely on the basis of orthography (although there often were additional grounds), it was possible to expose as fakes a number of alleged Daniel Boone inscriptions, including those on rifles, trees, and other artifacts—among them a notorious "Boon hut" that reposed in a rock shelter in the Daniel Boone National Forest. As investigation revealed, the "hut" was a children's playhouse fashioned about 1935 and the inscription on an accompanying board, "D. BooN," the product of a later schoolboy's pocket knife.[25] (See figure 4.4.)

The forgeries of Konrad Kujau often contained tell-tale misspellings. In his forgery of the Munich agreement between Chamberlain and Hitler, the text is filled with untenable spelling errors, including "an" for "and" and "againe" for "again."[26] Kujau fared little better with his forgeries in German. For instance, in a letter supposedly written by Hermann Goering in 1944 he badly misspelled the word *Reichsmarschall* as *Reichsmarsall*, an error that Goering would have been most unlikely to have made.[27]

Simple word choice can also betray an otherwise clever forger's work. In the Beale papers, for instance, the historical faker had his apparently fictitious character, Thomas Jefferson Beale, mention in a letter dated January 4, 1822, "stampeding" a herd of buffalo; however, the root word *stampede* (from the Spanish *estampida*) apparently did not enter into print before 1844, and the earliest known use of *stampeding* dates from 1883, some six decades later. Authoritative sources for dating such word usage include *A Dictionary of American English on Historical Principles, A Dictionary of Americanisms on Historical Principles*, and *The Oxford English Dictionary*.[28]

Of course, such sources are not infallible, and it may be that a word was in use well before its first known appearance in print. Anachronistic word usage, however, especially combined with other suspicious elements, can provide evidence that underscores the word *questioned* in the case of a questioned historical document, and in some cases the evidence can be decisive.

When a particular word seems highly evidential, however, it should be thoroughly researched so that the evidence is correctly understood. A good illustration of this point comes from the controversy surrounding John Demjanjuk, the Nazi war criminal. Whether he is the notorious "Ivan the Terrible" of one death camp, or an "Ivan the Less Terrible" of another, it is unquestionably his picture on an identification card issued by an S.S. training facility for death-camp guards. Nevertheless, Demjanjuk's defenders have tried, without success, to discredit the damning document.

One approach was to call attention to certain perceived errors in wording in portions of the four-panel card, including (in a list of clothing issued to him) the use of the feminine *Bluse* ("blouse") for the masculine *Hemd* ("shirt"). Actually, however, research established that *Bluse* was correct in German military usage for "field jacket." Therefore, rather than evidence of a Soviet forgery, as some imagined, the wording was entirely consistent with authenticity (a fact firmly established by forensic evidence).[29]

Beyond the occasional word, a writer's entire style—his or her identifiable writing habits—can be studied with a view toward identification. In his book *Literary Detection: How to Prove Authorship and Fraud in Literature and Documents*, A.Q. Morton describes a method called "stylometric analysis."

"Stylometry," writes Morton, "is the science which describes and measures the personal elements in literary or extempore utterances, so that it can be said that one particular person is responsible for the composition rather than any other person who might have been speaking or writing at that time on the same subject for similar reasons."[30] Stylometric analysis is based on such features as "words in preferred positions" (generally the beginnings or endings of sentences) and "collocations" (the placement of two or more words in immediate succession) as used in an undisputed text in comparison with positions and collocations in a questioned text. "The fundamental principle of stylometry can be set down thus," Morton observes, "the authorship of texts is determined by looking at habits which are common to all writers of the class under examination. The habits are used by each writer at his own rate. The different writers are separated by calculating the differences between their rates."[31]

Methods such as stylometry are potentially applicable in cases in which a writer's handwriting is unavailable, as in the Beale papers, the MJ-12 documents, and similar situations. There are many such methods of analyzing texts, including clause analysis or the so-called "structural fingerprinting."[32] More traditional linguistic studies attempt to assess a number of individual writing options.

In the Beale case, Jean G. Pival of the University of Kentucky, a specialist in English linguistics and rhetoric, performed an analysis of the "Beale" writings in comparison to James Ward, the author of the Beale pamphlet and the obvious suspect in the forgery. For controls, sample writings of other nineteenth-century Virginia gentlemen were used, including Chief Justice John Marshall, John Randolph of Roanoke, and Ward contemporary John Randolph Tucker. Pival's analysis (reported in detail elsewhere[33]) is summarized in the following table:

	Negatives	Negative Passives	Infinitives	Relative Clauses
Beale	24	6	44	30
Ward	36	7	40	39
Marshall	15	0	21	8
Randolph	29*	0	18	9
Tucker	14	0	16	34

* Ten of the negatives occur in one letter, in which Randolph tries to justify his participation in a duel.

As a result of her analysis, Pival concludes: "If it is true, as many linquists claim, that any individual's writing style is characterized by idiosyncratic choice of the various syntactical options available in language, then the striking similarities in the Ward and Beale documents argue that one author was responsible for both. Although two writers might share one idiosyncratic characteristic, the sharing of several extraordinary features constitutes, I think, conclusive evidence that the same hand wrote both documents."[34]

Pival has also done linguistic analyses in the case of Lincoln's letter to Mrs. Bixby (proving Lincoln's authorship over that of his secretary John Hay, as had been rumored) and in the case of one of the MJ-12 documents, the supposed briefing document for Eisenhower, the typewritten text of which was supposedly written by Rear Admiral R.H. Hillenkoetter.

Pival points out that while she could not say conclusively whether or not the admiral wrote the briefing document, she did find "some puzzling deviations from the style of the other manuscripts"; the exemplars, for example, included certain "syntactical structures fond sparingly or not at all in the other materials I examined." She adds:

Perhaps more significant is the inclusion of a contradictory mixing of the passive voice (elsewhere employed in relating second-hand information) and the uncharacteristic judgmental statements (found in the twenty-two Hillenkoetter memos and letters *only* in first-hand reporting). Phrases such as "highly credible military and civilian sources"; "a second object, probably of similar origin"; "the motives and ultimate intentions of these visitors remain completely unknown" probably would have been qualified in the same ways as these more characteristic ones which appear in the same document: "what appear to be a form of writing"; "it is assumed that the propulsion unit was completely destroyed"; and "It was the tentative conclusion of this group."

Pival concluded that if Hillenkoetter did write the questioned text, "the uncharacteristic judgments could have been added by a second party." She also said of the document, "certainly, it could have been written by someone sophisticated enough to emulate his style." This was consistent with the cumulative evidence that the MJ-12 papers were completely bogus.

A study of grammatical elements in a questioned document can have additional implications. For example:

The tense of verbs in a questioned document may have an unmistakable date significance. The verbs in more than one disputed will have indicated quite clearly that it was actually written after the death of the testator. In referring to services rendered the deceased, it is easy to understand the distinction in date significance of "taking care of" and "took care of," or of "caring for me" and "took care of me up to my death" which appeared in a contested will.

A careful analysis of the language of a disputed document, other than a will, sometimes will show quite clearly that it was written after and not before certain incidents or occurrences referred to in the document itself.[35]

In addition to orthography and linguistics, internal evidence can also consist of various matters of fact as they are given in a document. In the case of the Beale treasure papers, for example, the name of a hotel and the date of its acquisition proved significant. In the papers an alleged account by one Robert Morriss begins, "It was in the month of January, 1820, while keeping the Washington Hotel, that I first saw and became acquainted with Beale" (who supposedly lodged at the hotel that winter). In fact, however, Morriss did not become proprietor of the Washington *Inn*—its actual name while Morriss was its owner—until nearly four years later. This is shown by a notice from the *Lynchburg Virginian* dated December 2, 1823. Headed "Washington Inn" and signed by Robert Morriss, it reads: "the Subscriber informs his friends and the public in general, that he has rented the house known by the above name . . . and he is now prepared to accommodate BOARDERS"[36]

Another example comes from the case of the "Lincoln conspiracy" papers (mentioned earlier in the discussion of provenance). Since only transcripts were available—precluding an examination of handwriting, paper, ink, or other elements—the editors of *Civil War Times Illustrated* made use of internal evidence to assess authenticity. For example, they demonstrated that the content of certain "journals and cipher-coded manuscripts" was predicated on the modern presidential succession order, not the line of succession applicable in Lincoln's time, and that the papers were therefore obvious fabrications.[37]

Even such a rustic document as an old tree in Louisville, Kentucky—carved "D. Boone. Kill a Bar. 1803"—was revealed as spurious purely on the basis of the date: In that year the famed frontiersman was serving as a magistrate in Missouri. He had already resided there for a few years and did not revisit Kentucky until about 1810.[38] Similarly, a Madison County, Kentucky, rock was carved "D. BOONE" and above it the year "1765"—two years before Boone entered the Kentucky region for the first time.[39]

Without such use of internal evidence, historians would be at a loss to judge the authenticity of many writings. As the great English poet and critic Samuel Taylor Coleridge wrote: "Any work which claims to be held authentic, must have had witnesses, and competent witnesses; this is external evidence. Or it may be its own competent witness; this is called internal evidence."[40]

WRITING MATERIALS

Because they have evolved over time, writing materials have significant evidential value. Indeed, they can often be decisive in exposing a forgery, as in the case of a manuscript poem supposedly penned by Lord Byron (1788–1824) yet written on paper that gave the lie to the authorship: Held to the light the paper divulged a watermark that read "1834"—ten years after the romanticist's death![41] While not all instances of incorrect writing materials are so easily detected, with careful study the examiner can hope to spot the clues his quarry may inadvertently have left behind—clues provided by the choice of writing implement, ink, paper, and other materials.

Writing Implements

From the ancient stylus, brush, and reed pen of the ancients, writing implements have undergone a steady development, one that has been especially eventful during the past two centuries. (See figure 4.5.) The quill pen, the mainstay of penmanship through the middle ages, underwent a transformation from its old chisel-edge or "broad pen" form to the pointed nib of the Renaissance pen, which made possible the tapered shadings and hairline flourishings of the engravinglike script called round hand.

Although there are isolated references to metal pens over the centuries, the steel pens were not significantly used until after 1780, when they began to be manufactured in Birmingham, England. They were not produced on a large scale until 1824. By 1830 they had begun to be somewhat common in America but were not fully accepted until about 1845. By the end of the Civil War, the quill pen was little more than a brittle relic found in the neglected corner of an old desk drawer.[42]

Other durable pens included the gold nib, whose makers followed on the heels of steel-pen manufacturers. By 1810 gold nibs were being tipped with a hard substance, such as rhodium, to prevent them from wearing so quickly, and such perfected nibs continued into the fountain-pen era. So did glass pens, known for their smooth writing from at least as early as 1850, although their fragility made them so impractical that they saw comparatively little use.

Experimental fountain pens are known from the seventeenth and eighteenth centuries, but reservoir pens were not patented in England until 1809. From the 1820s, when metal nibs had completely supplanted quill ones, there was a proliferation of reservoir pens. These included the "stylographic" type (of which today's Rapidograph pen, used by artists and draftsmen, is an example), which began to be advertised in the 1870s. In 1884

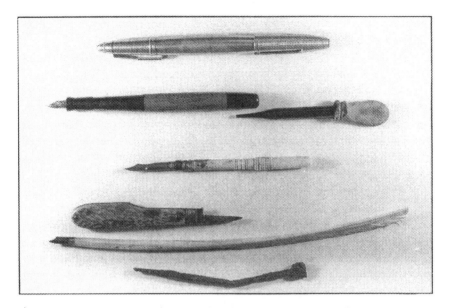

Figure 4.5. Writing implements have evolved over time. Shown from bottom to top are a Roman stylus, a Renaissance pointed quill pen (with late eighteenth-century pen knife), an early steel pen (on a bone penholder with cap), a nineteenth-century fountain pen (with its dropper filler), and America's first ballpoint pen, made by Reynolds and dated 1945.

Lewis E. Waterman marketed the first truly successful fountain pen having an effective "feed" (or flow mechanism), and fountain pens began to be sold in great quantities. (Again see figure 4.5.)

Fountain pens were largely displaced in the late 1940s by the ballpoint. Originally conceived in 1888 (as a rotatable-ball marking pen) and placed on the market in 1895, the ballpoint was first produced in its modern form in Prague in 1935 and (apparently independently) in Hungary in 1938. The latter makers moved to Argentina, where their invention was copied by others—notably Milton Reynolds who first successfully marketed his version in New York in 1945 (figure 4.5) Later developments included the Liquid Lead Pencil (a ballpoint with an erasable graphite ink), that was introduced in 1955 but was phased out during the early 1960s; the "roller ball" pen (a ballpoint with a free-flowing ink similar to that used in fountain pens), in the late 1960s; and the Eraser Mate pen (which had an erasable ballpoint-type ink), in April 1979.

Porous-tip pens, first manufactured in the 1940s as refillable "brush pens," are pens with nibs composed of some fibrous or other porous material, to which ink is fed, wicklike, from a reservoir. From a canister-type "marker," introduced in 1951, developed the fiber-tip pen, which was marketed in Japan and the United States beginning in 1964.

Although pens have always been preferred for preparing legal documents, because ink is not easily erased, pencils have nevertheless been used for much legitimate writing. The pencil developed from Renaissance artists' use of a silver, lead, or lead-alloy stylus for ruling lines and drawing. The true "lead" pencil was made possible by a freak event in 1564 at the town of Borrowdale, Cumberland, England: A great oak tree was uprooted in a storm, and in the resulting cavity was discovered what proved to be a vast supply of almost pure graphite. (Originally called Plumbus, "lead," in 1789 it was named graphite, after the Greek *graphien*, "to write.") Only a year after the mine's discovery, what may have been the first wooden pencil was described, incidentally, in a treatise on fossils. By 1662, cut-graphite sticks were being replaced by sticks molded from graphite dust and adhesives. Later clay was added and the sticks were fired in a kiln, a process that permitted the hardness of pencil "leads" to be regulated. Except for automation and some specific technical developments, the basic pencil-making process remains relatively unchanged. The "ever-pointed" or mechanical pencil dates from 1822, and "indelible" pencils or "ink pencils," which contained dyes and whose writing could be converted to a permanent inklike form by wetting, from 1866.[43]

Being able to identify each type of pen—which will be explained in the next chapter—enables the document examiner to determine when an instrument has been used that is inappropriate for the alleged time period or that may have been unlikely to have been used by the document's putative author at that time and place. For example, some forgeries of Benjamin Franklin lack the characteristics produced by the common goose quill of the period and instead have an ink trail indicative of the later steel nib.[44]

Again, some legal writings that were allegedly produced at different times between 1881 and 1886 all have evidence of a similarly defective steel-pen nib. As one expert observed, "It is highly improbable that this pen would have performed in the same way for five years," thus leading to the conclusion that the writings were all produced at approximately the same time.[45]

Inks

As far back as the third millennium B.C. the Egyptians were producing brush-drawn hieroglyphic writing on papyrus using a simple carbon ink. This was made by mixing lampblack or soot, collected from burning resinous wood, with a solution of gum or glue. A similar writing fluid was also used by the ancient Chinese. Such inks remain black for centuries, since carbon neither fades nor can be bleached by chemicals, but they have at least one liability: They remain largely on the surface of the writing material and thus are subject to easy erasure or accidental abrasion.[46]

This problem was eliminated by the development of a later ink, an aqueous decoction of an iron salt known as "copperas" (hydrated ferrous sulfate) and tannin (usually gallotannic acid obtained from nutgalls), with some gum added for viscosity. Such iron-gallotannate (or simply "iron-gall") inks may have been in use on Greek parchments as early as the second century, and they were the mainstay for writing during the quill-pen era. With age, the black iron-gall ink would eventually turn a rusty brown, the result of the oxidation of the iron. Its corrosive properties caused it to "bite" into the parchment or paper, thereby making it less subject to abrasion; however, with age, it frequently burned right through a page, producing holes where the ink was heavily applied.

In contrast, when first produced, iron-gall ink often appeared quite weak (although it would later blacken on the page because of oxidation). As a consequence, carbon ink was sometimes mixed with it (during the Middle Ages especially) and, during the eighteenth and nineteenth centuries, dyes such as indigo and logwood were commonly employed for the same purpose. Other substances were sometimes added, as indicated by this recipe of ca. 1840. *"To Make Black Ink:* 1-1/2 oz. Galls, 1 oz. Gum Arabick, 1 oz. Copperas, 6 cloves, 1 Drm. Indigo. Infuse these in a Jug wth 3 half pints Boilg. Water for 12 Hours, stir[r]ing it occasionally."[47] In addition to the indigo, which was added as a provisional colorant, the sugar candy would make the ink glossy, and the cloves would help prevent molding. Spirits (usually in the form of wine) could also be added to prevent ink from freezing. (See figure 4.6.)

Indigo was added in greater quantities to Henry Steven's patented Writing Fluid, a type of "blue-black" ink. The one-time roommate of poet John Keats, Stevens set up a factory in 1834 to produce this and a selection of other inks. Distinctly blue when first used, blue-black inks eventually blackened over time. Because of their greater proportion of indigo, these inks were less corrosive to steel pens than the common iron-gall variety.

Other less corrosive inks soon followed. These included a potassium chromate type of logwood ink, dating from about 1848; a synthetic indigo ink, introduced in 1861; certain other colored inks that were made possible by the discovery of aniline dyes in 1856; nigrosine ink, first produced commercially in 1867; and vanadium ink.[48] The coloring matter in most present-day inks is composed of synthetic dyes.[49]

Special inks were formulated for reservoir pens. For fountain pens, there were many varieties, notably Sheaffer's popular Skrip, formulated

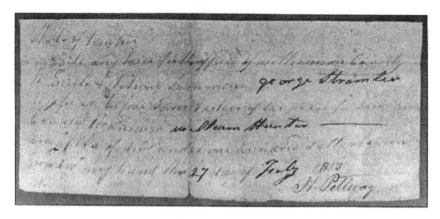

Figure 4.6. Inks of different composition age differently, sometimes as dramatically as in this 1813 document—one ink having been used to produce a formulaic text (with blanks to be filled in later) and another used to complete the document.

in 1922, and a blue "washable" ink, developed in the 1930s. Ballpoint inks (from about 1945) were viscous, oily varieties, more akin to printing ink than ordinary writing fluids. (Erasable ballpoint inks came with the Liquid Lead Pencil of 1955 and the Eraser Mate of 1979.) So-called "roller ball" pens (from the late 1960s) have a free-flowing ink that is similar to fountain pen ink, and porous-tip pens use inks that are loosely termed "washable" (water-based) or "permanent" (petroleum based, with solvents like benzene or naphtha).

Colored inks include the rather paintlike varieties used in medieval documents—notably vermilion (mercuric sulfide, either as powdered cinnabar or as a synthetic variety). Various other mineral, animal, and plant materials were also commonly used in inks from middle ages to the nineteenth century. For example, pokeberry ink was reportedly used on the American frontier. As noted earlier, colored inks made with analine dyes became available after 1856.

With varying degrees of success forgers have attempted to obtain— or simulate—suitable inks. Some, like the talented forger of Robert Frost manuscripts, Thomas McNamara, had a typical forger's outfit from which to select an appropriate writing fluid. In McNamara's possession when he was arrested were no fewer than fourteen bottles of colored inks, as well as some twenty pens. Thus McNamara could select a blue ink (and thick-nibbed pen) to produce fake Frost writings, and a bright green ink (with a medium-nibbed pen) to forge Langston Hughes's signature on typewritten poems.[50]

Of course, the chemistry was not always right. The ink McNamara used in his William Carlos Williams forgeries was not made until a year after the poet died.[51] Even more obvious anachronisms are the amateurish attempts by some criminal penmen to simulate the brown appearance of aged iron-gall ink by using modern brown fountain-pen ink or even tobacco juice![52]

Of course, Mark William Hofmann was a more determined chemist, following old recipes to produce genuine iron-gallotannate ink, then using special techniques, such as heating with a hand iron or applying chemical oxidants, to artificially age the writing.[53] Eventually, though, even he was uncovered, and problems with the ink played an important role in the detection of Hofmann's fakes. In some instances, evidence of the artificial aging itself (for example, the presence of ridges that had the appearance of scorching with an iron[54]) pointed to forgery.

As such cases illustrate, a knowledge of the history of inks, their chemical composition, and the means of identifying them can be of inestimable value. As one authority observes:

One of the most frequent and most important questions regarding ink is whether it is like or different in kind from ink on other parts of the same document or on other documents. This is a question that many times admits of the most positive and convincing answer. A second question of the same class is whether two writings made with the same kind of ink were made with the identical ink, or with inks of different qualities or in different conditions.

A third question is whether documents of different dates or a succession of differently dated book entries show the natural variation in ink writing, or whether the conditions point to one continuous writing at one time under identical conditions. The fourth inquiry, in some ways the most important of all, is whether an ink is as old as it purports to be.[55]

Being able to answer such questions gives the document detective added means of uncovering evidence of a forger's handiwork.

Paper

The papyrus plant provided the rather heavy, brittle material from which paper eventually took its name. Made by crisscrossing strips sliced from the plant's pith, then pounding and drying the two layers under pressure to bond them (the plant's own juice being used as an adhesive), the resulting papyrus sheets were finally polished on one side for writing. They were then glued end-to-end to form a scroll, an early form of the book.[56]

By later Hellenistic times, a more flexible writing material began to be used. Since it could be creased without breaking, it gave rise to the modern type of bound book—called a codex—which gradually displaced scrolls by the fourth century A.D. This new material was parchment, which derives its name from the ancient Greek city of Pergamum. It was made primarily from the skins of sheep—although calf and goat skins were also used. A particularly fine type of parchment, called vellum, was made from the skin of young animals (calves, particularly, as well as kids and lambs), but today the term vellum is often used merely as a synonym for ordinary parchment.

Parchment was prepared by alternate washings and scrapings, the latter scraping being done with the skin stretched over a frame. Then the sheet was dusted with chalk (to remove fattiness) and smoothed with a rubbing of powdered pumice. Both sides of parchment were used: the "hair" side being yellowish, comparatively rough, and marked with hair follicles; the "flesh" side being noticeably smoother and whiter. (In manuscript books the folded sheets were placed with like sides together to help minimize a mismatched appearance.) For writing, parchment was prepared with guidelines made by scribing with a stylus or drawing with a stick of silver, lead, or lead alloy.[57]

Paper eventually supplanted parchment for writing. First made, apparently, by the Chinese during the Han dynasty (206 B.C.–A.D. 221), paper spread to the Arabs in the eighth century and thence (largely via Constantinople) to Europe early in the twelfth century. The earliest known European document on paper is a deed made in 1102 by King Roger of Sicily. Subsequently, paper mills were established in various European countries by the following dates: Spain, 1150; Italy, 1276; France, 1348; Germany, 1390; and England, 1495. (Paper was first used in England in 1309 and soon became common, long before a paper mill was built in Hertfordshire.) England and Holland supplied paper to the American colonies, the first American paper mill being built near Germantown, Pennsylvania, in 1690 by William Rittenhouse.

The early paper was handmade, produced by dipping a framed screen-wire mold into a vat of stock (macerated rag fibers in warm water), allowing the nascent sheet to drain off its water, then flopping it deftly onto a sheet of felt where, after other sheets of felt and paper were alternately placed, the stack was squeezed in a press and the individual sheets hung to dry. If the paper was to be used for writing, it was dipped in size to minimize ink absorption.

The earliest European molds were in the "laid" pattern—the brass screen being composed of heavy, widely spaced "chain wires," each placed over one of several supporting ribs of the frame, and finer, more closely spaced "laid" wires crossing the chain wires at right angles. About 1755 a

Figure 4.7. Holding a sheet of paper to the light can provide important
evidence, in this case designation that the paper is "laid" pattern with an
identifying watermark.

second pattern of mold covering was introduced (although such paper was
not used appreciably in America before 1800[58]). This pattern is called
"wove." As its name implies, it was formed of wire mesh woven on a loom,
similar to today's window screening. These two patterns gave their name
to the paper they produced, and laid paper is easily distinguished from
wove by holding a sheet to the light.

Backlighting may also reveal the presence of a watermark. Originally
these emblematic devices were made by bending wire into the desired
shape and sewing it to the mold's laid or wove screen. As with the laid
pattern, the wires of the watermark device resulted in thin spots in the
paper, so that the design appears more translucent than the rest of the sheet
of paper (figure 4.7). (The wove screening leaves only a faint, if indeed
perceptible, pattern, since only very fine wire is used.)

Machine papermaking was patented in France in 1798, but the method was little used there. However, by 1809 a cylinder-type paper machine
was operating in England (the same type as America's first paper machine,
which was in operation by 1817), and by 1810–12 a wire-belt "Fourdrinier"
machine was operating there as well. (This was named for two brothers,
London stationers Henry and Sealy Fourdrinier, who financed its development based on patented improvements of the French model.)

Early machine-made paper necessarily lacked any watermark, but in 1825 a patented roller, later called a dandy roll, began to be used to impress a watermark and/or a pseudo-laid pattern into the tender, newly formed wove paper. Thus the mere presence of a "laid" pattern in paper no longer is proof that the sheet was handmade. However, handmade paper can still be distinguished from the machine-made variety, as discussed in the next chapter. Although linen and cotton rags were used for paper pulp in the early centuries, eventually other materials were employed. Straw paper was produced experimentally in 1765 and commercially in 1829 (at Chambersburg, Pennsylvania). Still later, esparto grass was introduced in England (1857) and in the United States (1869). Ground wood pulp was first produced commercially in Saxony in 1847, but its commercial production in the United States did not occur until 1867, when wood-pulp paper began to be made in Curtisville, Massachusetts. Chemical processes used to eliminate extraneous materials (primarily lignin) that are destructive to the cellulose in paper were first used in England in 1851.

Special techniques applied to paper manufacture include coloring (1687), machine ruling of lines (circa 1770), bleaching (1792), embossing (1796), rosin sizing (circa 1800), and "loading" with filler material (1807), all originating in England or on the European continent. Hot-pressing of paper originated in the United States in 1809. So-called "parchment paper" (vegetable parchment) was invented about 1857 and was first manufactured in the United States in 1885.[59]

A clue to a forged writing may come from the size of the paper involved. The folio sheet (a very large size) was common through the eighteenth century; the quarto (about eight by ten inches) was popular during the first half of the nineteenth century; and the octavo (half a quarto) was used during the second half for most correspondence—just as today an eight and one-half by eleven inch sheet is predominately used.

The flyleaves of books have commonly been a source of old paper tapped by forgers—ranging from the nineteenth-century forger Robert Spring, who was adroit in manufacturing George Washington fakes, to Mark William Hofmann himself. As Edmund Malone wrote in 1796, in exposing the productions of the Shakespeare forger, William Henry Ireland: "The true and natural paper-warehouse for such a schemer to repair to is, the shop of a bookseller, where every folio and quarto of the age of Elizabeth and James would supply a couple of leaves of white-brown paper of the hue required." Malone asked: "What would an author naturally do when he sat down to write a play, at least such an author as Shakespeare, who at the time *Lear* was produced was in the zenith of his reputation, and in affluent circumstances? Would he not purchase a paper-book or at least a quire of paper, which would be sufficient for the longest piece he ever wrote, and then could be procured for five pence?" As Malone continued, considering the forger's plight in obtaining suitable paper for a Shakespearean forgery: "But what would he do who set down to write a play for him near two centuries after his death? He would pick up as well he could such scraps of old paper as he could find, at various times, and in various places; he would, as in the present case, not be able to show any of his pretended originals except in the form of half or quarter sheets, and these single leaves having been collected from various quarters would exhibit more than twenty different papermarks."[60] In fact, in later confessing to his forgeries, Ireland stated: "I applied to a bookseller . . . who, for the sum of five shillings, suffered me to take from the folio and quarto volumes in his shop the fly-leaves which they contained."[61]

Stationery, especially the correct type known to have been used by a particular notable, is not usually easy for a forger to obtain, although occasional sheets and even rare, unopened packets of old paper are available to the collector and hence the determined forger. For example, a genuine sheet of old "Lincoln blue" paper (a variety especially common from about 1840 to 1860, and so-named because as an attorney Abraham Lincoln used it for many of his legal papers) was obtained by the unknown forger of the Gettysburg Address owned by Lloyd Ostendorf. (Despite credible paper—although there were questions as to whether it would have been available to Lincoln at the particular time and place the address would have been drafted—the forgery was easily exposed on other grounds.)[62]

Sometimes forgers err hilariously in their choice of paper, as when (in an instance mentioned earlier) a forger rendered a "Byron" manuscript on paper bearing a date watermark reading "1834"—ten years after the celebrated poet's death. Apparently the forger—De Gibler, alias Major Byron (he claimed to be the poet's illegitimate son)—had not troubled to give his paper supply even the minimal scrutiny of holding a sheet to the light. Neither did the dealer who attempted to market the manuscript (John Murray III, son of the publisher of Lord Byron's poetry).[63]

The paper of another bogus historical document, a forgery of the 1938 Munich agreement between Neville Chamberlain and Adolph Hitler, was similarly faulty. Fabricated by Hitler diaries forger Konrad Kujau, the document was typed on a letterhead that Hitler never used, and it contained other errors.[64] Similarly, a copy of Abraham Lincoln's celebrated letter to Mrs. Bixby, consoling her for the loss of her sons in battle, was easily spotted as a fake: It was imprinted with an engraved portrait of Lincoln, a form of stationery the Great Emancipator never used.[65]

Even more absurd were the productions of the French forger, Vrain-

Denis Lucas. According to Mary Benjamin, "So completely catholic was he in his forgeries that he had sold letters, all written in French and on paper made in France, of Julius Caesar, Cleopatra, Mary Magdalen and even of Lazarus—after his resurrection." Lucas's victim, whom Benjamin calls "one of the greatest dupes in history," was not an imbecile but actually a noted mathematician and astronomer—albeit one blinded by the passion of obtaining, seemingly, a succession of incredible rarities.[66]

Even though a forger may use a credible sheet of paper, he or she may then use it in an improper manner. For example, Mark Hofmann's notorious "white salamander letter" (one of several Mormon-related papers faked by the young forger) was folded and sealed improperly for a pre-envelope letter dated 1830, and there were still additional problems.[67]

Typical of the questions concerning paper that may arise in modern forensic work is one central to a case involving a disputed accounting sheet. The question was whether the disputed sheet had been ruled (by mechanical ruling machines) in the same order as a 1952 file sheet that was used as a known standard. Attempting to align the horizontally ruled lines revealed slightly unequal spacing—evidence that the pages had actually been ruled in separate runs. In other instances, differences in the tint of ink might indicate that such forms were ruled, say, some months apart.[68]

As illustrated by this brief historical overview of paper and its antecedents, along with a few cases of forgers attempting to secure or utilize credible writing material for a particular deception, the document detective does well to learn all he or she can about this important subject. As we see, there are many ways for a forger to err, and his use of paper alone contains many potential pitfalls.

Other materials

In addition to pen, ink, and paper, there are a variety of additional materials that can provide clues in questioned-document cases.

Take paper fasteners, for example. They include the old ribbon-and-wax method, which appeared by the thirteenth century, in which a ribbon is threaded through slits placed along the end of the pages to be secured and then held in place at either terminus by a blob of sealing wax. The wax itself has an even longer history, with green wax denoting the official Exchequer Court in medieval England, and black having long been used to seal mourning letters. Wafers (thin discs of flour, gum, and coloring matter) were moistened and used to close folded letters, fasten two sheets at a corner, or the like. (The term *wafer-seal* is mentioned as early as 1635.)[69] Staplers were introduced about 1875; practical, lever-action models (which did not need whacking with a mallet) appeared in the early 1900s. Previ-

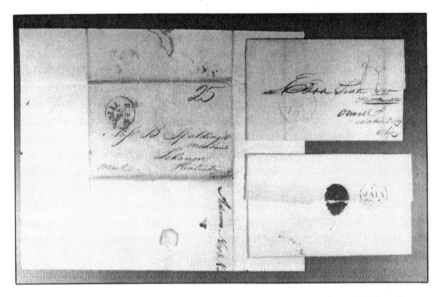

Figure 4.8. Pre-envelope letters were sealed with paste wafers or blobs of sealing wax. At left is an opened letter sheet showing the manner of folding. (At bottom center of the sheet is a piece of paper adhering to the wafer.) At upper right is a similar sheet folded into its packet, and below it is the reverse of another packet, showing how the wax seal was placed over the fold. Postmarks might be placed anywhere on either side of a letter packet, as shown by these examples.

ously, straight pins (also called "bank pins") were often used, especially for temporary fastening (on which use the stapler had little effect). Paper clips were a British invention of about 1900, and "Scotch" tape an American one of 1930.

While pre-envelope letters were usually sealed with wax or wafers (the latter placed under the flap) (figure 4.8), envelopes invited a variety of closing devices. Not common until the 1840s, envelopes were closed with mucilage; "motto seals" (small printed stickers occasionally used circa 1850); imitation seals made of embossed, glossy red paper; and other devices. The adhesive or "self-sealing" envelope (of about the late 1840s) eventually prevailed, but the clasp envelope (patented in 1879) also remains common.

Since the pre-envelope covers also bore postmarks (figure 4.8), they represent another challenge for the forger. Hofmann, for example, faked a postmark on the address panel of his folded "white salamander" letter but, as an expert reported, "the flatness, vagueness, and ink distribution of the postmark differ from genuine postmarks of the period."[70] For an address-leaf of a forged letter by Abraham Lincoln, Joseph Cosey created a postmark by using an inked bottle top to produce the circle, and printing the wording, "ALTON 7 CENTRAL ILLINOIS R. R. DEC. 6, 1847," with a child's rubber-stamp outfit. (In places the letters overlapped the circle, a tip-off that the postmark was produced in two stages.)[71]

After adhesive postage stamps were introduced (in Britain in 1840 and in the United States in 1847), cancellation devices joined postmarks on address leafs (and later envelopes). Eventually the two were combined, but early stamps were typically canceled with pen and ink (with an "X," slash marks, etc.) and are known as "pen cancellations." "Cork cancellations" (improvised from a cork stopper into the end of which a simple design, such as a cross, was cut) were also much used. "Target cancellations" (a simple design of concentric circles) were common throughout the latter half of the nineteenth century. "Flag cancellations" were produced by canceling machines and first appeared in 1894.

In addition to the type of fakery produced by the likes of Cosey and Hofmann, forgers are now using phony postmarks and cancellations to create bogus postal collectibles. For example, a particular Confederate stamp is more valuable in used rather than mint condition (since it was produced at the end of the Civil War and few were actually used). By investing several dollars in an unused specimen, affixing it to an old envelope, and adding the address and fake postal marking, the forger has attempted to triple his investment.

Similarly, penny ante fakers are also enhancing the value of "patriotic covers." (Common during the Civil War, these are small envelopes printed with decorative cachets, most commonly expressing proloyalist or antisecessionist sentiments.) Invariably, these covers are more valuable if used, so one forger obtained an inexpensive supply, which he then converted to "used" specimens. For each, he affixed a canceled stamp, then used a felt pen to draw the remainder of the postmark onto the envelope, and finally penned an address in brown ink. However, his fakes were not skillful enough to get past the experienced eye of Abington, Massachusetts, manuscript dealer K.C. Owings.[72]

The document detective should also become familiar with the various implements that have been used as an adjunct to writing, particularly those that leave their marks upon paper. They include the paper knife, whose origins may be as old as paper itself. To cut the large sheets of handmade paper, one would fold the sheet, insert the paper knife (which typically had a rounded blade rather like a tongue depressor), and slit open the fold. As a "library knife" it is still used in libraries and archives to "open" the inadvertently uncut pages of old volumes. About the middle of the

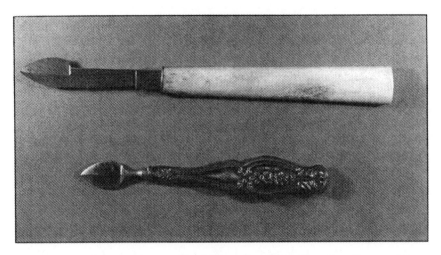

Figure 4.9. Ink-eraser knives (like the bone-handled and sterling silver models shown here) were used throughout the dip-pen era to scrape mistakes from parchment or (with more care) from paper. Such erasures are, naturally, easily detected.

nineteenth century, with the advent of the envelope, the paper knife became more slender and tapered to a point, being known in its new guise (somewhat incorrectly) as a "letter opener."

Another type of knife, once found in most desks, was the ink-eraser knife (figure 4.9). Often misidentified as a "bleeder" because of a similar blade (although it is not at right-angles to the shaft as in blood-letting knives), the knife was used to scrape off mistakes—first on medieval parchments, then on paper throughout the "dip"-pen era. (Often the roughened area that resulted would be polished by rubbing with a burnisher of some sort to minimize the spreading of ink in rewriting.) Another eraser of sorts was even more readily at hand—quite literally: If the mistake had just been made, many writers (including Thomas Jefferson) simply used their little finger to wipe off the ink. This worked best with a highly "calendered" paper (paper given a polished finish by rollers during machine papermaking).

Ink erasers of gray "sand rubber" have been sold since as early as 1867 and were later modified to become typewriter erasers. A special ink-eraser brush was advertised about 1925, and today's electrically powered rubber or vinyl eraser may eventually be supplanted by a "laser eraser"—a beam that vaporizes ink. Chemical "ink erasers," or so-called ink eradicators, were merely bleaching solutions (usually chlorine bleach); the "eradication" was usually followed by application of a second solution (typically lime-water) to neutralize the first. This process was common from the late nineteenth century until it was effectively rendered obsolete by the advent of the ballpoint pen, whose oily ink repelled the eradicator liquid. More recently, correction fluid or "white-out" has been used to paint over unwanted typewritten or pen-written text.

In addition to erasure, blotting was another function that left its mark, so to speak, on old documents. While the medieval scribe typically let his ink dry in leisurely fashion, from the sixteenth century sand was often dusted on wet writings to dry them. (This immediately gave the effect of coagulating the ink and prevented its running; also, by thus increasing the surface area of the ink that was exposed to the air, it facilitated the drying.) Traces of writing sand (or a speckled appearance where it was lodged before sloughing off) are occasionally seen in old documents. However, by the mid-nineteenth century blotting paper (known from 1465 but not much used until about 1800) had effectively supplanted sand, and the machine manufacture of blotting paper (begun, in America, in 1856) caused its use to soar. Blotters, however, eventually succumbed—like inkwells and certain other accoutrements—to the ballpoints.

Additional implements and materials could easily be mentioned, including bill spindles (upon which receipts and the like were spiked, thus punching a hole in the paper), various embossing devices (such as notary seals and check writers [again see figure 3.9]), rubber stamps (including signature stamps), scissors, and many others.

All the elements that have gone into creating a document, or that have left their mark thereon, should be carefully examined with a view toward discovering any anomalies, anachronisms, or other revealing evidence. Even a microscopic clue can sometimes reveal unmistakably the imitative handiwork of an interloper.

SCIENTIFIC ANALYSES

Properly carried out and correctly assessed, scientific evidence can be conclusive in many forgery cases. Why the caveats? Is not science, by its very nature, characterized by objectivity and precision? Ideally, that is so, but in cases of forgery, the perpetrator has often taken means to subvert scientific testing. Consider, for example, the notorious art forger, Han van Meegeren.

Called "the forger supreme," van Meegeren produced paintings in the style of the Dutch old master, Jan Vermeer (1632–75). Van Meegeren, spurned by the art critics of his day and contemptuous of what he perceived as their unfounded arrogance, embarked on a course of revenge. Exactly why he chose Vermeer as his subject is uncertain, but he learned that art experts theorized Vermeer had once produced pictures with religious subject matter, which had become lost. Van Meegeren decided to "discover" such a painting, along with some more typical genre paintings.

To circumvent the experts van Meegeren conducted extensive research and experimentation so he could give the experts just what they were looking for. They would expect genuinely old canvas and stretcher bars, so van Meegeren chose old, but relatively worthless, paintings of Vermeer's time and removed the paint. The experts might test the pigments to see if they were the natural ones—including genuine ultramarine—that Vermeer had used, so van Meegeren obtained and hand ground his colors. They might even analyze a stray bristle caught in the paint, so he collected badger hair shaving brushes and used the hair to make his own brushes.

The experts would also expect old, hardened paint and the craquelure of age, so van Meegeren substituted less fatty oils, thinned his paint with quick-drying solvents (formaldehyde and phenol) and developed a special technique for producing not the modern cracks of mere baking but a credible "age-crackle." He simulated the grime of centuries by applying india ink over the cracked surface, then removing the varnish layer, so that a small amount of the ink penetrated into the cracks of the underlying paint. Finally realizing that a valuable seventeenth-century canvas would have been unlikely to have been spared restoration, van Meegeren tore the canvas of his large, masterful "Christ at Emmaus," then repaired it with more modern materials.[73]

Van Meegeren enjoyed the newfound wealth that came from producing an occasional "Vermeer" or "Frans Hals" or other "old master." But with the end of World War II, one of his paintings having ended up in the collection of Nazi Air Marshal Hermann Goring, van Meegeren found himself confessing his forgery to avoid a charge of collaborating with the enemy. To prove to skeptical art experts that he had indeed forged the paintings, he produced another "Vermeer," *Young Christ Teaching in the Temple*, from his jail cell!

Belatedly, the experts re-examined the paintings—this time much more extensively. Additional microscopic and microchemical tests were carried out, together with radiographic, spectroscopic, and other analyses. These revealed tell-tale traces of formaldehyde and phenol, the residues of black ink, and even the presence of cobalt blue, a pigment not used before 1802. Van Meegeren received a relatively light sentence but soon died of a heart attack.[74] Yet his legacy remains: a lesson for today's histori-

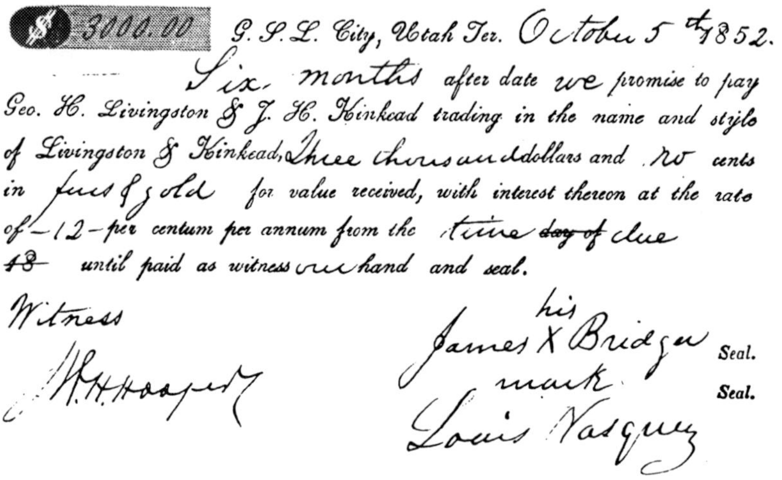
$3000.00 G. S. L. City, Utah Ter. October 5th 1852.
Six months after date we promise to pay Geo. H. Livingston & J. H. Kinkead trading in the name and style of Livingston & Kinkead, Three thousand dollars and no cents in fine gold for value received, with interest thereon at the rate of 12 per centum per annum from the time ~~day of~~ due ~~18~~ until paid as witness our hand and seal.

Witness
W. H. Hooper

his
James X Bridger Seal.
mark Seal.
Louis Vasquez

Figure 4.10. Forger Mark Hofmann created all types of fake American documents—including this bogus promissory note supposedly "signed" by famed mountain man Jim Bridger—before turning to bombing murders in an attempt to conceal his crimes. (The document is courtesy of Steven Barnett, who donated it to the author's collection.)

cal sleuths on the value of a complete examination of a questioned work and a weighing of all the evidence relating to it.

In the realm of manuscript forgery, Mark William Hofmann followed the example of van Meegeren. He built on his own background as a document dealer. He did historical research, obtained antique paper, made ink from old recipes, cut quill pens, took a course in calligraphy and practiced early penmanship, and conducted experiments in artificially "aging" ink—even applying suction from a vacuum cleaner to the back of a sheet (supported by screen wire) to draw a chemical oxidant deep into the paper and thus simulate the effects of time.

Hofmann's excellent reputation and the superb quality of his fakes enabled him to elude exposure by experts as he created hundreds of sensational manuscripts: rare printed documents and currency; letters and other autographic material from such figures as Daniel Boone, Betsy Ross, Charles Dickens, Mark Twain; and other productions. (See figure 4.10.)

A book on Hofmann's crimes made much of the fact that a certain manuscript expert, one of many who had been deceived by Hofmann, "was not a trained forensic document examiner."[75] Yet the FBI laboratory had been equally unable to uncover evidence that the "white salamander letter"

Figure 4.11. The questioned document examiner has at his or her disposal many modern techniques, such as electronic static detection analysis (used to detect very slight impressions in paper) illustrated here. The author is assisting noted forensic examiner Maureen Casey Owens in applying the technique to the alleged Jack the Ripper diary at Owens's Chicago laboratory.

was a forgery. Eventually that letter and other Hofmann forgeries were examined by forensic experts who had been extensively assisted by manuscript experts—an effective combination that resulted in detection of the forgeries. Based on their often suspicious provenance, their incredible rarity, and the sensational content of some papers, they came in for deserved scrutiny.

As a result, flaws were detected in printed documents, letter paper was discovered to have actually been purloined from old books, the ink and paper showed signs of artificial aging, linguistic analysis indicated the text of one letter was authored by someone other than its putative author, and so on. Even earlier, of course, circumstantial evidence had begun to point toward Hofmann, and a search warrant had uncovered incriminating evidence in his possession. (Hofmann eventually confessed and provided additional details of his work.)[76]

The effective combination of manuscript specialists and forensic experts recalls a passage from Mary Benjamin's *Autographs* (1986). As she wisely wrote:

To differentiate the natural handwriting of an individual from that of another is not too difficult a task for the adept, but to detect forgeries is a very different matter, requiring greater alertness, patience, study and skill. The professional expert, for instance, has at his disposal fairly well perfected, modern and scientific devices, such as measuring instruments, light rays and chemical tests with which he can make a thorough analysis of all materials. The dealer-expert, on the other hand, is equipped with the complementary advantage of long experience. In addition to a subconscious guiding instinct, he draws on a heterogeneous fund of information. Generally he possesses such a photographic memory that without ever seeing the signature he can recognize at a glance the handwriting of hundreds of famous men and women. He is, moreover, familiar with those personal affectations which led them to select a particular type, color and size of paper, a particular kind of ink or a thick or thin pen. He knows certain eccentricities which distinguish an individual's script—the size of strokes, how letters are looped, how "t's" are crossed and "r's" formed, how words are spaced and many other revelatory features. This is a special knowledge gained by years of handling thousands of miscellaneous letters, which even the professional expert does not have. That each one can happily supplement the work of the other is obvious, and on many occasions they have pooled their resources.[77] (See figure 4.11.)

That is as it should be, a concept we should keep well in mind in the chapters that follow.

5
Macroscopic and Microscopic Study

A careful study of any questioned document begins with a thorough examination of its elements, conducted in good light. Sometimes this is but a preliminary to a further examination of the document, including a detailed study of the handwriting or sophisticated scientific analyses of the paper, ink, and other components. However, quite often the visual inspection alone is sufficient to reveal that a document is not genuine. Such inspection may consist either of *macroscopy*, the scrutiny of things visible to the naked eye (or with an ordinary magnifying glass)[1] or *microscopy*, investigation by means of the microscope.

MACROSCOPY

Macroscopic examination, or ordinary visual inspection, may be conducted by reflected light, oblique light, and transmitted light.

Reflected light

The usual viewing of a document, in which light falls normally on the viewing surface, is known as reflected-light examination. In some cases, a mere glance at a document reveals that it is spurious. For example, even from across the counter of a shop that dealt in antiquarian books, it was possible to identify as a fake a Daniel Boone document that the bookseller sought to authenticate. Although a closer inspection was needed to reveal that it was a mere photocopy—"antiqued" by what were probably tea stains —even at a distance one could see that the ink was positively black—unlike the rusty brown color of the oxidized iron-gall ink of genuine Boone writings.

Although positive identification of ink depends on chemical or instrumental tests (discussed in later chapters), some inks do have a charac-

        Detecting Forgery

teristic appearance that may provide a clue to the experienced examiner. For instance, the most common ink of pre–twentieth-century writings is iron-gallotannate ink, the properties, of which are well known. Over time the once black writing fluid will have oxidized to a brown or reddish-brown color. (A staff member in a Kentucky county court clerk's office was once overheard telling a patron, with hilarious inaccuracy, "They used brown ink for writing back then.") Iron-gall ink is also highly corrosive and has sometimes burned through the page it was written on, leaving browned spots or even holes, or possibly offsetting onto paper in contact with it (as by a document being folded on itself) so as to leave faint, brown mirror-imaged traces of the writings, resulting from cellulose degradation.

The "blue-black" type of ink may also yield a characteristic appearance over time, with the writing having a distinctively spotty appearance, rather as if the writing were alternately penned in a brown and a blue ink. The brown is the color of the oxidized iron and the blue the indigo showing in places where the ink is both thin and faded.

Still another ink that may have a distinctive appearance is nigrosine ink, which can show "a peculiar metallic luster and also a distinct secondary color when observed at a certain angle of light."[2] This ink, an aniline type, was first produced commercially in 1867, and so nigrosine-ink writing dated before that time "is either fraudulent or incorrectly dated."[3]

India ink, sometimes used by forgers to simulate printed matter or to make alterations in it, may be distinguished by its sheen. Its shiny surface stands in contrast to the matte finish exhibited by most printing inks.[4]

A fuzzy appearance of any ink writing, whatever its chemical composition, should be noted. As Mary Benjamin observes:

When paper, acting in a manner somewhat similar to that of a blotter, unduly absorbs ink, there is cause for suspicion. A good grade of freshly manufactured paper, of any period, is rarely soggy. Ink used on it leaves a fine, clean impression. This same paper in aging, however, and especially if subjected to dampness and mildew, becomes readily absorbent. Ink of a later date, when applied to it, tends to spread in being absorbed, but it will for this very reason not run. The effect differs widely in appearance from the clearly defined pen stroke made by the original signer at a time contemporary with the publication of the printed material or not too long thereafter. Forgeries may often be spotted because the fraudulent overlook these facts.[5]

This increased absorbence of old paper occurs because of a loss of the paper's sizing. It is for this reason that forgers are sometimes careful to re-size their paper, as, for example, Mark Hofmann did for his forgery of the "Anthon Transcript" (a bogus Mormon document displaying characters like those reputed to have been on the gold plates of the Book of

Mormon). Obtaining a suitable sheet of old paper, he dipped it in a solution of hot gelatin to prevent the ink from "feathering," then after writing the text he ironed the document to "age" it. Finally, he applied a solution of hydrogen peroxide to further oxidize the ink and also to remove the gelatin (except where it was protected by the ink) so that the paper would once again look like that which had lost its sizing.[6]

Another cause of ink feathering, and one that can also raise suspicions, is writing done over an erasure. The roughened surface—whether resulting from an ink-eraser knife, a rubber eraser, or even chemical "eradicators" (which on some papers can completely remove the sizing)—can cause the ink to spangle and be drawn into the paper fibers.[7]

Of course, while erasures may indicate fraudulent changes in a check or other document, they do not necessarily indicate forgery. A case in point was a land grant ostensibly signed by President Monroe but at the top showing a noticeable alteration. The original printed name had been scraped from the parchment with an ink-eraser knife and "James Monroe" penned over the roughened area. Examination, however, revealed the document and the quill-written signature to be genuine, and the date of the document—in the first days of the president's term—provided an explanation for the change: Monroe's own land-grant forms had yet to be printed, so one of his predecessor's was modified and pressed into service.[8]

Ink that has been blotted can also have a distinctive appearance. If sand was used for the purpose, traces may still be embedded in the ink, or there may be a speckled appearance where the sand sloughed off. As to the use of blotting paper, it may be evidenced by writing that is progressively dimmed at the end (since the freshest ink was more readily absorbed by the blotter than that which had had longer to dry). Blotted writing may also be slightly smudged, in a characteristic way, as well.

Blotting, or its absence, may be associated with particular authors or circumstances. For example, although there was no rule against blotting President Franklin D. Roosevelt's signature, his secretary, William D. Hassett, who stood by while Roosevelt affixed his name to official documents, often avoided the blotter and instead spread the papers about to dry. He explained that, in the case of parchment documents, the blotter would almost completely remove the ink, and in the case of government papers that were to be photographed by the National Archives, the ink went unblotted so it would photograph darker. (For the same reason, during his last ten years President Roosevelt used India ink in signing official document.)[9]

In some instances, blotters or writing pads discovered in the possession of suspected writers of anonymous letters have borne actual impressions of portions of the writing. In this way the suspects were linked to the writing, even though the penmanship may have been greatly altered.[10]

As the foregoing illustrates, the wrong ink for a period or even for an author—or a credible ink improperly used—may be detected by simple visual observation. For example, in forging holograph checks of George Washington (again see figure 3.7) Robert Spring invariably used a reddish-brown ink, quite unlike that actually employed by the first president.[11] And Joseph Cosey forged Benjamin Franklin Revolutionary War pay warrants using ordinary Waterman's brown ink without any aging improvements.[12]

Poor attention to ink was also a major reason for the downfall of the forger Alexander Howland Smith, popularly known as "Antique" Smith. Although his freehand penmanship was superb and he was "one of the most able script forgers," he blundered badly in his attempts to produce "old" inks by doctoring modern ones, as well as in other technical ways. (After he went to prison in 1893 to serve a year for forging numerous letters by Robert Burns, Sir Walter Scott, and other notables, Smith readily admitted that he was the author of what he termed his "facsimiles."[13]

Paper was also a problem for Antique Smith, as it has been for others of his ilk. Although Smith chose paper that was correctly watermarked for the period in question, it was usually wrong in other respects. Moreover, he was careless in attempting to "antique" it with tea and other substances, and he made further mistakes in the way he used the paper for letters.[14]

The notion of "antiquing" paper is ancient. In his scholarly work *Forgers and Critics: Creativity and Duplicity in Western Scholarship*, Anthony Grafton states: "It would be hard to venture a guess as to the earliest practitioner of 'distressing,' as this art is called in the theater and the antique furniture business." However, Grafton suspects it was as familiar in classical times as it was in fifth-century China, where forgers altered the color of paper with drippings from thatched roofs and otherwise mistreated their fake documents to simulate the supposed effects of age. Concludes Grafton: "The effort to imagine the world that produced one's text and the effort to give it a patina of age are not something new to the Enlightenment but part of the *longue durée* of literary fraud."[15]

Some forgers go to great lengths to age their paper. According to one investigator:

Paper, parchment, and vellum can be aged artificially quite easily, and all forgers have their own special brews and techniques for doing so. A weak tea solution can render a uniform brown tint. Licorice, tobacco juice, coffee, certain leaves and nut husks, and some kinds of soil have a similar effect. These substances are applied frequently to old maps, which fakers (and some buyers) seem to associate with browned paper and other damage—such as burns, wine stains, and candle wax—as if they have been pored over during the midnight watch by ancient mariners.

In fact, many of the "antique" maps on sale are modern reproductions given a rapid aging before being placed in a truly old or artificially aged frame. A few fly spots here and there and a bit of rough treatment can soon add a hundred years to the proposed age—and several hundreds (or thousands) of dollars to the price—of a map. Cigarette ash is one popular medium for adding in five minutes the appearance of many years' worth of slowly accumulated grime.[16]

Genuine historic documents are occasionally soiled and in poor condition, but that is the exception rather than the rule, and forgers often add ridiculous elements of damage (like the bullet-riddled message for help that Custer allegedly wrote from the battlefield of the Little Big Horn) or of age (like the seashell encrustations on the "Secrete Log Boke" of Christopher Columbus). As manuscript expert the late Forest H. Sweet wrote to one would-be forger: "Your stains don't match either in the folds or against the envelope. The only clown act you didn't try was boring a worm hole or two into it."[17]

A novice forger's wrong choice of paper can serve as a warning flag to the experienced manuscript sleuth. Just as a nineteenth-century letter-sheet bearing a stationer's embossed crest (common from about 1835 to almost the end of the century) would be inappropriate for a letter from Daniel Boone, Forest Sweet noted anachronisms in the letter the novice forger had dated 1858, including "Letter paper wrong size, wrong folds & wrong texture & wrong mfg. for 1858." The envelope was "wrong even in design & adhesive for 1858," and it bore a stamp of the wrong denomination—one dating in fact, from 1883.[18] Erring somewhat in the opposite extreme, one forger produced a receipt for a slave written out by George Washington on parchment. Parchment was seldom used at the time except for certain legal and official documents; only a forger would have used it for a receipt, letter, or the like.[19]

Then there is the imitation parchment that is so often encountered in myriad reproductions of the Gettysburg Address, copies of U.S. Grant's will, and other historic documents—including various denominations of Confederate currency. None of these would have been penned on genuine parchment, let alone the antique brown, crinkly variety of parchmentized paper that is typically employed for such documents. Although they are not forgeries but facsimiles, they are sold by the millions in gift shops and historic sites, and are responsible for a good deal of mischief. Fortunately, anyone familiar with genuine documents can spot them at several paces. Almost as obvious is the brown, brittle old paper that is made of cheap wood pulp. Since such paper was not common until the second

half of the nineteenth century and in fact was never even produced commercially before 1847 (in Saxony),[20] a document on such paper that bore
the date "1793" was obviously a fake.[21]

Beyond the ink and paper, other errors that may be spotted by mere
visual examination include those made in using sealing wax. Such a blun-
der, which Mark Hofmann made with his "white salamander" letter, was
mentioned in the previous chapter. Another example was a letter of James
Madison forged by Joseph Cosey, bearing a misplaced, double wax seal
and lacking the folds needed to create the requisite address leaf.[22] Also,
Antique Smith, in fabricating pre-envelope letters of Burns, folded and
sealed them incorrectly, signaling the bogus nature of his productions to
anyone with an experienced eye.

Many other potential blunders may be revealed by a careful, thoughtful examination of a questioned document in good light. The use of oblique light and transmitted light, however, easily increases the range of
observations that may be made.

Oblique light

A valuable mode of visual examination is what is termed oblique-light
examination. Also called side-light or grazing-light examination, it is conducted with light striking the document's surface from one side at a low
angle.[23] This technique takes advantage of the shadows that are thus produced by any surface irregularities, notably erasures, indentations, embossments, and the like.[24]

Although erasures may be observed by reflected light, by transmitted light (discussed later), or by ultraviolet or infrared inspection (treated
in a later chapter), oblique lighting may easily reveal the roughening of
the surface that results from erasures. Varying degrees of magnification
should be used (including use of the stereomicroscope, discussed later)
and with light striking the paper at various angles. According to one authority: "The slightest disturbance of the surface of smooth paper even by
an ordinary rubber eraser can readily be detected by holding the sheet so
that the angle of reflection from the portion in question is exactly on a
line with the eye. The portion disturbed will look darker simply because
it will not reflect as much light as the smoother portions of the paper."
Specifically,

In order to make this surface examination of paper for the purpose of discovering
erasures, the paper to be examined should be taken to a door opening into a dark
closet or room and opening *toward* the light, or taken to the darkest portion of a
room lighted from one side, and observed at just the proper angle looking toward

the light. This method of examination sometimes will show unmistakable evidence of erasure which cannot be discovered in any other manner. This condition of a paper surface cannot be seen even by the use of the microscope under the highest power.[25]

While complete erasure of carbon ink may be beyond recovery, special techniques (such as infrared photography or chemical treatment) may help restore erased writings. Erasures of ballpoint, erasable ballpoint, and pencil writing may leave indentations that may be deciphered by visual or photographic examination with oblique illumination.[26]

This approach may be useful not only in the case of ordinary erased writings but in some instances of traced forgeries. Forgers sometimes use a pencil to trace the writing they wish to copy, then retrace the pencilings with ink and afterward erase the pencil marks. Sometimes this last step is carelessly omitted—as in the case of a "Mrs. A. Lincoln" signature on a mourning card (again see figure 3.6)[27] and the artist's signature on a fake Utrillo gouache painting—in which case the penciling may easily be spotted. Otherwise, oblique lighting may reveal the indentations. The verso of the document should also be examined in this way, since the indentations may penetrate the sheet of paper.

Similarly, "indented writing" may be discovered and deciphered. The indenting occurs when writing is done on a sheet placed over another, leaving traces on the latter that may be enhanced by oblique-light examination. Such writings, as left, say, on the topmost sheet of a pad of paper, represent an especially common document problem in police work.[28] Impressed typewriting, either on a backing sheet or on carbon paper, may similarly be discovered and deciphered.[29]

Forgers have deliberately produced indented writing by using heavy pressure to trace a signature, then using the imprints on the underneath page as guidelines for final tracing in ink. Of course it is difficult to follow such guidelines exactly, and the mismatching of the ink lines and the indentations may be detected and even photographed for evidence.[30]

The specialist in historic documents is especially likely to encounter various embossments—such as embossed seals and stationers' embossments—that need to be read and studied. For example, Mark Hofmann reproduced an embossed seal on each of several early Mormon currency notes he forged. Obtaining a copy of the genuine Seal of the Twelve Apostles, he was able to make a reproduction that he used to emboss the forged notes.[31] In other cases, one forger produced counterfeit seals on a series of forged railroad bonds,[32] and another obliterated the date on a notary seal.[33]

Figure 5.1. Oblique light (in this case, from a simple penlight) is used to enhance an embossment in a nineteenth-century letter. A stand magnifier is most convenient for such examinations.

Figure 5.2. Stationers' embossments—common to nineteenth-century letter sheets—are successfully enhanced by oblique lighting, as illustrated here.

Some forgers, rather than attempt to make a fake embossing device, say, for a corporate or notary seal, simply employ a similar seal and use it to make a weak impression in hopes that no one will detect the subterfuge. Although inspection by oblique light could uncover such forgeries, according to one authority, "actually, it seems, few persons ever bother to try to make out the design of the seal, its presence being regarded sufficient to authenticate the document."[34]

Other embossed markings that are commonly encountered in old documents are stationers' embossments. Impressed in the upper left corner of sheets of nineteenth-century stationery, these were small, embossed, crestlike designs, featuring the name or monogram of a stationer or papermaker (for example, "H & L" or "Eagle Mills") or the locale of manufacture (such as "Bath") or even an indication of the type of stationery (as in "Commercial Superfine White Laid"); some have intricate pictorial designs, with or without lettering. Popular from about 1835 until almost the end of the century, these can often be identified and approximately dated, and some may be associated with a particular author at a certain place and time. Although some notesheets are both watermarked and embossed, the latter occurrence is more common during the relevant time period. Therefore the crests may represent significant evidential value that might otherwise be overlooked.[35]

During a study of hundreds of such embossments, a technique was found that facilitated reading the sometimes weak impressions. This involved observing the design through a magnifying glass (one mounted on a stand was especially convenient) while directing illumination from a penlight at a very low angle to the paper and plying it from different directions. (See figures 5.1 and 5.2.) When the embossment was especially faint, use of this technique in a darkened room seemed to produce better results.[36]

In addition to embossments, indentations, and the like (see figures 5.3 and 5.4), the relative sheen of certain writing features may be enhanced by oblique lighting. This was inferred in the previous section of this chapter, concerning the luster of nigrosine ink and the difference in appearance of India ink and printing ink.

Writing or typewriting on a charred document may also be deciphered in this way. The sheen of the ink relative to that of the blackened paper may provide suitable contrast under side lighting (analogous to the difference between India and printing inks) so that the writing can be read and photographed. However, since charred paper is exceedingly fragile and necessitates extraordinary care in handling, such work should be undertaken only by an experienced person.[37]

Figure 5.3. Oblique lighting is the most effective technique for viewing or photographing raised or depressed areas, such as the decoratively embossed paper of this 1850s envelope.

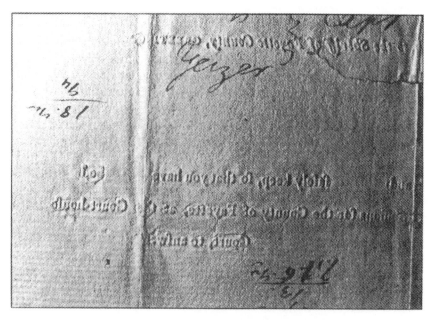

Figure 5.4. Indentations of all types—such as indented writing or, in this instance, the deep type impressions often left on the back of paper during the hand press period—are enhanced by oblique lighting.

Transmitted light

The examination of a document by transmitted light involves illuminating it from behind, as by holding it up to a window or placing it on a commercial light table so that light passes through the paper.[38] Such an examination facilitates identifying the type of paper (i.e., whether "laid" or "wove," handmade or machine made), studying any watermarks that might be present, and detecting erasures or other alterations.

Transmitted light immediately reveals whether paper has the distinctive pattern of lines (heavy, vertical wide-spaced "chain" lines together with finer, horizontal, narrowly spaced "laid" lines) that are produced by the screen of the laid paper mold. Back lighting shows these lines to be more translucent than the rest of the sheet of paper, since those areas are naturally thinner (the result of the thickness of the wire, which prevented the paper pulp from settling as heavily in those areas).[39]

The absence of such lines denotes wove paper. This was introduced about 1755, apparently at the behest of John Baskerville (1706–75), the celebrated English printer and type founder whose name designates a typeface widely used in book printing.[40]

The value of this quick identification of paper type, made by transmitted light, is illustrated by a typical case. A dealer in antiquities had acquired what appeared to be an etching by Titian (1477–1576) that was (in the jargon of printmaking) "signed in the plate."[41] Was it an original, as the dealer fervently hoped, or—as it appeared from other indications—merely a plate from an old book? Holding the small sheet of paper to the light instantly settled the matter: the paper was wove and therefore dated not from the sixteenth century but the eighteenth at the earliest. (Further examination was not made, since any more precise age determination at that point would have been academic.)

Occasionally, early handmade paper exhibits small, round translucent spots, especially near the corner of a sheet. These "accidental watermarks" were caused by drops of water falling from the papermaker's hands onto the freshly dipped layer of paper pulp (a nascent sheet of paper). These may appear in either laid or wove handmade paper.[42]

Early paper made by hand exhibits an added feature when held to the light. In laid paper, along either side of each heavy chain line is a noticeable darkening (figure 5.5). (This resulted from the chain wires being sewed to the rib-supports of the mold, thus causing the paper pulp to lie more heavily along them.) Paper with such "bar shadows" is termed "antique laid"—or "antique wove," since the early wove paper mold also had its wire covering sewed to the mold ribs. This feature continued until about the end of the eighteenth century, when it began to be eliminated.[43]

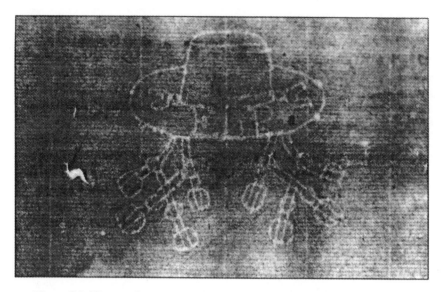

Figure 5.5. Watermarks in paper are known from 1282 and have considerable evidentiary value for the historical document examiner. Transmitted light (backlighting) not only reveals watermarks but other identifying features, in this case the pattern of fine wire lines that identifies this as "laid" paper and a striped appearance due to darkening along the chain lines (the heavier, vertical lines) that is characteristic of "antique laid" paper.

The later handmade paper that lacks the bar shadows is said to be of the "modern" pattern, and it is not so readily distinguishable from the still later machine-made paper. While the latter variety (produced on a continuous screen-wire belt) is necessarily of the wove variety, after the first practical paper machine began operating in England (being in full commercial use at the beginning of 1812), there came a means of impressing the paper with a pseudo-laid pattern (and/or a watermark). This was accomplished by a "dandy roll," a cylinder affixed to the paper machine. It was patented in 1825, and continues in use today.[44]

Therefore, it is necessary to be able to distinguish handmade wove or laid paper of the modern pattern from machine-made wove or "laid" (actually pseudo-laid) paper. Occasionally, this is easily done since the early machine wove paper may have a row of stitch marks running across it, caused by the seam in the machine's wire-screen belt being impressed into the continuous web of paper at every complete revolution.[45] But since this feature appears relatively infrequently in old documents, a better means is needed of differentiating between hand- and machine-made papers, and this is accomplished with the microscope (discussed later).

In addition to the features already mentioned, watermarks are also revealed by transmitted-light examination. (Again see figure 5.5.) The genuine early watermarks—known from as early as 1282 and lasting until the advent of the paper machine—were fashioned from wire and sewn to the screen cover of the paper mold. Therefore, like the lines of laid paper, these wires leave thin spots in the paper and show up as bright lines when the sheet is held to the light. The later watermarks produced by the paper machine's dandy roll are not true watermarks in the strict sense, yet the term is still used.[46] (Machine-made watermarks, like the paper in which they appear, are identified by microscopic observation, as discussed later.)

Obviously, watermarks have considerable potential for dating paper. Some actually provide dates, while others can be identified with specific historic periods. For example the "post horn" was common during the fourteenth to sixteenth centuries and the "fool's cap" (i.e., profile of a jester), although known from 1479, was especially popular during the sixteenth and seventeenth centuries. A "cardinal's hat" was in use for a relatively limited period from about 1649–52.[47]

Changes in watermarks can provide a means of dating a document. For example, some of the molds of Joshua Gilpin (a Quaker merchant who established a paper mill on Brandywine Creek, a few miles north of Wilmington, Delaware, in 1787) were watermarked "JG & Co"; however, after 1800 Joshua's initials were replaced by those his younger brother, Thomas.[48] As another example, in 1976 Trojan Bond paper underwent a subtle change in its watermark that provided significant date evidence, and even flaws in a particular watermark have been used to date documents or to prove their dates fraudulent.[49]

A number of standard guides are available to help identify and date watermarks. These include Briquet's *Les filigrantes*, which covers European marks from 1282 to 1600;[50] W.A. Churchill's *Watermarks in Paper in Holland, England, France, etc. in the XVII and XVIII Centuries;*[51] and Heawood's *Watermarks, mainly of the 17th and 18th Centuries.*[52] For American watermarks, the standard treatise is Gravell and Miller's *A Catalog of American Watermarks, 1690–1835,*[53] together with their supplementary volume on foreign watermarks found in historical American documents.[54] Modern watermarks are also cataloged according to manufacturer.[55]

Unlike the line drawings and tracings of most compendiums, which lack the precision needed to make precise identifications of particular marks, and in contrast to the technique of beta-radiography, which made excellent reproductions but was laborious, expensive, and generally inaccessible, Gravell and Miller employed an improved technique. Developed

Figure 5.6. Antique newspapers—like this one, purportedly the *Ulster County Gazette*, dated January 4, 1800, and relating the death of George Washington— often prove to be reproductions. In this case the absence of a double fleur-de-lis watermark was a fatal flaw.

by Gravell in 1970, it utilizes a photosensitive paper—Du Pont's DYLUX 503—and transmitted light to make a contact-print image of a watermark. (A sheet of DYLUX 503 is placed on top of the watermarked paper; exposed to a high-output Diazo fluorescent lamp for one to five minutes; and then exposed briefly to ultraviolet light, which causes the unexposed portions of its special coating to turn bright blue. Finally the blueprintlike result is photographed with a red filter and printed on high-contrast paper.) The process reproduces even minor flaws in the watermark (or other features revealed by transmitted light), thus providing an accurate means of recording and examining them.[56]

As valuable as watermarks are, however, a cautionary note should be sounded. Many have been used for long periods, thus lessening their effectiveness in dating a sheet of paper. As well, some hand papermakers purchased and used old molds that had been discontinued by others, and some even engaged in deliberate deception. For example, one American papermaker is known to have ordered a mold with a British watermark and a date of two years previous, apparently to give his new paper the appearance of seasoned, imported stock.[57]

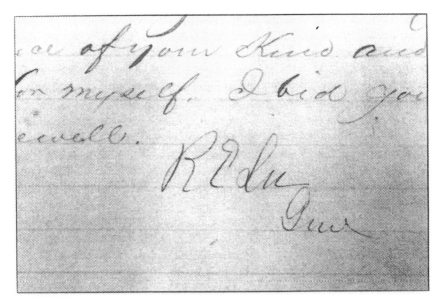

Figure 5.7. This signature of Robert E. Lee appears genuine, as does the entire document (written in a clerk's hand). Unfortunately, it is a halftone printed reproduction of the document, a copy of General Order No. 9, relating to the surrender of the Confederate Army. Magnification reveals the mechanical screenlike pattern of dots that is characteristic of the halftone process.

Even so, watermarks often provide valuable clues (figure 5.6). Many forgers give no thought to watermarks, while others may be unable to obtain the correct paper and thus may be forced to hope their purchasers are ignorant of watermarks' potential evidence. Considering even the most negative view of their potential, Mary Benjamin states: "Nevertheless, if a forger is careless to the point of using a water-marked paper that came into being long after the alleged writer's death and it is so dated, it is not necessary to explore further to establish the fraud."[58]

Neither was further investigation necessary in what we may call "the case of the vanishing watermark." A young speculator had purchased an apparently old and valuable document, discovered folded in an antique volume from an estate sale. At first glance it appeared valuable indeed, a clerical copy of General Order No. 9, relating to the surrender of the Con-federacy and signed by Robert E. Lee (figure 5.7). On "Lincoln blue" paper, it bore a large watermark that invited closer inspection. However, when held to the light, the expected translucent design was nowhere to be seen. A quick check with a loupe revealed that the document was a very detailed photographic reproduction (made by the halftone process, with a very fine halftone screen). Even the back of the document had been printed! Its appearance on a list of commonly encountered facsimiles indicated that the deceptive copies had been around for some time.[59]

Finally, something should be said about false watermarks. Forgers and counterfeiters have devised various means to produce them, including rubber-stamping them with various preparations (such as Canada balsam thinned with turpentine) so as to render the paper translucent. Another method is to place a sheet of paper over a wet sheet smoothed onto a piece of glass and then tracing firmly over the design with a suitable implement (such as a ballpoint), thus using pressure to create the desired thin spots in the paper, imitating the impressing technique of the dandy roll in machine papermaking.[60]

More successfully faked watermarks were those produced by counterfeiters of forged Treasury Department prescription blanks, used to prescribe legal alcohol during the Prohibition era. In 1922, posing as representatives of a nonexistent "League for the Enforcement of National Prohibition," the counterfeiters duped a Chicago paper manufacturer into printing large sheets having the "league" name watermarked across the top, followed by the desired "PROHIBITION-PROHIBITION" pattern over the rest of the sheet. With its top cut off, the sheet provided a deceptive facsimile of the genuine security-watermarked Treasury paper. Some of the counterfeit forms were actually used before T-men exposed the plot.[61]

Even more determined was the notorious British counterfeiter Charles "Old Patch" Price, whose moniker stemmed from the black eyepatch he wore as a disguise. About 1780—despite the earlier imposition of the death penalty for even copying the "Bank of England" watermark—Price actually set up his own small papermill. He thus produced credibly watermarked paper, which he printed from his own engraved plates. Although he was eventually apprehended, Price even beat the executioner by hanging himself in his prison cell.[62]

Careful examination of suspect watermarks, in comparison with genuine specimens of the targeted mark, should uncover the deception. As with most forgeries, even if the falsifier approaches perfection in one area, he or she is unlikely to succeed everywhere with the same degree of excellence.

As with watermarks, transmitted light will also reveal thin spots in the paper caused by erasures. The abrasive, gray "sand rubber" type of eraser, designed to remove ink writing (including ballpoint ink and typewriting), and the older ink-eraser knife, whose presence can be detected throughout the dip-pen era, are both likely to leave thinned areas in a document. Transmitted light (or backlighting) can sometimes show clearly the actual scrape marks produced by the eraser blade.[63]

Backlighting will also reveal the opposite effect—in which there is increased opacity rather than translucency. This can be caused by application of various types of "correction" materials, including typewriter correction tape and the correction fluid that is painted on with its bottle's self-contained brush. (The latter type of "white out" also comes in formulas especially developed for use with pen and ink or with photocopies.) The presence of such materials is so easily detected by other techniques (oblique-light examination, ultraviolet light, and microscopy) that they can scarcely go undetected. In fact, text typed or written under such areas can often be read by transmitted light or by using infrared film and filters to photograph the reverse side of the sheet.[64]

Another use of transmitted light that is invaluable to the document examiner is the ability to superimpose one signature—or even a printed document—over another. This technique is used, in the former instance, to demonstrate that one signature has been traced from another, and, in the latter instance, to demonstrate that one printed text is spurious in comparison to another.

Let us consider the signatures first. As is well established in the forensic literature, one does not sign his or her name precisely the same way twice.[65] According to one authority, "By comparing a great number of signatures of a free, skillful and rhythmic writer, there can be found some closely resembling each other, but even with an exceptional writer exact identity is extremely improbable."[66] Thus in the case of the Truman signature on one of the MJ-12 crashed-saucer documents (as discussed in the previous chapter), it was possible to demonstrate that the questioned signature precisely superimposed over a genuine Truman signature from a 1947 letter in the Manuscript Division of the Library of Congress. The signature was exact even as to an anomalous pen stroke, thus demonstrating that the genuine signature had been photocopied, then used in a cut-and-paste manner to produce a fake document. (Recall that the "original" MJ-12 papers were unavailable, having been sent anonymously in the form of a roll of photographic film.)[67] Such exact matching of signatures in the case of a later president, could, of course, indicate that they were produced by an autopen.[68]

A traced signature may not precisely superimpose over its model. However, "close similarity of a suspected signature to a possible model in design, size, proportions and position is always a suspicious circumstance, especially if the resemblance is very close and similar to a rubber-stamp impression, or there is reproduced an accidental or unusual feature in the

particular model signature selected. Under these last named conditions
the identity or close similarity may be very strong evidence of forgery."[69]
A case in point is the "lost" draft of the Gettysburg Address owned by Lincoln collector Lloyd Ostendorf (also mentioned in the previous chapter).
The text suspiciously superimposes over a genuine copy of the address
known as the Hay copy. In one place, where the Hay copy features a distinctive, anomalous act of the president's pen (a too-heavy downstroke that
prompted Lincoln to lift his pen, then sweep across the stroke to continue
writing), the Ostendorf "draft" reproduces the exact flaw at the same point
in the text![70]

Routinely, traced signature forgeries are encountered, as in the New
Bedford, Massachusetts, case of a disputed codicil to a will. The codicil
signature was of poor quality and it superimposed so perfectly over the
genuine will signature as to indicate that it was a tracing.[71] Herein is a cautionary note, however: for the hypothesis of forgery to be maintained, the
line quality of the alleged tracing must be consistent with tracing (which
typically produces a hesitating and unnatural line quality) rather than with
freely penned script.[72]

The superimposition technique has also been used to reveal forged
printed documents, notably what purported to be an original broadside
printing of the Texas Declaration of Independence. A dealer in rare books
had asked William R. Holman, an experienced rare-book librarian, to as-
sist her in comparing the broadside with an original in the Barker Texas
History Center of the University of Texas. What happened is described by
W. Thomas Taylor in his admirable book *Texfake: An Account of the Theft
and Forgery of Early Texas Printed Documents*:

They carefully compared the two documents, and all seemed fine until Holman
laid one copy on top of the other. At that moment he noticed that on the collector's
copy the type area was perceptibly smaller—2 to 4 percent, he estimated. Combined with the fact that the printing of the collector's copy was noticeably fuzzy
compared with the crisp blackness of the copy in the university's collection, this
caused Holman to conclude that the collector's copy was probably a fake. He theorized that it could have been made by photographing a genuine copy and making a
zinc printing plate from the negative—fuzzy printing is a common characteristic
of printing from zinc plates—and the difference in size was probably the result of
the camera being slightly miscalibrated, so that the negative was not a 100 percent
image of the original.[73]

As it happened, numerous copies of the forged declaration broadside
turned up over the years, along with other fake printed documents—all
displaying "anomalies in the type matter explainable only by touching-up
of a photographic negative."[74]

MICROSCOPY

There is a limit to what the naked eye can see—hence the use of various magnification devices that are useful to the document specialist. Magnification that is more powerful than necessary, however, is a hindrance rather than an assistance. Just as it is said that one cannot see the forest for the trees, one may fail to see the tree for the leaves or a leaf for its microscopic cells. In document examination, for example, if one wishes to study a pen stroke to see what type of pen produced it, one obviously does not wish to magnify the stroke to the extent that bacteria are seen; rather, one would probably want the entire width of the stroke to be visible in the viewing field, at least for the initial look.

Generally speaking, the larger the magnification, the smaller is the area that can be viewed at one time. That is why an ordinary magnifying lens (or "reading" glass) is appropriate for studying many macroscopic features of a document. The approximately two- to four-power magnification provided by such a single lens, together with its relatively large field of view, may be ideal for comparing, say, two watermarks.

For greater magnification, there are magnifiers and loupes—usually with double lenses or a single, thick lens—that are convenient for fieldwork. For example, a 10-power penlight magnifier, a Bausch & Lomb "illuminated Coddington" magnifier, features a single thick lens that is especially effective when used not like a magnifying glass but as a loupe (against the eye). It thus provides an exceptionally clear, bright image.[75]

For higher magnification in document work, microscopes are used, usually a relatively low-power stereoscopic or "stereo" microscope for direct inspection of a document and the more familiar laboratory microscope for certain specific analyses. Other types, including the comparison microscope, also have many forensic applications.

Stereoscopic microscope

This instrument is a standard one for scientific document examination. It is quite different from the type of microscope that is found, say, in a medical laboratory, by which tiny specimens on glass slides are viewed by transmitted light at rather high magnifications. Instead, the stereo microscope uses comparatively low magnification (usually 10 to 60 power, with 20 to 30 power being especially useful for document work) in direct light (either reflected or oblique) to view relatively large objects such as mineral specimens or—by transferal of the microscope's body from its usual base to one with an adjustable extension arm—large documents or paintings (figure 5.8).

Although medical-type microscopes may also have binocular eyepieces, such eyepieces in the low-power stereo microscope provide a high-

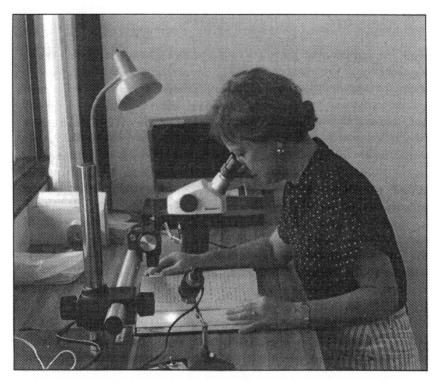

Figure 5.8. The stereomicroscope is the document examiner's basic instrument. Here Maureen Casey Owens, who for twenty-five years was the Chicago Police Department's questioned document expert, uses the binocular instrument to examine the handwriting of the purported Jack the Ripper diary.

resolution, three-dimensional image. This enables the document examiner to more accurately view such subtle, depth-related features as nib tracks (furrows in paper left by steel or other hard-nibbed pens), crossed strokes, and erasures.[76]

The stereo microscope is ideal for identifying the type of pen used to produce a given writing. Although macroscopic observation is suited to distinguishing the writing produced by a "dip" pen from that of a fountain pen (since the former tends to exhibit dark-to-light ink trails as the pen is freshly dipped, then redipped), higher magnification is needed to study the subtle features that nibs produce. These features are best observed where the ink is somewhat thin, as for instance where it has been blotted or where the pen is running out of ink.

The quill pen typically produces a line that is of uniform density across its width, although a fire-hardened (or "Dutched") quill may have dark margins like those produced by a steel pen. The quill's flexibility yields writing characterized by considerable contrast in thickness of strokes, usually hairline upstrokes and "shaded" (thickened) downstrokes. Quills wore quickly and, rather like pencils, were frequently sharpened or recut with the penknife; this means that blunt pen strokes may change abruptly to sharper ones during the course of a document.[77] (See figure 5.9.)

Metal pens produce similarly contrasting strokes, but with the heavier strokes having darker, sharper outlines. This results from the nibs separating under pressure and leaving distinct scratches—called "nib tracks"— which retain additional ink. Thus, as the ink fades over time, the tracks often show up as dark margins framing the stroke (figure 5.10). Although nigrosine ink also tends to produce dark margins, irrespective of any nib tracks, the difference should be apparent with the stereomicroscope.[78]

A distinctive type of metal pen nib is the "stub" pen, a nib with its tip clipped off (comparable to a narrow, chisel-edge calligrapher's pen). It thus leaves a distinctive, ribbon-like line, although some other steel-pen writing may often resemble it. To distinguish them, one should carefully examine the tops of rounded letters like the *e*, where the pen moves to the left. Because of the different widths of the two pens, the stub will produce a broad stroke at places where the ordinary pen will yield a thin stroke.[79] (See figure 5.11.)

The stylographic fountain pen (figure 5.12) produces a continuous ink flow like other reservoir pens (figure 5.13), but with a line of near uniform width on both upstrokes and downstrokes—rather like the ballpoint pen. The latter is readily identifiable by the distinctive line produced by the viscous ink and rotating ball application—often with a characteristic "skipping" line and/or blobbing of ink (figure 5.14).[80] Typically, there are also ink-free striations (fine, white lines in the stroke) that are caused by failure of the ink to fully cover the ball's surface. (In curved strokes it is possible to determine the directions of pen motion, since the striations run toward the outer edge of the curve in the same general direction as that in which the pen traveled. This has obvious importance to handwriting comparison since—for example—one writer may make an O in a counterclockwise direction, another in a clockwise one.[81]

The more recent "roller ball" or "floating ball" type of ballpoint uses a free-flowing ink, like that of fountain pens, thus producing "a mark that falls somewhere between the ball-point and the fountain pen."[82]

Fiber-tip or porous-tip pens—developed in Japan by Pentell in 1962 —are made of felt, nylon, or other porous material. They produce bold lines with relatively uniform width and lacking nib tracks and roller striations. They tend to leave ending strokes that have a somewhat "dry" ap-

Figures 5.9-5.14. From the ancient quill to the modern ballpoint, pens leave
evidence of their form in the lines they trace.

pearance. Since the fiber tip wears readily, "the writing stroke becomes
wider and wider until it has the appearance of a marker pen."[83]

Although extensive illustrations could represent many of the line
characteristics and potential defects of the various types of pens, perhaps
the best instruction comes from obtaining and writing with each type, then
carefully studying the results under the microscope. (Even an impover-
ished graduate student can afford one of the small "pocket" microscopes,

which can teach several lessons before being replaced by a more expensive stereo microscope. Even the latter, however, is available in a choice of good, economy models.)

Microscopic examination is also essential for detecting and studying "patching" (or retouching) of writing. Although some writers habitually retouch their letters in a characteristic manner—as, for example, by more clearly shaping the loops of tall letters,[84] such patching is usually done boldly, whereas careful patching is a defect symptomatic of much forged handwriting.[85] The distinction can be critical, as illustrated by the case of John Demjanjuk, the former Nazi death camp guard who claimed his S.S. identification card (discussed in the previous chapter) was a forgery. The signature of an S.S. commandant Karl Streibel did exhibit one retouched stroke, but it was a bold retouching and the signature everywhere was consistent with a freely written, authentic signature, as determined by the distinguished expert, Gideon Epstein. Microscopic inspection revealed that a fiber in the coarse paper had caused the pen to skip, prompting the hasty retouching stroke.[86]

Other features that are suitable for microscopic examination and that may reveal the forger's handiwork are suspicious pen lifts (those extraneous, often frequent liftings of the pen that occur when a forger seeks repeatedly to check his progress in tracing or copying a signature or other writing).[87]

Another feature suitable for microscopic study is tremor, defined as "a writing weakness portrayed by irregular, shaking strokes."[88] It may occur in genuine writing as the result of age, illness, or other debility, including illiteracy. However, as indicated in chapter 3, spurious writing is often characterized by what is termed forger's tremor—shaky handwriting that results from the slow, careful drawing or tracing of script, in contrast to handwriting that is smoothly, rapidly, and otherwise naturally executed.[89] The microscope makes even the most delicate tremor readily apparent, although interpretation of the evidence is still left to the eye and judgment of the investigator. For example, tremor in the Ostendorf "draft" of the Gettysburg Address was dismissed by some (who had apparently not studied it) on the grounds that Lincoln was ill at the time. However, in the inscription on the document's verso (the nontraced portion) the tremor was also accompanied by a tell-tale instance of incorrect pen pressure (lack of shading on a downstroke) and other clear symptoms of forgery.[90]

Stereomicroscopic examination is appropriate for many other writing features, including erasures; corrections or other alterations; sequence of pen strokes, where one crosses another (usually, in the case of fluid inks, the second line tending to spread into the first at the intersection); the

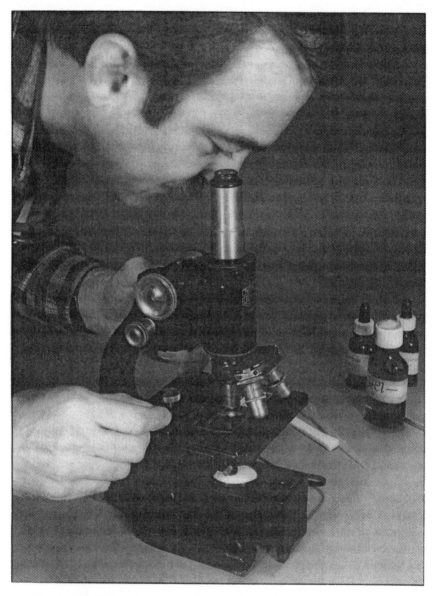

Figure 5.15. The author uses a standard laboratory microscope to conduct a microchemical test of ink.

identifying features in typewriting; and many additional elements, including recent trimming of the edge of an old sheet of paper.

Microscopic examination also provides the best means of distinguishing machine-made paper from the handmade variety. This allows the examiner to see that the lines impressed by the paper machine's dandy roll—pseudo "laid" lines or watermarks—are pressed into the upper side of the paper while the wove wire marks of the continuous wire-screen belt are visible on the lower side. Even plain wove paper produced on the old paper machine can readily be distinguished from that which was handmade. In the latter case, the screen pattern of the wove-wire paper mold is naturally a grid of tiny squares, whereas that produced on the old paper machines has a diamond-shaped grid pattern (because of distortions caused by tight stretching of the belt).[91]

Standard laboratory microscope

The standard laboratory microscope—typically with three or four objective lenses, offering a range of powers such as 40X, 100X, and 400X—is generally unsuitable for examining documents as such (figure 5.15). However, for examining minute traces removed from a document—a tiny sample of ink or paper—this instrument is ideal. For ink examination, the microscope is used in conjunction with chemical reagents (discussed in chapter 7). The requisite microchemical tests can be performed on a microscope slide (preferably a "well" slide, one having a central recess in it). The reagents are applied with a bulb pipette (eye dropper) or a hypodermic syringe, and the reaction, if any, is observed with the microscope. In this manner, extremely small amounts of material can be analyzed—an important advantage in examining potentially valuable historic documents.

Similar microchemical tests can be used with paper. A tiny sliver is excised from an edge using a scalpel. This is then placed on a microscope slide, moistened with distilled water, teased with a needle, and blotted. Again, the reagents are added and the reaction observed microscopically.

Also, using standard techniques,[92] the types of fiber (linen, wood, straw) in paper can be determined and if there are mixtures the percentage of each type can be determined. The procedure involves using special fiber-staining techniques and observing the fibers' morphological characteristics with the microscope.[93] For example, in rag paper, the twisted, ribbonlike appearance of cotton fibers is distinguished from that of linen fibers, which resemble slightly knobby tubes; in wood-pulp paper, gymnosperm cells (spruce, pine, fir) are long and narrow, in contrast to the smaller and broader cells of angiosperms (birch and poplar); and straw and other grass fibers are long, slender, and knotted at regularly spaced intervals.[94]

Other microscopes

At least two other types of microscopes are used by some document scientists. One is the comparison microscope, a specially constructed instrument that permits the simultaneous comparison of two specimens. The instrument is constructed so that it brings two separate, magnified images side by side in the same field of view. The examiner is no longer forced to shift back and forth from specimen to specimen, relying on memory for specific details.[95]

Another type of microscope that may be used in larger forensic laboratories is the polarized light microscope (PLM), which uses polarizing light filters as an aid in the identification of substances, such as pigment particles in a specimen removed from a questioned oil painting.[96]

PHOTOGRAPHY

Both macroscopic and microscopic features can be photographed. For the former, a good quality copy camera is used, one that is able to photograph details from 1-to-1 to 10-to-1 magnification and that is capable of photographing either a whole document or any portion of it.[97] This camera can be used in conjunction with flanking lamps and an ordinary copy stand that secures the camera and permits it to be moved up or down.

Photographing an embossment, impression, or other feature that is enhanced by oblique lighting may be accomplished by illuminating one of the copy stand's two flanking lamps.[98] However, in many cases (such as an entire sheet of typewriting indentations), a series of oblique-light photographs may be necessary, with the light being directed from various angles and directions. Sometimes results are improved if the light is admitted from a very narrow slit.[99]

For specialized work, one has recourse to professional photographic laboratories. According to one authority:

Although private processing firms can be used to process photographs made by the document examiner, the well-equipped laboratory has ready access to a well-equipped photolab. The totally equipped photolab with specially trained photographers can be an invaluable aid to the document examiner. These photographers have specialized training to deal with document problems and, in some cases, are more qualified than the document examiner on the most effective photographic techniques. In addition, the totally equipped photolab has the variety of camera

arrangements necessary to handle every conceivable problem the document examiner might encounter. Such problems might include the photography of a blue
ink check endorsement covered by a red ink bank stamp, photography of a typewriting defect using photomicrography techniques, contact prints of watermarks
and photography of alterations using infra-red techniques.[100]

In addition to photomacrographs (enlarged photographs made with a
lens having a short focal length), photomicrographs (photos made through
a microscope) may also be made.[101] Some 35mm cameras have special
adapters that enable them to be mounted onto a microscope,[102] while some
cameras—including a special Polaroid model—are designed to fit most
standard microscopes (whether monocular or binocular) and utilize the
microscope's own optical system.[103]

Photographs enable the examiner to properly document his observations and to utilize them appropriately either as evidence in courtroom
presentations or as illustrations in scholarly publications.

6

Spectral Techniques

———◆❖◆———

Occasionally one may notice that an article of clothing or other item has a slightly different color under fluorescent light than it does under incandescent light, or that a spot on a shirt or blouse is more noticeable in one light than another. By taking advantage of the different properties of the visible spectrum—as well as those of the invisible—the forensic document examiner greatly augments his or her ability to detect forgeries as well as to handle other document problems that may be presented.

Visible light is simply one portion of what is known as the electromagnetic spectrum (that is, the range of all known radiation). It is the portion that normally stimulates the sense of sight, which perceives the continuous range of frequencies and wavelengths as a gradation in color: from red, through orange, yellow, yellow-green, green, blue-green, and blue, to violet. Beyond this range—that is, beyond the visible red at one end and violet at the other—are invisible portions of the spectrum: respectively, infrared and ultraviolet radiation.

The properties of all of these bands of the spectrum are utilized by scientific investigators in interesting and often dramatic ways. For example, ultraviolet light is used in some cases of questioned sculptures and other artifacts to detect a false patina, as in the case of a bronze Chinese vessel; it was genuinely of the eleventh century B.C. but had been severely damaged and crudely repaired, with the repairs disguised by a false patina.[1]

Infrared photography has been similarly used to detect restoration on tapestries, for example, and to reveal designs on pottery and other artifacts that have become invisible over time.[2] Aerial infrared photography has also been used by archaeologists to detect certain land scars that are indicative of ancient village sites but that cannot be seen by the naked eye or revealed by ordinary photography.[3]

Laser technology has also been employed in many innovative, investigatory ways. As examples, forensic applications include detecting minute blood traces, matching or reconstructing fractured glass fragments, and developing latent fingerprints. For instance, at the scene of a triple slaying in Aurora, Colorado, in 1984, a portable laser picked up latent prints that had been missed with conventional fingerprint-development methods.[4]

These spectral techniques are also employed by the document examiner—often utilizing the latest computer-enhancement technology—in a variety of impressive ways: to enhance dim ink writing; to lighten the color of obliterating markings to reveal what is underneath; to decipher the text on charred documents; to restore writing that has been effaced by chemical eradicators; and to use the fluorescing properties of paper to compare different sheets. These and other techniques are described in the following discussions of ultraviolet light, infrared radiation, laser technology, and photographic processes. Like those in the preceding chapter, these also are nondestructive techniques.

ULTRAVIOLET LIGHT

An invaluable tool for the document investigator is an ultraviolet light. Simply by darkening a room and switching on the lamp, one is able to perceive certain things that are otherwise invisible, as well as to enhance certain others that may barely be perceptible by the unaided eye. As one police-science text explains: "When ultraviolet radiation strikes a surface it is absorbed by some substances and its energy transformed and radiated back in light of different colors. Thus, although the original ultraviolet is invisible, its effects on an object as observed in a dark room are distinctly visible. The object is then said to *fluoresce*. This interesting phenomenon is useful to the investigator who may in this manner detect stains on a garment, alterations on a check, or secret writing in a letter."[5]

To be useful for such work the lamp must be a special ultraviolet lamp (not merely a source with incidental ultraviolet output).[6] Such models are readily available from science supply houses and include convenient portable lights. The effects of ultraviolet radiation may be photographed (as described in the later section on photographic techniques).

One use of ultraviolet radiation is to study the paper on which a questioned document is written. The rays can reveal differences in various types of paper. For example, the sizing in one type of paper may have a reddish fluorescence, whereas another may fluoresce green. In this manner, the counterfeiting of some tickets and coupons has been detected. Certain tickets—notably parimutuels—have been specially impregnated with fluorescent substances to facilitate their identification.[7]

Old paper has relatively little fluorescence in comparison with modern bond and other papers that often contain optical brighteners. These cause the paper to emit a strong white fluorescence. The presence of such brighteners in the "Hitler diaries" was an early indicator that the diaries were not genuine, since such whitening agents were not used prior to the 1950s.[8]

Similarly, the absence of optical brighteners in the identification card of the Nazi John Demjanjuk (as well as the lack of synthetic fibers and other materials that would not appear in paper until a later date) was consistent with authenticity—according to the testimony of Dr. Antonio Cantu, the renowned U.S. Treasury document chemist who performed extensive tests on the Demjanjuk identity card.[9]

Conversely, in the case of the Ostendorf draft of the Gettysburg Address, the paper's fluorescence was highly suspicious. Although the paper was determined to be a genuine sheet of Lincoln blue paper (common from about the 1840s through the 1860s), its bright fluorescence under ultraviolet light was inappropriate, as shown by comparison with several authentic sheets from a document reference collection.[10] Since the document is obviously forged, yet the ink passed one scientific dating test, the fluorescence raises the distinct possibility that it is related to the faulty ink dating—that is, that the paper may have been treated in some way so as to artificially age the document and the fluorescence is simply a by-product of that treatment.[11]

This situation is reminiscent of the Mark Hofmann case. According to forensic expert George J. Throckmorton:

Entire Hofmann documents were found to exhibit a certain discoloration under ultraviolet light. Our questions thus became: Why had these documents been chemically treated and with what chemical(s)? Many possible answers were considered. In the end it was determined that hydrogen peroxide and ammonium hydroxide could cause the characteristics exhibited by these Hofmann documents. These two chemicals cause a rapid oxidation of the iron in iron-gall ink and also cause a slight blue-hazing effect on the paper itself. There is no reason why genuine nineteenth-century documents would legitimately be treated with these chemicals. However, such chemicals artificially age the appearance of iron-gall ink. Only those documents . . . coming from Hofmann among the over 6,000 documents examined exhibited this blue-hazing effect.[12]

Some inks fluoresce under ultraviolet illumination. For example, in February 1955 the manufacturers of Sheaffer's Ink added a fluorescent additive, RC 35, to their washable inks. Although erasure and soaking in water effaced the visible ink, because of the additive the writing could still be read under ultraviolet light. This was fortunate in the case of a will that had suffered considerable water damage. Since it had been written with Sheaffer's green fountain pen ink, which contained RC 35, decipherment of most of the original text was eventually accomplished.[13] Certain other dyestuffs used in inks and colored pencils can be differentiated to some extent by ultraviolet illumination.[14]

Faint writing done with certain inks may be enhanced by ultraviolet illumination—even though the inks do not themselves fluoresce. In the case of faded iron-gall ink or weak carbon ink, for example, the light makes them appear black by causing the background (paper) to fluoresce slightly. The rejuvenation can sometimes be dramatic.[15] (See figures 6.1 and 6.2.)

Just as the art expert employs the ultraviolet light to detect newly painted areas of a canvas,[16] the document specialist uses the special illumination to detect various erasures and corrections. As E. Patrick McGuire writes in his book *The Forgers*: "Nearly all papers exhibit a degree of fluorescence when exposed to ultraviolet light. The forger may have made a skillful alteration or addition, even tinting the background as required, which escapes detection under ordinary light radiation. However, this alteration often becomes quite visible when exposed to ultraviolet radiation."[17]

As McGuire notes, ultraviolet illumination may even reveal the original writing.[18] For example, in one case the endorsement area of a questioned bank check showed suspicious loss of background printing that was suggestive of chemical eradication. Photographing the area using ultraviolet light revealed the faint outline of another endorsement followed by a passbook number.[19] The same technique applied to a signed, typewritten note revealed that above the signature had originally been a handwritten message. It had been effaced by the eradicator and then typed over.[20] Fortunately, the ink most effectively bleached by such chemicals, and thus most likely to escape notice, is an iron-base ink, one that is also the best candidate for restoration.[21]

Another effect of old iron-gall ink writing that may be seen under ultraviolet inspection is that of the ink's age migration: a radiating outward in all directions. This occurs naturally over time, but it may also be produced by chemical treatment. However, many of the Mark Hofmann forgeries exhibited "a unidirectional running" of the ink that betrayed the process Hofmann had employed to age his creations; he had used liquid chemical oxidants to treat the forged documents and then hung them up to dry. Thus gravity caused the ink to run in a downward direction rather than to radiate in all directions as it should in a genuine document.[22]

Just as the corrosiveness of iron-gall ink can cause it to "burn" through a page, such ink sometimes leaves traces on paper that it is in con-

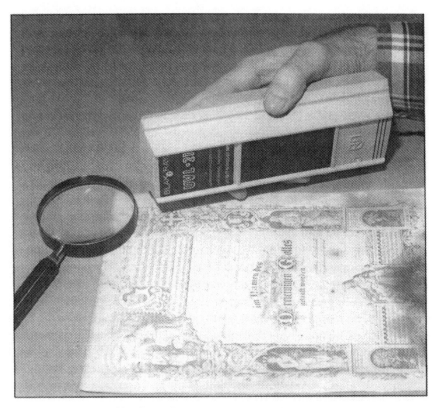

Figure 6.1. Portable ultraviolet lights (suitable for fieldwork) are available for use in enhancing dim writing, detecting alterations, and other forensic uses.

tact with, and these may be enhanced with ultraviolet radiation. The effect may be present on a document that has been folded, the acidic ink producing offsetting onto portions it is thus impressed against. The resulting traces—which are typically faint brown in appearance, if they are visible at all—are the result of degradation of the cellulose in the paper. The ultraviolet radiation causes the offset writing to appear as white-fluorescing script or "ghost writing."[23]

This is normally a sign of age in a document since such offsetting (as distinguished from that caused by wet ink when a document is folded prematurely) is expected to occur over time. "Lincoln blue" paper, like that used for the Ostendorf "draft" of the Gettysburg Address, seems especially conducive to such an offsetting effect. Although its absence is not an indication of spuriousness in documents, nevertheless it could have been expected to appear in a document that had supposedly been folded in a book

Figure 6.2. Although not always successful, the enhancement of faded ink by
ultraviolet light is often quite striking. (Photos by Robert H. van Outer.)

over a long period of time. Yet inspection of the "draft" showed no signs
of the anticipated brown traces. (Ultraviolet detection of very faint traces
was precluded by the suspicious fluorescence of the paper, mentioned
earlier.)[24]

Ultraviolet inspection may also be used for many other document
purposes. For example, the fluorescence may reveal two dissimilar glues
in the case of an envelope that has been opened and resealed. Again, in
case of a wax seal that has been transferred from a genuine to a forged
document, which may cause cracking and patching of the seal, the repair
may result in the presence of two different waxes, "which may be disclosed
by examination under ultraviolet light and the microscope."[25] Because of
its nondestructive nature, coupled with its extreme ease of use and high
potential for revealing clues in documents, the ultraviolet lamp is an essential weapon in the document examiner's arsenal.

Infrared Radiation

At the opposite end of the visible spectrum from ultraviolet radiation, lying between visible light and radio waves, is that portion of the electromagnetic spectrum comprising infrared rays. Whereas ultraviolet rays have wavelengths shorter than those of visible light, infrared wavelengths are longer than visible light rays and so are not detected by the eye. Also called heat or thermal rays, they do provide the sensation of warmth.[26]

Infrared radiation does not offer the simplicity of use, convenience, and low economy of ultraviolet light. To be utilized for investigative purposes, infrared rays must not only be emitted by a particular source but the effects must be viewed by special optical means. The source—an infrared-emitting lamp—is easily obtained in the form of an infrared heat lamp, but it is also available in other forms, such as a solid-state infrared flashlight-style illuminator that is particularly convenient for some uses and eliminates the risk of heat damage that the common lamps offer. For observation of the effects it is necessary to use a special infrared viewing device that is capable of close-up focus. Such viewers convert infrared radiation to a green light that is visible to the eye. They are sold by scientific equipment companies, are somewhat expensive, and warrant professional advice before purchase.[27] Alternatively, the effects of infrared radiation can be photographed, but a special filter and film are required (as discussed in the later section on photographic processes). (See figure 6.3.) Despite these practical limitations, infrared illumination offers a panoply of remarkable investigative possibilities. It has application in many fields, including hydrology, geology, plant pathology, and animal studies, as well as its previously mentioned role in aerial archaeological surveying.[28]

It is also extensively used by art experts in studying paintings and detecting forgery. One important capability of infrared radiation is in revealing undersketchings in paintings. The black charcoal lines that artists typically use for their preparatory drawings on canvas, which do not show up in x-rays, are revealed by infrared radiation. They may have important information to impart in cases of questioned authenticity. According to writer Ann Waldron in *True or False? Amazing Art Forgeries*, "The sketches are valuable to the detective because each artist's sketching style is different— one artist used a network of fine hatching lines, another used outlines— and sometimes the sketch beneath the paint gives the forgery away."[29]

In one case, the mere presence of apparent undersketching—as revealed by infrared photography—cast further doubt on one "miraculous" picture: the Image of Guadalupe in Mexico City. Dating from 1531, it is the conventional artistic likeness of the Virgin Mary rendered on a peasant's

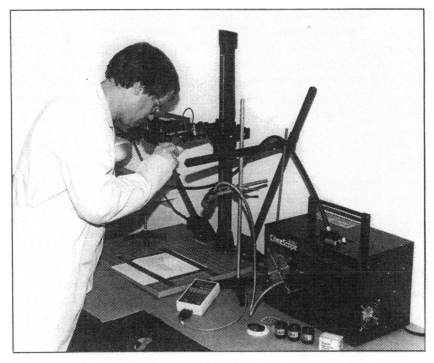

Figure 6.3. Forensic analyst John F. Fischer illustrates a crime laboratory setup for infrared photography, using a "Crimescope" infrared output (right) and a Nikon camera equipped with an infrared lens and filter.
(Photo by Bill Schulz.)

cactus-fiber cloak. Although it is obviously covered with paint, miraculists claim that certain portions are original and that underneath others remains the original *acheiropoietos* image (one that, to translate from the Greek, is "not made with hands"). This, they say, was bestowed as a sign by the Holy Virgin. Actually, infrared photographs reveal what appear to be sketch lines beneath the robe. They also show that the hands have been modified (outlined and some fingers shortened)[30]—indicative of the modifications typically made by artists in the course of creating a work.[31]

In addition to detecting undersketching in paintings and alterations in paintings and other artworks and artifacts, infrared radiation may sometimes be used for restorative work. An interesting example is provided by an antique icon, badly damaged in a fire, that was examined by forensic analyst John F. Fischer. Although the icon was said to have depicted the Virgin Mary, infrared photographs yielded a remarkable restoration of the image—a picture, actually, of Jesus.[32]

In a like manner, museum artifacts are examined with infrared radiation—often with extremely rewarding results that can readily be appreciated by the document specialist. In one case, infrared rays penetrated the patina and salt encrustations on a stone fragment to reveal a carbon-ink inscription.[33] In another, illegible stenciled markings on a Civil War canteen's fabric cover were revealed by a pair of photographic techniques:[34] infrared-reflection (in which the object is photographed in reflected infrared illumination) and infrared-emission (in which the object is caused to emit infrared radiation and so expose the film).[35] In addition, "Badly discolored, faded, or dirt-covered photographs, daguerreotypes, engravings, drawings, maps, and other such items, have been successfully photographed by infrared."[36]

Similar dramatic effects result from infrared applications in document investigation. As with damaged artworks, one important use is in restoring texts. For example, some portions of the ancient Dead Sea Scrolls—a group of Hebraic and Aramaic manuscripts discovered near the Dead Sea in the 1940s and 1950s—were so badly blackened by age that they were utterly illegible. However, infrared photography was astonishingly effective, revealing writing that in most places was virtually as clear as if it had just been written.[37]

Infrared also permits deciphering of charred documents. In one criminal case, in order to destroy incriminating evidence, a suspect threw some bonds into a fire. However, the charred remains of the papers were collected and photographed, using infrared film and the requisite filter. This process rendered the printing and writing on the bonds legible.[38] In another case, four Maryland bookies attempted to destroy the evidence of their criminal gambling activities in a furnace. However, the charred scraps were recovered by law-enforcement personnel and sent to the Document Section of the FBI Laboratory. There, infrared photography of the evidence revealed the scribbled names of racehorses and numbers that listed betting odds.[39]

Erased writings represent another class of document problems that may be solved by use of infrared rays. With erased ink or pencil, enough residue may remain so that it will appear in contrast to the paper or other background when it is subjected to infrared photography.[40] Carbon ink is difficult to erase, as is ballpoint ink and typewriting done with a standard record ribbon. However, if expunged completely—as by scraping with a knife or rubbing with an abrasive rubber eraser—decipherment may prove exceedingly difficult. Even so, indentations of ballpoint writing and impressions of typewriting may remain even when the pigment has been completely removed.[41] Of course, the mere presence of an erasure may in some cases be suspicious and even a small portion that is restored may be evidential. Illustrating these two points is a grand larceny case in which the suspect's alibi was that, at the time of the crime, he was hundreds of miles away. A hotel registration card showed the check-in time as "9:30," and morning was indicated by the printed "P.M." being struck out so as to leave "A.M." showing. However, heavy roughening of the area gave evidence that the time had been altered; also, while the only portion of the original writing that could be recovered with infrared was a groove through the "A.M.," that was sufficient to show that the original registration time had been in the afternoon, not the morning. Expert testimony thus demolished the alibi, and subsequent plea bargaining resulted in the accused pleading guilty to second-degree larceny.[42]

In certain instances a combination of oblique lighting (as discussed in the previous chapter) and infrared photography produced results in detecting and deciphering erasures. In one such case, concerning ballots in a union election, erased cross marks were revealed in several instances, demonstrating that those ballots had been altered.[43]

Among the important qualities of infrared radiation, insofar as document examination is concerned, is its ability to differentiate between certain types of ink. Upon exposure to light energy in both the visible and near-infrared portion of the spectrum, inks exhibit different qualities when observed with an infrared viewing device. Some inks absorb infrared radiation, and thus darken; others reflect the infrared rays, and consequently lighten; still others transmit the infrared, and thus disappear.[44]

Inks that are opaque to infrared (i.e., that darken and are described as infrared-absorptive) include carbon inks (such as Chinese and India inks), iron gallotannate ink, and chrome logwood ink. (The latter is made from a saturated solution of logwood extract to which a small amount of potassium chromate is added; it was first used commercially about 1848.[45])

Among the inks that are transparent to infrared (that is, that disappear and are described as infrared-transmissive) are colored inks that contain aniline dyes. (The first aniline dyestuff—Perkin's mauve—was discovered in 1856; such synthetic dyes were later used in colored inks.[46])

By this means it may be possible to distinguish between two different inks used for a document, even though the inks appear the same by ordinary observation.[47] For example, a scholarly argument over some alleged Charles Dickens notes in the flyleaf of an old dictionary raised the question of whether one or more blue inks was used. In fact, contrary to the opinion of one Dickens scholar, two inks were actually employed, one being absorptive (and thus darkening when viewed under infrared), the other transmissive (those portions that were written with it vanishing from

the page when observed with an infrared viewer). (As it happened, however, the matter had little bearing on the larger question of authenticity.
The presence of "forger's tremor," unnecessary and non-Dickensian pen
lifts, and careful retouchings—together with several other factors including a suspicious provenance—established that the notes were bogus.)[48]

In the event that writings are deliberately obliterated, infrared may
enable the obscured text to be read easily—given that it is opaque to infrared while the overlying ink is transparent to it. Just this type of infrared
decipherment was done by L. Bendikson at the Huntington Library at San
Marino, California, in 1932. Certain passages in a collection of travel volumes, dating about 1600, had been censured by a member of the Spanish
Inquisition, who had covered the offending passages with ink. Fortunately,
according to one source: "The ink used in the expurgation was transparent to infrared, whereas that employed by the author absorbed infrared.
The resulting infrared records [i.e., Bendikson's infrared photographs]
revealed the censured lines as clearly as the untouched ones."[49]

Similarly, a mystery concerning Charles Dickens was solved when
several of his letters were subjected to infrared photography. Unlike other
letters that his family had destroyed, these simply had the offending passages inked out. And since Dickens's ink was opaque to infrared while that
used by protective family members was transparent to it, Dickens scholars were able to read the obliterated portions. These contained revealing references to "Nelly," thus confirming what was long rumored: During the
last dozen years of his life, the great English novelist had kept a mistress
named Ellen Ternan, a young actress the same age as Dickens's youngest
daughter.[50]

By this same method, ancient palimpsests (manuscripts of papyrus,
parchment, or other material that have been erased and written over) may
have their original text restored. Again, however, "when two inks are involved, the ink applied last has to be entirely transparent to infrared or has
to have some transparency and more infrared reflectance than the ink covered up."[51]

The same principle is again used in revealing some suspected forgeries. For example, in the case of one questioned signature (which bore
many of the symptoms of forged handwriting), an infrared photograph
disclosed that underlying the (infrared-transparent) ink was a pencil (carbon) tracing of the signature. Proof of forgery was thus clearly established
and documented for courtroom presentation.[52]

Two further reactions of ink to infrared rays can occur when the
document is exposed to a more specific wavelength and a "long-pass" filter is used with the infrared viewer. Some inks absorb energy in this por-

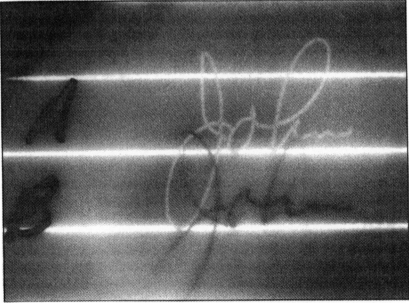

Figures 6.4 and 6.5. Two common black inks are indistinguishable by the unaided eye (above) but appear quite different when an infrared luminescence analysis is conducted (below). Photos courtesy of John Fischer.

tion of the spectrum and emit what is known as "infrared luminescence." Whether the ink luminesces or does not provides two additional reactions to those of the three already mentioned (absorptive, reflective, and trans- missive). (See figures 6.4 and 6.5.) Regarding these reactions to infrared IR, one authoritative source states: "It is recognized that, within these five broad categories, observable variances occur from one ink to another. However, these variances must be evaluated with caution, since many are functions of the storage conditions and handling of the document prior to its examination rather than of ink composition. Most notably, some inks can be induced to luminesce by moisture, the presence of transparent tape, perspiration, and so on. Because of this, IR luminescence may not be to- tally reliable as a method of categorizing inks."[53]

Nevertheless, falsified checks that are raised by using some cleverly added pen strokes to alter, say, the "5.00" and "five dollars" to read "50.00" and "fifty dollars" may be detected if the original ink and that used by the forger are of different types with regard to infrared response. So may simi- lar alterations, such as that of a postal-meter stamping that bore a re- touched, raised figure for the amount.[54]

Infrared radiation may also be used for other document purposes, including detecting and reading secret writing, reading unopened letters (when the paper is transparent to infrared and the ink opaque to it), de- tecting and differentiating stains, and performing other investigatory tasks.[55] So varied are its applications in regard to document examination that one authority terms it "the most fruitful field" among the forensic sciences, to which infrared radiation can be applied.[56]

LASER TECHNOLOGY

A more recent spectral weapon in the fight against forgery, one that is ad- ditionally an invaluable tool for investigating other document conun- drums, is truly a space-age creation. It began at the turn of the century as a science-fiction notion: a powerful light beam, capable of piercing iron. It was further envisioned by the great physicist Albert Einstein, but the first working model was not built until 1960, when it was assembled from a flash lamp and a synthetic-ruby rod. Termed the *laser*—an acronym for *light amplification by stimulated emission of radiation*—it produces what is called "coherent" light. Unlike ordinary light, which radiates in all di- rections, that from a laser is beamed so that all its waves are parallel as well as in phase with one another.[57]

Such electronic light-amplification may extend from the (invisible) ultraviolet portion of the electromagnetic spectrum, through all the colors of visible light, to the (again, invisible) infrared band. This makes the laser an extremely utilitarian instrument, existing in a variety of models and types that range from large laboratory instruments to portable models. As they become more common, they are becoming increasingly affordable, but they do still represent a potential safety hazard, requiring the user to wear special protective goggles whenever the device is in operation.

Today lasers are employed in an impressive variety of military, industrial, medical, and other technical and scientific uses. They range from mundane chores such as drilling metal, scanning product codes at supermarkets, and serving as essential components of laser printers, to such unique and dramatic functions as cleaning art masterpieces and performing delicate eye surgery.[58]

The laser is also now increasingly used in the detection of crime. The forensic sciences, which have typically lagged behind the other sciences, have—with the use of such state-of-the-art technological weapons as the laser—finally caught up with the space age. Lasers offer an impressive panoply of techniques—both in the crime lab and at the crime scene. Portable models have facilitated the latter use. By means of a "wand" and fiber-optic cable, laser light may be directed into difficult-to-reach areas. Whether in the laboratory or in the field, however, the subject area may be viewed or photographed directly, or it may be displayed on a television monitor, which permits enlarging and refining the image as well as recording it on a videocassette.

Forensic applications include the matching or reconstruction of broken glass fragments, the detection and enhancement of body fluids, the identification of various dyes and drugs, and other applications. Employed in various spectrographic techniques—such as emission spectroscopy—laser technology is also increasingly helping to identify the elemental composition of tiny specimens, such as a speck of paint.[59]

One of the most extensively used forensic applications of the laser has been in detecting latent fingerprints, an application that should be of interest to the document examiner since it is possible that a forger has literally left his mark (i.e., a thumb mark) upon his creation. So too might a passer of counterfeit currency or some other criminal—from the bookie to the confidence man—with whom documents may be associated in different ways.

Various deposits or traces upon the fingertips (natural oils, sweat, foreign substances) can leave latent traces that are nevertheless capable of being rendered legible. However, the old powder method of "dusting" for fingerprints was never very suitable for fingerprints on paper, instead working best on hard, glossy surfaces. Also, chemical development (discussed in the following chapter) might interfere with other analyses and could damage a document.[60]

The laser provides an excellent, nondestructive technique for detecting latent prints. Typically the document or other item of evidence is exposed to argon laser light, which may cause fingerprint residue to fluoresce. Sometimes the resultant visibility is sufficient for the print to be photographed as is; in any event, once a fingerprint has been located, any development powders or chemicals that may be required can be limited to a specific area.[61]

Lasers have also proved effective following conventional fingerprint-development techniques, according to E. Roland Menzel, who pioneered in the laser detection of fingerprints. Menzel demonstrated that certain materials that themselves fluoresce strongly under laser light (brown cardboard, for example) and that are therefore generally unsuitable for such examination, may nevertheless be examined effectively by laser light after the material is first treated with ninhydrin (a chemical developer discussed in chapter 7).[62] Menzel has also reported that by adding a dye laser to the usual argon laser and using the combined instrumentation together with ninhydrin treatment, fingerprints may be successfully developed on certain surfaces (such as metals) that are usually unsuitable for ninhydrin development.[63]

It is not only with fingerprints that the laser may prove more effective than usual methods. Other traces that one might anticipate discovering by ultraviolet or infrared inspection may be revealed by the laser's "coherent" light. An illustration of this was provided by a unique case involving "spirit precipitations on silk." So termed by the mediums who produce them in dark-room seances, these are small portraits—gullible attendees are told—of their very own "spirit guides." Approximately a hundred percent of the time these are fake, the pictures being transferred onto the cloth swatches from newspapers and similar sources. In a case I investigated, John F. Fischer discovered tell-tale solvent stains around the "spirit" images and photographed them by argon laser light. That technique was utilized after both ultraviolet and infrared examination failed to reveal the traces.

Such potential is offered in the field of document examination. For instance, in a fraud-theft investigation involving postal-meter impressions, the first digit of the amount had been obliterated with a date stamp (in fact had been further obscured with a black felt-tip marker). The suspect maintained that the hidden digit in each instance was a *9*, whereas a *0* or * would represent a discrepancy of nine dollars for each of the obliterations. Standard techniques were employed, including microscopic and photographic examinations, utilizing ultraviolet and infrared techniques, and chemical solvents were even resorted to in an attempt to remove the obliterating ink. When all of these methods failed, an argon laser examination was conducted on another group of similarly obliterated postal impressions from the same investigation. By means of an appropriate filter, the hidden digit was revealed as an asterisk in thirty-one of thirty-six obliterations. As a result of this scientific evidence, a suspect was convicted in the case.[64]

The laser was also effective in a case involving an altered lottery ticket. A person had submitted the ticket and claimed a prize for matching the final three digits in the winning number. However, the ticket's apparent last three digits had been very heavily circled with a ballpoint pen, so heavily as to raise suspicions that the true final digit had been deliberately obscured by the circle. When visual examination and even an ordinary laser inspection using special filter goggles proved unsuccessful, the argon laser was used in conjunction with a camera fitted with a special filter, and an infrared luminescence recording was made on high-speed infrared film. The photograph revealed the final digit (a 4) under the heavy ink circle.[65]

Laser light has also been used successfully in the detection of "ghost writing"—the often invisible offsetting of old ink writing mentioned earlier in the discussion of ultraviolet light. Using illumination from an argon laser, John F. Fischer detected such offsetting in various old documents—photographing one typical manifestation of the phenomenon in a legal document of 1842.[66]

With reference to inks, sophisticated laser technology has been utilized to discriminate between similar inks when other, conventional methods may prove unsuccessful. This involves using what is known as laser-luminescence spectroscopy, and using this technology it is possible to analyze very small amounts of ink.[67] Briefly, "the idea is to excite ink luminescence emission in situ by focusing a laser beam onto an area about the width of an ink trace (on the order of 1 by 1/2 mm) and to measure the ink luminescence spectrum using well-known spectroscopic techniques."[68] Obviously, such analyses are available only to the most sophisticated forensic laboratories—in this case, the Center for Forensic Studies at Texas Tech University. (Spectroscopy is discussed further in the following chapter.)

As these examples demonstrate, laser light is increasingly being applied to document problems hitherto confined to ultraviolet and infrared examination—often with greatly improved results. In addition, specially filtered high-intensity light is being utilized as a less expensive alternative to the laser.[69]

PHOTOGRAPHIC PROCESSES

Photography represents an important aspect of document investigation—not only to record that which is gleaned from macroscopic and microscopic observation (discussed in the previous chapter) and as an adjunct to ultraviolet, infrared, and laser examinations but as a technique in its own right. (See figure 6.6.)

Prior to photographs being taken showing any special results—such as the effects of oblique light, or ultraviolet, infrared, or laser illumination —photographs should be taken of the entire document and any important details as they appear normally. In other words, "before" photographs should be taken as well as "after," so that evidence may be properly recorded and placed in proper context. (If the document cannot suitably be copied in a single frame of film, the multiple frames must be certain to overlap, so that no detail is either lost or may be construed to be omitted.)

Either black-and-white or color photographs may be made, depending on the requirements of a given case. Black-and-white photos will suffice if the writing is only in blue or black. Except for photographing special details in order to enhance them, film offering a moderate contrast should be used rather than high-contrast film. The latter may cause very fine details—such as hairline pen strokes—to disappear, or to appear intermittently as if they were broken. (This problem should also be avoided, to the extent possible, when making photocopies.) If the document contains features in colors other than blue or black, then panchromatic film is recommended.[70]

The basic set-up described in the previous chapter may be used. Often, a sheet of optically clear glass (sold as an accessory to copy stands at photographic supply houses) is used to hold the document flat. A small ruler or special scale made for the purpose should be placed in the camera's view, both as part of the photographic record and to indicate the degree of enlargement of the resulting print. The fine markings of the scale can also help insure accurate focus of the lens (figure 6.7).

As to illumination, a standard text offers the following advice: "Illumination of the document during film exposure is a critical consideration. Good photographs can be made with natural daylight from a north window, and this lighting method has been employed by many document examiners. If artificial illumination is used, for best results the lights should be arranged so that about 60% comes from one side and 40% from the other. Either technique gives the desired slightly uneven negative, which brings out details of the ink and pencil strokes or of the typewriting as well as the paper texture."[71]

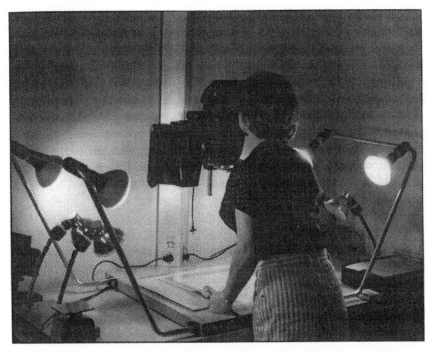

Figure 6.6. Photography is an important aspect of the document examiner's work, as Maureen Casey Owens demonstrated with the alleged diary of Jack the Ripper, photographing each page of the document—which was available only for one day—for further extended study.

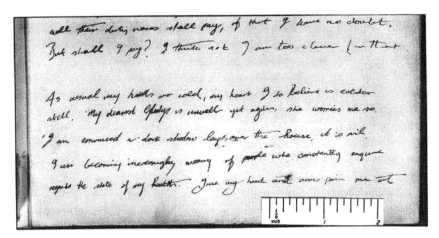

Figure 6.7. When photographing a document, the examiner places a small scale in the camera's view as part of the photographic record.

A document on white paper will reflect too much light for the light meter to give a correct reading. In such instances, one should take the reading from a standard photographic "gray card" (or from the base of the copy stand, if as is sometimes the case it has been supplied with a base of the requisite gray tone). "Bracketing" (providing a range of exposures) is added insurance. In bracketing, in addition to making exposures at the optimum aperture setting indicated by the light meter, the photographer makes one or more additional exposures that are deliberately overexposed (by adjusting the aperture accordingly, say, one major f-stop) plus one or more that are underexposed. Bracketing thus increases the likelihood of obtaining a picture—or permitting a detail thereof to be enlarged—with the desired exposure.[72]

Ultraviolet photography

As we have seen, the effects of ultraviolet light can be photographically documented. According to Elbridge W. Stein, who was a pioneer in the application of ultraviolet light to forgery and other document problems: "A valuable part of a fluorescence study of a document is making the effects permanent by means of photography. Fluorescence not only can be recorded on the photographic plate but these effects can be enlarged and put into such concrete form that anyone can see them and, when they are properly explained, understand them. An additional and highly important value of photography, as stated above, is the fact that certain details can be recorded on the photographic plate which are not actually visible to the eye even under the ultra-violet rays."[73]

Ultraviolet photography is usually accomplished with a special filter that admits only ultraviolet light. By this means, it was possible to restore the writing on a testimonial scroll. Written with a black dye-type ink, it had faded as the result of sunlight falling on the document over a long period as it hung on its owner's office wall.[74] Similarly, the faded ink on an 1876 German-American baptismal certificate was enhanced so that it could easily be read.[75] This means of photographing such a document—if necessary, using a series of overlapping, close-up exposures—will often prove to be effective to some degree.

Another type of photography involving ultraviolet radiation is ultraviolet fluorescence photography. In this method the document is illuminated with ultraviolet rays and the camera is provided with a filter that absorbs (or filters out) the ultraviolet rays. Thus, only the visible fluorescent light reaches the film.

By use of the appropriate filter, ultraviolet photography can be applied to a host of document problems as already indicated, including detecting erasures and revealing "eradicated" writing. In one case investigated by the FBI, for example, ultraviolet photography rendered legible the eradicated writing on a Tennessee automobile registration form; the fraudulent certificate had been used to sell a stolen vehicle. Another case, an early one reported by Elbridge W. Stein, concerned a will that was apparently signed in 1931; however, photography by ultraviolet rays revealed that beneath the "31" was "16," proving that the date had been altered.[76]

Infrared photography

Photography in the infrared region of the spectrum involves both a special filter (to block unwanted light rays) and a special film (sensitized to infrared radiation). An ordinary, good-quality camera is loaded in the dark with a high-speed infrared film (which, since it must be kept refrigerated, is allowed about two hours to reach room temperature, or, if it is kept in a freezer, about four to six hours). A Kodak Wratten Filter No. 87 is standard for document work (or a No. 87C if a greater infrared effect is required) and, for lighting, tungsten photoflood lamps are used in the copy-stand holders.[77]

Focus is critical. After the camera is focused without the Wratten filter, the filter is affixed over the lens and the camera is refocused. Most lenses have a red dot on the focusing scale to indicate the average recommended correction for infrared photography. (Consult Kodak's *Applied Infrared Photography* for additional information.)[78]

We have already discussed the application of infrared radiation to many specific document problems. Generally speaking, according to *Applied Infrared Photography*: "The most important application of infrared photography in copying is the deciphering of indistinct writing. The text may have been made illegible by charring; deterioration as a result of age or the accumulation of dirt; obliteration by application of ink by a censor; invisible inks; deliberate chemical bleaching; or mechanical erasure and subsequent overwriting."[79] All invite the use of infrared photography in hopes of rendering the illegible legible. In one interesting case, involving a date that had been altered by a heavy overwriting of the final digit, the infrared photograph could not penetrate the ink, so the photograph was made from the reverse side (with the negative "flopped" for printing). The photo did penetrate the paper successfully, and the obscured digit was rendered visible.[80]

Similarly, infrared photography is used in investigative work with paintings. For instance, one painting was believed to have an inscription that was overpainted by the artist. Indeed, "infrared photography provided conclusive information that proved the existence of the legend, indicated the ground upon which it was painted, and thus justified uncovering the text."[81]

Infrared photography is also an invaluable tool in the investigation of various philatelic matters. Forgeries of rare postage stamps, the addition or removal of postal cancellations, and similar deceptions may all leave evidence that can be detected and preserved by infrared photography.[82] So may altered postmarks, as in a case from the files of Elbridge W. Stein. Microscopic inspection of "JUN" in the postmark disclosed an abrasion in the area of the *U*, suggesting erasure, and also revealed that the *U* was done in pencil rather than stamping ink. Subsequently, infrared photography revealed a trace of the tip of the erased A of "JAN."[83]

Laser photography

As briefly mentioned in the earlier discussion of laser technology, laser images can be viewed on television monitors from which videocassette recordings can be made. As well, a Polaroid photograph may be taken of the image as it appears on the monitor.[84]

For infrared luminescence recording using laser light (as in the case of the altered lottery ticket mentioned earlier) successful photographs have been made by using a Kodak high-speed infrared film, with an exposure time of twenty minutes.[85] For additional information, the technical and scientific literature should be consulted.[86]

Other photographic techniques

As we saw in the preceding chapter, visible light can be deployed in various ways—reflected, transmitted, or directed obliquely—to examine documents. It can also be employed in ways that are analogous to the uses of ultraviolet, infrared, and laser techniques. Just as special films and/or filters are employed with them, so can they be utilized with ordinary light.

For instance, one can increase contrast—the tonal difference between a photograph's light and dark portions. Even without using special films or filters, this can be accomplished in ways we have already discussed: oblique light can enhance (emphasize the contrast of) indentations, and transmitted light (backlighting) can intensify watermarks and similar features. Also, special high-contrast papers are available that may be helpful in emphasizing some document details.

Another means of boosting contrast is by using high-contrast film—film with a special contrast-intensifying emulsion. For example, typewriting produced by a standard record ribbon that has been erased but not completely expunged (or, similarly, typed text erased from a carbon copy) can often be intensified photographically by means of a high-contrast film. Such a technique is termed "contrast photography."[87]

Conversely, contrast may be lessened at any stage of the photographic process. A means of selectively doing so is called "dodging" and is usually accomplished during the printing process. As the light of the enlarger projects the image from the negative onto the photographic paper to make a print, the photo technician typically passes his hand over the area to be lightened, thus briefly interrupting the flow of light. This results in that area of the paper being slightly less exposed and therefore lighter. In addition to the hand, paddles of black paper, supported on wires, have been used for dodging, as have black cards with holes in them.[88]

Instead of being done during printing, dodging may also be accomplished during camera exposure, as was done during some infrared photography of the Dead Sea Scrolls. One fragment was relatively light in one half but comparatively blackened across the other. To solve the problem a paddle was employed to withhold illumination from one of the lamps that would otherwise have irradiated the lighter portion of the fragment. Thus that area received only half the exposure of the dark portion, balancing the contrast of the two halves so that they could be printed uniformly. (In dodging during camera exposure the paddles must not encroach on the field of view or they will cause blurred streaks to appear in the photograph.)[89]

Another method of affecting contrast is by means of filters placed over the camera lens during exposure. One use is to enhance writing, as for a courtroom exhibit. For instance, if the writing in question was on a green registration form, then a green filter would be used to subtract the background color. In a black-and-white photograph the form would thus appear white rather than gray, and the writing would consequently be more legible as a result of the improved contrast.[90]

Similarly, if a medieval parchment had yellowed with age, a yellow filter might prove effective in lightening it for a photograph. Or if a document bore a yellow stain (which would tend to photograph too dark and thus possibly obscure some critical feature), a yellow filter would lessen the intensity of the stain, perhaps eliminating it entirely from the copy photograph.[91]

Another example of the use of filters subtractively is in the case of a check endorsement lightly penned in a common blue ink but overprinted with a bank's heavily red-inked rubber stamp. To filter out the unwanted imprint, the document photographer uses a red filter. Correctly done, this procedure should yield a photograph of the signature that is suitably legible for study.

Conversely, just as filter photography can be used to lighten a color, it can be used to darken one. For instance, in his *Scientific Examination of Questioned Documents*, Ordway Hilton illustrates a document having a partially erased date that had been written in red pencil. Photographic decipherment was effected by photographing the erasure through a green filter, thus intensifying the remaining faint strokes so that "July 24" could easily be read.[92]

As the foregoing illustrates, by proper choice of filters, film, illumination, and attendant factors, the document investigator can frequently triumph over those problems—frequently small in scale but as frequently large in their import—that fall within his or her province.

7
Chemical and Instrumental Tests

Thus far we have discussed only nondestructive tests. Because of the inherent value of documents—their legal or historical or collectible worth—it is usually important that they not be damaged or defaced. Horror stories about documents that have been ruined as a result of carelessness, ignorance, or lack of appreciation are all too common.

In addition to the mishandling of documents that are not properly protected, the result, say, of excessive handling by jurors,[1] amateur investigators have defaced many documents. For instance, one attempted to read erased pencil writing by the Dick Tracy approach to enhancing indentations: rubbing the document with the side of a pencil lead. He then wreaked added destruction by scrubbing away the defacing graphite coating with an eraser, further destroying the original pencil traces and rendering infrared photography useless.[2] In a similar way, papers needlessly blackened with a sootlike coating of fingerprint powder—as in the case of a robbery note written in pencil—have been effectively given the coup de grace, insofar as evidence is concerned.[3]

In light of such ruination, custodians of documents need to be mindful of the vast array of nondestructive techniques—described in the preceding chapters—that may be used in investigating documents. Also, among the panoply of sophisticated chemical and instrumental analyses that we now consider are many (such a microchemical tests of ink) that may cause little appreciable damage if carried out properly. Of course, in a case like that involving Mark Hofmann—in which outlandish fraud is coupled with serial murder—the examiner will understandably be allowed considerably more latitude, and techniques that may to some extent damage a document may be permitted.

In addition to emphasizing nondestructive techniques (or at least urging their use before more extreme measures are resorted to), it seems advisable to emphasize the types of comparatively easy-to-perform tests that are often carried out by historic document specialists and conservationists. While not neglecting to mention some of the more advanced procedures that may be available, these will naturally be treated in more detail than the more exotic—and frequently prohibitively expensive—analyses.

One shudders to think, for example, of a potentially valuable historical document being defaced by tests that only confirm, sadly, that prior to the tests it *was* valuable. Such a possibility recalls the poet Wordsworth's lament that we "murder to dissect."[4]

These concerns aside, scientific tests that are properly administered and correctly interpreted can provide powerful evidence to the investigator of forged documents and artworks—evidence that may be decisive in exposing the forger's illusory work.

CHEMICAL TESTS

A variety of chemical tests are available for analyzing paper and inks and for investigating other document problems.

Paper

Among the useful tests that may be applied to paper are "spot" tests in which reagents (special chemical reactants) are used to identify its constituents. The presence of lignin, for example, while not an "infallible indication that paper is machine-made" (as has been asserted),[5] does nevertheless indicate that the paper post-dates the advent of the paper machine (the first "useful" paper having been made from chemically processed wood fibers in 1851, well after the paper machine was in common use).[6]

To indicate the presence of lignin and other substances that commonly comprise paper, a tiny sliver should be removed from an edge and moistened with distilled water; its fibers should then be teased on a microscope slide and blotted. The addition of Herzberg's Stain as a reagent will yield the indicative color reactions: wine red indicates cotton and linen; a blue, gray, or blue-violet color indicates purified cellulose (chemically processed wood fibers or bleached straw); and yellow-green changing slowly to blue-green indicates lignified cellulose (ground wood, straw, manilla).[7]

Used with the microscope, this procedure permits estimation of the relative percentages of mixed fibers. The fiber content offers significant dating potential (discussed at some length by Grant[8]). The presence of synthetic or glass fibers, of course, is not indicated by this method, but they can be identified microscopically and can provide an indication that the paper was not manufactured until the 1950s or later.[9]

It is also possible to test a tiny sample of paper as to the type of sizing used in its manufacture. To differentiate between vegetable and animal size, iodine solution is used as a reagent, a drop being placed on the specimen. Vegetable size will turn blue, animal sizing brown.[10]

More sophisticated chemical tests can be carried out. According to an authoritative forensic source:

Paper products contain a large variety of chemical ingredients such as sizing and loading materials, fillers, whiteners, plasticizers, and waxes. Examples of such components are starch, glue, clay, calcium carbonate, titanium oxide, talc, and paraffin wax. These components can be present in a large number of different combinations and provide useful characterizing information. The results of the analysis of these components can serve to indicate similarity or dissimilarity of paper samples and can also serve to determine the earliest date of production of a paper sample, providing the paper manufacturer has been identified and has maintained accurate records of the changes in his product.[11]

(For further forensic discussion of paper, the investigator should consult more specialized sources.)[12]

Differentiating between paper samples can be important, as in demonstrating that the paper for a document is correct or incorrect for the time period in which it was allegedly produced or in determining whether a questioned page in a multipage will or contract is consistent with the other pages. Additionally, paper comparison is used in the detection of counterfeit lottery tickets, food stamps, and, of course, currency.[13]

Brown staining of a document suspected of having been aged with tea can be tested by a saturated solution of hydrated ferrous sulfate, which will cause tea stains to turn black. Of course, as discussed in chapter 5, other substances have been used to give the appearance of age, so a negative response to this test means little. Other examination and analyses should readily uncover a forgery of this type.

Ink

Spot tests of ink can also be conducted. One forensic source advises making the tests directly on the document, followed by careful washing and blotting.[14] Another suggests lifting off a "pinhead-size spot of ink" with a scalpel,[15] and still another recommends applying a drop of 5 percent acetic acid onto the tail of a letter, letting it stand briefly, then lifting it off with blotting paper, on which the tests are performed.[16] Less destructive is a technique that lifts off a tiny amount of ink onto a piece of chromatogra-

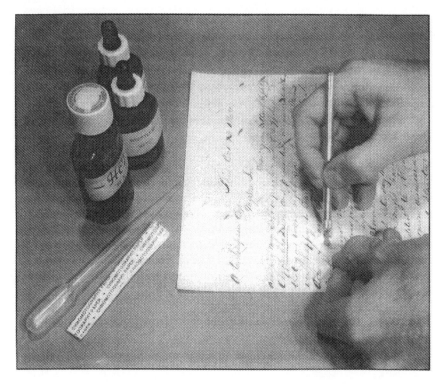

Figure 7.1. A tiny amount of ink from a document is carefully transferred to a
strip of special laboratory paper. "Spot tests" (based on the reaction to a drop
of reagent) can then be performed without harming the document.

phy paper (or laboratory filter paper or similar paper that has been tested
with reagents for neutral reaction). The paper is dampened with distilled
water and blotted to remove excess water, then placed over a heavy pen
stroke and carefully rubbed with a blunt instrument using moderate pressure.[17] (See figure 7.1.)

This technique has been used on eighteenth-century archival records
as well as on medieval book manuscripts without any noticeable defect or
damage. Although the old inks are insoluble, the rubbing procedure does
transfer a small amount of ink to the chromatography paper upon which
the reagents are then applied.

For identifying black inks (including brown-appearing inks), three
reagents are used, all of them easily obtainable chemicals. The first is a 20
percent solution of hydrochloric acid (laboratory grade, not "muriatic
acid," as hydrochloric acid is labeled for industrial use). A drop of this is
applied to the ink specimen on the chromatography paper and the reac-

tion carefully noted. An iron-gallotannate ink is bleached to a light yellow color; a blue reaction indicates an iron-gall ink to which a blue colorant such as indigo has been added. A red reaction indicates a logwood variety, either logwood ink per se, or an iron-gall ink to which logwood dye has been added. Carbon ink and nigrosine ink do not react to the hydrochloric-acid reagent. (Should the ink be partially bleached but black particulate matter remain, carbon ink was added as a provisional colorant.)

After the first reaction has been carefully noted, a drop of a second reagent is added to the same spot. This is a saturated solution of potassium ferrocyanide. The reaction, if any, of this reagent should be interpreted in light of the first one: If the first reagent bleached the specimen but the second one produced a prussian-blue color, iron-gall ink is thus indicated; if the first reaction was red and remains red, logwood ink is indicated, but if it turns blue the ink is demonstrated to be an iron-gall ink that contains logwood dye.

The third reagent is used only if the ink specimen remains black during application of the first two chemicals. This final reagent is a solution of sodium hydroxide (caustic soda), and it causes nigrosine ink to run dark violet. Carbon inks are impervious to this or any chemical reagent and thus are identified by negative evidence.[18]

Similarly, differentiation tests of the old blue inks that were used during the late dip-pen era may be conducted. Ordinary ink eradicator will bleach prussian blue ink but not two other common varieties: methylene blue (a thiazine dye) and acid blue (one of several "acid" dye colors). These two are differentiated by using a 1 percent solution of sodium hydroxide, which turns acid blue ink a brown or yellowish brown color but has little or no effect on methylene blue. Also, a 10 percent solution of ammonia bleaches acid blue ink (leaving little if any blue color), but it does not bleach methylene blue (although it causes it to run).[19] As mentioned in chapter 3, ink eradicator is sometimes used to differentiate writing ink from printing ink.[20]

The current standard forensic procedure for identifying inks is by a process called chromatography, usually thin-layer chromatography. The term *chromatography* is applied to a number of methods by which the components in some chemical mixture (such as ink) are separated by a means of extraction involving percolation through a suitable adsorbing medium. If there are differences in the solubility or adsorption between the components, then some components will lag behind others, thus effecting a separation.[21]

Thin-layer chromatography (TLC) is presently the "most useful laboratory tool for comparison of writing inks." By comparing the resulting chromatogram with reference chromatograms of standard writing inks, the analyst can distinguish different types of ink.[22]

Briefly, to conduct a TLC examination, the analyst uses the blunted point of a hypodermic needle to punch out about ten tiny plugs from the written lines and an additional number—to be used as a control sample— from a blank area of the same document. (See figures 7.1 and 7.3.) These are placed in separate vials. The ink is extracted by means of a solvent (usually ethanol-water for fountain-pen, fiber-tip, and roller-ball inks, and pyridine for ballpoint inks and for water-resistant fiber-tip and roller-ball inks). The dissolved ink is next spotted onto a silica-gel chromogram sheet, which is placed in a developing tank for thirty minutes and then allowed to dry.

The thin-layer chromatograms of the questioned ink are then compared with those of standard inks of the same type and color. This method distinguishes between inks that have different dye compositions. To distinguish between inks that have similar compositions, an alternate is run. If still further scientific data should be needed to distinguish them, the TLC plates are scanned on an instrument known as a spectrophotometer. This permits the relative dye concentrations to be more accurately determined.[23]

As well, document chemist Antonio A. Cantu of the U.S. Secret Service has developed a method of determining the relative age of an ink on paper. It is based on the principle that the longer an ink has had time to dry on a document, the slower it will react to a solvent. Therefore, solvents such as water, ethanol, methanol, and pyridine can be used to extract a very small amount of ink and a spectrophotometer used to measure the optical density at various times. This allows the analyst to obtain an extraction-versus-time curve and so determine the approximate age of ink.[24]

Minus the spectrophotometer, this same principle was used as a test of age—and therefore authenticity—in the case of Mark Hofmann's "salamander" letter and other "historic" documents. As forensic document examiner George J. Throckmorton explains:

It was discovered that a 15 percent solution of ammonium hydroxide in distilled water would eventually cause iron-gall ink to become soluble. When small portions of such a solution were placed on genuine nineteenth-century documents, very little reaction occurred—even after as much as three minutes. Application of this test to more than 200 documents ranging in age from 100 to 200 years old showed this resistance to the solvent. However, when the solvent was placed on the Hofmann documents it caused an almost immediate reaction—always within 15 seconds. Even acknowledging a wide tolerance for error in the test, it was ascertained that the Hofmann documents are significantly newer than their claimed 100 years.[25]

Figures 7.2 and 7.3.
Ink chemist Robert Kuranz demonstrates the technique for removing core samples of ink from a questioned document for testing, by thin-layer chromatography (above). Using a device similar to a hypodermic needle, Kuranz carefully samples ink from the alleged Jack the Ripper diary (right).

(As well, microscopic examination showed that when the crusted ink was scraped away with a sharply pointed instrument, the paper beneath was not stained brown as it was in the case of the genuine, early-nineteenth-century documents used for comparison.[26])

Latent marks

Certain hidden features in a document—such as erasures and fingerprints—may be rendered visible by chemical treatment. This usually involves spraying the document or exposing it to fumes. For example, in erasures of indelible pencil writing, any remaining traces of the aniline dye may be enhanced by moistening the area with a fine spray of alcohol.[27] As well, there are chemical solutions that may intensify ordinary pencil traces.[28] In one case in which a date was erased and overwritten, the chemical staining solution was applied to the back of the document and the results photographed (the negative having been "flopped" to effect the necessary reversion).[29]

A chemical solution, applied to paper with a piece of cotton, may emphasize the alterations in paper fibers that may be present in indented writing. (The solution is made with 8cc of water, 4 grains of potassium iodide, and 20cc of glycerine. If removal of the developed traces is subsequently desired, this can be done with a 1 percent solution of "hypo"—i.e., sodium hyposulfite.)[30]

Iodine fuming may also enhance indented writing, and it may reveal chemical and other erasures as well as develop latent fingerprints. This process can take place in a developing tank with the document suspended over a crucible containing iodine crystals. Heat accelerates the process. The technique does have two drawbacks: the developed traces usually fade, and the document is likely to be defaced by the process.[31]

Fingerprints on paper can also be developed by spraying with a solution of ninhydrin with ethyl alcohol (0.2 to 0.4 percent). (Commercial aerosol sprays of ninhydrin are available from forensic supply houses.) This is the standard method of developing fingerprints on paper, and it is effective even on old prints. The solution does, however, stain the document, and some ballpoint and typewriter inks can be obliterated.[32]

Ninhydrin development was the method of choice in a check robbery and forgery case investigated by the U.S. Secret Service's Special Investigations and Security Division. The robbery netted the gang a thousand Federal pension checks—ranging in value from two hundred to seven hundred dollars and totaling about a quarter of a million dollars—all stolen from the mails. Using counterfeit identification cards and forging the necessary endorsements, gang members managed to cash approximately

$100,000 worth of the stolen checks before they were caught. However, none of the accomplices would incriminate the ringleader.

Soon, though, the recovered checks were sent to the division's Identification Section, where lab technicians decided to use their special ninhydrin facility. This is an oblong glass cabinet topped with a fume hood. The recovered checks were hung on lines with spring-type clips, much like laundry on clotheslines, and sprayed with ninhydrin solution. After several hundred checks were thus processed and the myriad of developed prints identified and eliminated, finally a single thumbprint of the ringleader was developed. As it happened, he had only once handled the checks, picking them up as a bundle before they were distributed to the other members of the ring. But once was enough, and he was sentenced to fifteen years in a Federal penitentiary.[33]

Another chemical, ammonium hydrosulfate, can restore the iron of old iron-based ink—whether it is faded or even bleached with "ink eradicator." This chemical is best applied in the form of fumes, "so that it will thoroughly penetrate but not stain the paper."[34] Since the restored writing gradually fades, it should be photographed promptly.[35]

INSTRUMENTAL ANALYSES

In addition to chemical tests, an array of sophisticated scientific instruments can be employed in detecting forgeries and addressing other questions. It often seems, however, that the more sophisticated the instrumentation, the more controversial the results may become, and some questioned documents and artworks are the subject of conflicting scientific claims, as well as outright acrimony. Overall, however, most serious investigators desire to correct any problems that may attend instrumental analyses rather than disavowing or discarding the technology.

Radiocarbon dating

Because of its considerable potential in dating antiquities, the scientific technique of carbon dating is deserving of at least a brief discussion. This method compares radioactive carbon-14, which breaks down at a known rate, with the stable isotopes of carbon. By this means, ancient organic materials—wood, cloth, and other carbon-based materials—can be successfully dated. However, the accuracy is only to about a century or so; therefore the technique is only recommended for artifacts and artworks that are a few hundred years old. Also, a small amount of the material, about the size of a postage stamp, is destroyed in the process.[36]

The technique was applied to the Shroud of Turin, supposed by some religious believers to be the burial cloth of Christ but widely held by others to be a medieval forgery. Proponents tout the perceived realism of the "blood" flows and anatomical and crucifixion details, plus the image's photo-negative properties (darks and lights approximately reversed) as well as the presence of Palestinian pollens on the cloth. Skeptics, on the other hand, cite the shroud's thirteenth-century lack of provenance, a medieval bishop's report that the forger confessed, various supposed errors (including anatomical flaws and "blood" that is still red) plus an artistic technique that reproduces photo-sensitive images and suspicions about the pollen study (other scientists failing to confirm the findings).[37]

Finally, three small swatches snipped from the shroud were radiocarbon dated by laboratories at Oxford, Zurich, and the University of Arizona, using a sophisticated carbon-14 procedure known as accelerator mass spectrometry. All three labs obtained dates in very close agreement: The age span was circa 1260–1390, or about the time of the reported forger's confession (circa 1350). Although shroud proponents raised a number of objections to the technique, the accuracy was in fact underscored by correct dates that the laboratories obtained on several control samples (that is, ancient cloths of known date).[38]

Carbon dating has been used to establish the age of many artifacts, and it has been considered for the controversial "Vinland Map" (discussed later). However, citing the opinion of the map's custodian, the *New York Times* reported: "Not only would a carbon 14 test destroy a fragment of the map, he said, but the analysis probably would prove nothing. At best, it might authenticate the age of the parchment, but since a clever fraud would undoubtedly use genuine medieval parchment to make a forgery, the map would still be suspect."[39]

Trace elemental analysis

Scientific attempts to establish that two paper samples are similar, or to date the approximate time a given sheet of paper was produced, are often based on trace elemental analysis—i.e, methods for determining the precise composition of materials. Such methods include emission spectroscopy and neutron activation analysis and are used to determine the material's trace elemental composition. According to an authoritative source, "studies have verified that there is statistically little chance that any two manufacturers will produce a paper product containing the same relative concentrations."[40]

Emission spectroscopy is also often used in analyzing sculptures and other artifacts and artworks when only a tiny amount of the material can be spared. The sample is heated to the glowing point, then the resulting light is passed through the prism in a spectroscope so that its distinctive spectrum can be identified. In this manner, an "ancient bronze" was discovered to have been made of almost pure zinc, a metal that was unavailable to the Romans who supposedly had made it.[41]

Lasers are also employed in such spectroscopic analysis. A minute sample of paint is vaporized with a laser beam, then analyzed by the spectroscope so that the constituents in the sample can be analyzed. This method was used to expose a forged painting owned by the Boston Museum of Fine Arts. Allegedly from the sixteenth century, the painting, depicting an old woman, drew suspicion on stylistic grounds. As a result, pigment analysis was undertaken, the laser vaporization of the sample being directed by use of a microscope. Since only a microscopic area was thus affected, the damage was negligible—an important consideration in case the portrait proved to be genuine. As it happened, however, the resulting spectrogram showed the sample contained zinc, which was not used in pigments until about 1820. This confirmed the suspicions that the painting was a fake.[42]

Neutron activation analysis is a nuclear—as opposed to chemical or spectroscopic—method of analyzing samples for the elements that comprise them. It involves irradiating a sample with an intense stream of neutrons, causing most of the elements in the sample to become radioactive. These disintegrate with the emission of gamma rays, which can be analyzed in such a way as to permit the elements to be identified. The method, said to be 99.99 percent reliable, has been used to analyze such diverse materials as paper, wheat paste, and paints.[43]

X-ray photography

Used with paintings and other artifacts, x-ray photography provides the museum laboratory with an invaluable method of nondestructive examination. In one important case, a triptych (or tri-panel picture) that was painted and gilded in fifteenth-century Sienese style had modern hinges and machine-made nails. As well, the radiograph showed that underneath the painting and gilding was wood that was worm-eaten before those materials were applied.

Sometimes x rays reveal an entire painting lurking beneath the surface. This is possible because the different paint pigments vary in their ability to absorb x rays. In this way a painting purporting to have been produced by the great Spanish master, El Greco (1541–1614), showed that underneath was a different painting in a style incompatible with his. Investigation revealed that the "El Greco" was, in fact, a modern forgery.

A similar discovery, but with a different outcome, characterized another case. The painting was *Adoration of the Maji* by seventeenth-century artist Jacob Jordaens. When the painting was undergoing routine cleaning and restoration in the laboratory of the Louvre in Paris, it was x-rayed as part of the usual preliminary examination. The radiograph revealed that beneath the *Adoration* was another painting by Jordaens that art experts have appropriately titled *Holy Family*. Unfortunately, although the experts agree that this hidden, earlier painting is superior to the *Adoration*, the paints in the two layers have fused together, making it impossible to separate them.

Again, the status of Raphael's portrait of Pope Julius II, long thought to be a copy, was revised after x-ray photography revealed various artistic experiments and reworkings that are typical of an original creation but would not be expected in a copy. Subsequent analysis of the paint revealed that the painting medium had been walnut oil—just as had been used by Raphael himself.[44]

According to art authority John FitzMaurice Mills:

X rays can further give some idea as to the chemical composition of a picture by the difference in tone values; for example, the trained eye can pick up a light tone value in the developed plate that will indicate the presence of lead. There is no doubt that from the forger's point of view the X rays have been in many ways one of the biggest snags. There have been actual cases in which the forger has attempted to cheat the X-ray camera by inserting a thin lead sheet between the priming and the support, but this is not a very wise course, because the very fact of a blank photograph coming through raises suspicion right away. X rays can also be useful to help determine the authenticity of ceramics and furniture. Here again an X-ray photograph would show up details underneath the surface glazes, patinas, or finishes that the eye would not see.[45]

Other x-ray analyses

X rays are also employed in a technique called x-ray fluorescence spectroscopy. In this technique, an object is bombarded with a primary beam of x rays, resulting in the emission of secondary x rays—the so-called x-ray fluorescence. By comparing these secondary emissions from the unknown material with emissions from known standards, the analyst can identify and quantify the elements that are present. This has been used for such exotic purposes as analyzing the amounts of manganese and cobalt in the blue glaze on some pieces of Chinese porcelain. This revealed that during the fourteenth century only cobalt ore imported from Persia (which contained no manganese) was used, that during the fifteenth and sixteenth centuries both imported and native ore were used, and that subsequently only native cobalt was used.[46]

Figure 7.4. Walter McCrone, regarded by many as the world's leading microanalyst, discovered paint pigments on the Shroud of Turin and subsequently examined pollen specimens allegedly removed from the same linen cloth. His motto is "Think small." (Photo by Joseph Barabe, copyright McCrone Scientific Photography)

One series of x-ray-based analyses—applied to the controversial Vinland Map—have themselves become the subject of controversy. Using a nondestructive, multi-elemental technique called particle induced x-ray emission (PIXE), a group of scientists from Crocker Nuclear Laboratory challenged the earlier findings of McCrone Associates, the Chicago laboratories founded by famed microanalyst Walter C. McCrone (figure 7.4).

McCrone had conducted tests on the parchment map after it had been questioned on a number of historic and other grounds. Although the document purportedly dates from the mid-fifteenth century, supposedly as a copy of an earlier map, its provenance cannot be established earlier than 1957, when the map appeared under what the *New York Times* called "clouded circumstances."[47] The book dealer who brought it to light repeatedly refused to disclose his source. A Latin inscription on the map says that "Bjarni and Leif Eriksson as companions discovered a new land, most fertile and even bearing vines, which island they named Vinland." "Unfortunately for historians, the Viking explorers left no known charts of their own. They lacked compasses, and their rough-and-ready navigation apparently depended mainly on the positions of the stars. All the geographic descriptions provided by the classic Norse sagas are suspect, moreover. For instance, the Vikings gave Greenland its wildly euphemistic name purely to dupe potential settlers from the mainland, knowing full well that most of Greenland is a barren ice cap."[48] Indeed, the geography of the map seems suspect, a number of the details being surprisingly "modern." For example, it correctly depicts Greenland as an island, whereas other maps of the time showed it attached to Europe, and its shape has been perceived as amazingly—hence suspiciously—accurate. Some scholars also perceived "errors in Latin grammatical construction," and other problems.[49]

Enter Walter McCrone. He carefully studied the map and found that underneath its black ink outlines were lines of a yellow-brown ink, apparently used to simulate the effect of age. He also removed minute particles of the ink, which he subjected to transmission electron microscopic analysis. This disclosed, in the yellowish brown ink, traces of anatase, a pigment that had not been synthesized until the twentieth century. McCrone therefore concluded that the map was a modern forgery.[50]

In 1986, however, Thomas Cahill and his colleagues from the Crocker Nuclear Laboratory at the University of California conducted their PIXE technique on the map, making 159 elemental analyses of the parchment and ink. They concluded that the titanium, which McCrone determined was the titanium dioxide of anatase pigment, occurred only in trace amounts, consistent with authenticity. However, they ended one article they published by stating: "In conclusion, we must stress that, while our work argues strongly against the specific McCrone Associates proof that the Map is fraudulent, we do not claim therefore that the Map is authentic. Such a judgement must be based on all available evidence, cartographic and historical as well as compositional."[51]

McCrone's response was swift and pointed, and it sheds light on the technical aspects of such controversies:

PLM [polarized light microscopy] shows narrow yellow lines for the map outlines centered on top of which are remnants of a finer black line. This simulates an old map on which some organic components of the black ink vehicle soak very slowly into the parchment and darken with age (like varnish on an oil painting). But, on the Vinland Map, this yellow line is not a darkened ink vehicle component but a thin ink layer itself, the main component of which is TiO_2 in the crystalline form of anatase and in the size and shape of modern (post–1917) pigment produced by Titanium Corp. of America about 1920. The black ink contains no Ti. Every one of the 16 yellow ink samples from different areas of the map contained this specific type of TiO_2 pigment particle in percentages ranging from 3-4% to 40-45% and averaging 14-19%.

McCrone added:

Our physicist friends using only PIXE found concentrations of Ti 5000-10,000X greater than the few μ^2 analyzed by PLM [polarized light microscopy] and EMA [electron microprobe analysis] in which we find an average 14-19% Ti. This is the difference between trace analysis using PIXE and ultramicroanalysis as done by PLM and EMA. If they understood the problem and their instrument they wouldn't have to publish their erroneous results in Time Magazine. . . . Incidentally, the Turin Shroud controversy is an identical problem and STURP, with their milliprobe and 1 cm² areas, are just as misguided as those who used PIXE on the Vinland Map.[52]

Thermoluminescence testing

Another means of testing certain types of artworks and artifacts depends on a phenomenon called *thermoluminescence*. Since most mineral substances contain traces of radioactive materials—such as uranium or thorium salts—they may be induced to release this energy in the form of luminescence (visible light). Most thermoluminescent substances need to be heated to more than 640 degrees Fahrenheit before producing the desired glow and, even then, it is often quite weak. However, sensitive devices are available to detect and measure the intensity of the light. Broadly speaking, the older the mineral substance, the brighter will be the thermoluminescence.

This principle is used in dating pottery. Since the firing of clay to produce pottery causes the previously stored energy to be released, the clay must begin to rebuild its store of energy from that time. Therefore, an ancient piece of pottery will have significant thermoluminescence, while a modern forgery will not. This proved valuable in proving the dates of hundreds of Chinese ceramic figures from the Sui and T'ang dynasties (A.D. 589–907).

Conversely, thermoluminescence testing was instrumental in exposing as forgeries some "Neolithic" ceramics supposedly excavated at a site in Turkey. The site dated from the New Stone Age, and authentic painted-pottery figures and vessels had been discovered there that were dated to

5,500 B.C. Subsequent to these discoveries, which began in 1956, however, there began to appear certain pieces that raised doubts on the basis of style as well as technique. Museum scientists then conducted thermoluminescence tests that revealed that a number of the pieces were modern fakes, and in 1971 Turkish police arrested a suspect in the case, charging him with forging the bogus artifacts.[53]

Thermoluminescence testing was also instrumental in establishing as forgeries several "ancient" sculptures that turned out to be modern works by the versatile Italian genius Alceo Dossena (1878–1937). One was a terracotta figure of "Diana the Huntress" supposedly unearthed in twenty-one fragments from an ancient Etruscan site. Evidence that it was a fake came in the form of a photograph taken by Dossena in his studio, showing the statue after he had broken it and then consolidated the pieces by tying them with rope. Unfortunately, the photograph was a double exposure, causing some defenders of the work's authenticity to brand the picture a "photographic trick." Finally, in 1968 a small amount of powder was taken from the specimens (using a dental-type drill) and subjected to thermoluminesce testing. This showed the piece was only about forty years old, consistent with forgery by Dossena but nearly two millennia too recent to be Etruscan.[54]

Scanning auger microscopy

A relatively new technique to determine the age of ink was developed by Roderick J. McNeil, an analytical biochemist who is director of his own Rocky Mountain Research Laboratories in Polson, Montana. The technique grew out of McNeil's interest in the Shroud of Turin (which he reportedly believes genuine, despite the scientific tests to the contrary), and is based on the concept that "the migration of ions from the ink is directly proportional to time."[55]

McNeil's technique, "scanning auger microscopy" (SAM) measures the ion diffusion of certain inks—especially iron-gallotannate ink—in paper and parchment. This migration of ions is extremely minute, only 1/2,000 of an inch in a thousand years,[56] yet SAM is reputedly highly accurate.[57] Some consider the technique virtually infallible and point out that it succeeded in proving Hofmann's "The Oath of a Freeman" was a forgery when other analyses indicated that the ink was appropriately old.[58] McNeil himself states:

The majority of documents submitted to the author are from the American revolutionary-constitutional period, 1760–1820, and a surprising number of forgeries have been detected. Of the 122 documents submitted from this time period, twenty-six were forgeries. While these might have been detected by some other subjective technique, all of these documents had been authenticated by handwriting analysis or paper or historical analysis, or all three. One of the most surprising aspects of this work to date has been the discovery of readily available paper from the late 1600s to date. Certainly paper of the proper date is readily available to the well-informed forger, making paper dating a poor choice in document authentication.[59]

Drawbacks to the techniques are that it is "extremely costly" and that—according to document examiner George J. Throckmorton—"few laboratories in the United States have the necessary equipment, and only McNeil is considered an expert in the technique."[60] Also, that SAM is not infallible is indicated by the "draft" of the Gettysburg Address owned by Lloyd Ostendorf.

According to NcNeil's report to Ostendorf, "the body of the document showed a median age of 1869, plus or minus 10 years, based on seven samples measured in triplicate." (The inscription on the verso showed a slightly later median age, 1875, plus or minus fifteen years, probably because of sampling problems.) McNeil stated: "My overall conclusion regarding the document is that it is genuine; that is, that it was created in the time period purported by the document." He added, "Obviously, this type of testing can draw no conclusions about who created the document, only when it was created."[61] Nevertheless, Ostendorf concluded that McNeil's tests proved the document genuine, since nineteenth-century forgers lacked access to the Hay copy (not released until 1916) to which the Ostendorf document bears a most suspicious resemblance.

Actually, however, the handwriting evidence is decisive. A noted forensic document examiner, Maureen Casey Owens, who had twenty-five years' experience as an expert with the Chicago Police Crime Laboratory, stated, "The uncanny similarity in handwriting characteristics is evident not only in form and proportions, but also particularly significant in writing movement, beginnings, endings, and pen emphasis throughout the writings. Even margins and line spacings are close." She concluded: "These similarities are too striking to be coincidence and are highly suggestive of simulation."[62]

Exactly where McNeil's technique failed remains to be determined. Perhaps the faulty SAM date had something to do with the suspicious ultraviolet fluorescence of the paper (mentioned in earlier chapters); that is, possibly some artificial aging technique was employed by the forger. As McNeil later told the *Manuscript Society News* (somewhat lamely): "It is unfortunate that I had a situation before me where there was no adequate coordination of all the information. I did not have access to other information I wish I had such as that the paper fluoresced. Dr. Joe Nickell was good enough to contact me on his own about this. Overall, I stand behind my results. I am fairly confident the paper is from the right period."[63] Actually, the *paper* is from approximately the right period, but the *ink* was clearly applied in this century—probably as recently as the document's nonexistent provenance suggests.

The erroneous SAM date might also have been in part because of difficulties McNeil had in performing the tests. As he reported to Ostendorf: "Since you desired that the document not be harmed in any way, sampling for Scanning Auger Microscopy (SAM) was quite difficult due to grounding problems. The sample was rolled around a two inch diameter metal bar and rotated in sequents to locate adequate concentrations of ink for sampling." Also, he reported, "a very high angle of incidence relative to the surface had to be maintained to minimize noise and optimize grounding."[64]

This one error should not cause us to dismiss McNeil's scanning auger microscopy dating method. Unfortunately, current evidence shows he also obtained an erroneous date (1921, plus or minus 12 years) for the forged Jack the Ripper diary, one potential problem having been the diary's unsized (and thus extra absorbent) paper.[65] In contrast, a British examiner used the relatively simple ink-solubility test to determine that the ink was barely dry on the pages.[66]

Such errors were almost inevitable—even predictable. As James Gilreath of the Library of Congress' Rare Book and Special Collections Division asked in his book *The Judgment of Experts* (which is about Hofmann's "The Oath of a Freeman"): "Who can doubt that an enterprising and knowledgeable (or even lucky) forger might beat the McNeil test at some time in the future?"[67] As Gilreath told Ostendorf: "McNeil's test, like every other analysis, must be used in conjunction with the full range of information about the document, and considered with a clear and open understanding of the manuscript's provenance."[68]

Other analyses

Additional methods of scientific analysis are available, among them x-ray diffraction analysis (important in identifying crystalline materials)[69] and infrared image conversion microscopy (the use of a special microscope that electronically converts infrared light into the visible light range thus enabling the examiner to compare inks as to infrared absorbence, reflectance, and transmission).[70] Although this survey far from exhausts the scientific possibilities insofar as the scientific detection of forgery is concerned, it does encompass many of the techniques that are actually being used and suggests some of the types of discoveries that may be made. These should alert the investigator to further possibilities and perhaps inspire further research.

Already, determined forgers are seeking to circumvent the latest laboratory techniques. One Italian forger of antiquities, for example, has reportedly claimed to have "figured out a method of defeating the thermo-luminescence test."[71] Those who would attempt to thwart the forgers' endeavors must redouble their own efforts to keep—so to speak—a watch-ful eye.

Notes

INTRODUCTION

1. L.W. Yaggy and T.L. Haines, *Museum of Antiquity* (Nashville: South Western Publishing House, 1880), 237.

2. John I. Thornton and Edward F. Rhodes, "Brief History of Questioned Document Examination," *Identification News* (Jan. 1988): 7.

3. Ibid.

4. *Encyclopaedia Britannica* (hereafter *Ency. Brit.*), 1960, s.v. "forgery."

5. Quoted in ibid.

6. *Webster's New International Dictionary of the English Language*. 2d ed., s.v. "counterfeit."

7. Charles Hamilton, *Great Forgers and Famous Fakes* (New York: Crown, 1980), 6; Kenneth W. Rendell, "Great Forgers: Their Successes and Downfalls," in *Autographs and Manuscripts*, ed. Edmund Berkeley Jr. (New York: Scribner's, 1978), 92-; *Ency. Brit.*, 1960, s.v. "Chatterton, Thomas."

8. Curtis D. MacDougall, *Hoaxes* (New York: Dover, 1958), 212.

9. Ibid., 212-14.

10. Hamilton, *Great Forgers*, 44-61, 88-120.

11. Irving forgery discussed in ibid., 166-71; Charles Hamilton, *The Hitler Diaries* (Lexington: Univ. Press of Kentucky, 1991); Steven Naifeh and Gregory White Smith, *The Mormon Murders: A True Story of Greed, Forgery, Deceit, and Death* (New York: Weidenfeld and Nicolson, 1988); Shirley Harrison, *The Diary of Jack the Ripper* (New York: Hyperion, 1993); Maurice Chittenden, "Scrap Dealer Confesses He Faked Jack the Ripper Diary," *Sunday Times* (London), July 3, 1994.

12. *The Young Christ* is also known as *Jesus among the Doctors*; see Piero Bianconi, Appendix: "Fake Vermeers and the Van Meegeren 'Affair,'" *The Complete Paintings of Vermeer* (New York: Harry N. Abrams, 1967), 101.

13. MacDougall, *Hoaxes*, 87.

14. Mary Benjamin, *Autographs* (New York: Dover, 1986), 88.

15. Denis Dutton, "Art Hoaxes," in Gordon Stein, *Encyclopedia of Hoaxes* (Detroit: Gale Research, 1993), 24.

1. THE WRITTEN WORD

1. This section is adapted largely from the author's *Pen, Ink, and Evidence: A Study of Writing and Writing Materials for the Penman, Collector, and Document Detective* (Lexing-

ton: Univ. Press of Kentucky, 1990). Except as otherwise noted, information is taken from that source and/or from the following: Alexander Nesbitt, *The History and Technique of Lettering* (New York: Dover, 1957); Diana J. Rendell, "The Development of Writing," in *Autographs and Manuscripts*, ed. Berkeley; Oscar Ogg, *The 26 Letters* (New York: Crowell, 1948); Donald Jackson, *The Story of Writing* (New York: Taplinger, 1981); Joyce Irene Whalley, *The Student's Guide to Western Calligraphy* (Boulder, Colo.: Shambhala, 1984); and Edward Johnston, *Writing and Illuminating and Lettering* (1906; reprint, London: Pitman, 1979).

2. Jane Polley, ed., *Stories behind Everyday Things* (Pleasantville, N.Y.: Reader's Digest, 1980), 244.

3. Ogg, *26 Letters*, 106.

4. See n. 1 above; see also Herman Degering, *Lettering: Modes of Writing in Western Europe from Antiquity to the End of the 18th Century* (New York: Pentalic, 1965), 709.

5. The quotation is from *Twelfth Night*, 3.4.30. The letter is illustrated in Joyce Irene Whalley, *English Handwriting, 1540-1853* (London: HMSO, 1969), plate 7.

6. D. Rendell, "Development of Writing," 27.

7. Whalley, *Student's Guide*, 53.

8. Albert S. Osborn, *Questioned Documents* (1910; 2d ed. Monclair, N.J.: Patterson Smith, 1978), 167.

9. Marvin Morgan, "Handwriting Systems and Penmanship," *Identification News* (July 1985): 2; Osborn, *Questioned Documents*, 173.

10. Morgan, "Handwriting Systems," 11; see also Osborn, *Questioned Documents*, 179, 186.

11. *Compton's Encyclopedia*, 1991, s.v. "handwriting."

12. Osborn, *Questioned Documents*, 177 (photo).

13. Quoted in Ray Nash, *American Penmanship, 1800-1850* (Worcester, Mass.: American Antiquarian Society, 1969), 47.

14. Benjamin, *Autographs*, 155.

15. Osborn, *Questioned Documents*, 139, 191.

16. Ibid., 139.

17. See Lois Harting, "The Art of Fraktur," *Early American Life* (April 1977): 48-49 and front cover.

18. Osborn, *Questioned Documents*, 168-69, 178, 408; Ordway Hilton, *Scientific Examination of Questioned Documents*, rev. ed. (New York: Elsevier Science Publishing, 1982), 143.

19. James Munves, *Thomas Jefferson and the Declaration of Independence* (New York: Charles Scribner's Sons, 1978), 103; for a similar memo book, see Nickell, *Pen, Ink, and Evidence*, 163, fig. 13.40.

20. Catalog of Robert A. Siegel Auction Galleries, New York, N.Y., Nov. 19, 1992, 288 (photo).

21. See, for example, the catalog of Historical Documents International, Bedford, N.H., Mar. 19, 1994.

22. Henry Petroski, *The Pencil: A History of Design and Circumstance* (New York: Knopf, 1989), 22-23, 324.

23. Joe Nickell, "Examination of a Helen Keller Letter," prepared for the Museum of the American Printing House for the Blind, Louisville, Ky., May 1, 1994.

24. Kenneth W. Rendell, *Forging History: The Detection of Fake Letters and Documents* (Norman: Univ. of Oklahoma Press, 1994), 13, 33.

25. Osborn, *Questioned Documents*, 565.

26. Norma Levarie, *The History of Books* (New York: Da Capo Press, 1968), 69-81. See also Nickell, *Pen, Ink, and Evidence*, 127-28, 217 nn 55-57.

27. See Nickell, *Pen, Ink, and Evidence*, 166-68; *Compton's Encyclopedia*, 1991, s.v. "duplicating machine"; *Oxford English Dictionary*, 1989, s.v. "carbons," "hectograph," and "Photostat."

28. This and the following section are adapted from the author's two chapters in *The Write Stuff: Evaluations of Graphology*, ed. Barry L. Beyerstein and Dale F. Beyerstein (Buffalo: Prometheus, 1992), 23-29, 42-52.

29. Ketuboth, 2.10. See Herbert Danby, *The Mishnah, Translated from the Hebrew* (Oxford: Oxford Univ. Press, 1933), 247.

30. Seutonius, *History*, 2.87 (cited in *New Catholic Encyclopedia*, 1967, s.v. "graphology," 6:704); quoted in Huntington Hartford, *You Are What You Write* (New York: Macmillan, 1973), 43.

31. Quoted. in *Ency. Brit.*, s.v. "handwriting."

32. Ibid.; Werner Wolff, *Diagrams of the Unconscious* (New York: Grune & Stratton, 1948), 5, 357;Hartford, *You Are*, 49.

33. Margaret Gullan-Whur, *The Graphology Workbook* (Wellingborough, England: Aquarian, 1986), 11.

34. Klara G. Roman, *Encyclopedia of the Written Word* (New York: Frederick Ungar, 1968), 175.

35. *Ency. Brit.*, 1960, s.v. "handwriting."

36. Roman, *Encyclopedia of the Written Word*, 175-76.

37. Gullan-Whur, *Graphology Workbook*, 12.

38. See also Oskar Lockowandt, "On the Development of Academic Graphology in the Federal Republic of Germany after 1945," *Graphologist* 4:1 (spring 1986): 2-8.

39. Martin Gardner, *Fads and Fallacies in the Name of Science* (New York: Dover, 1957), 296-97.

40. Beyerstein and Beyerstein, *Write Stuff*, 16.

41. Adrian Furnham, "Write and Wrong: The Validity of Graphological Analysis," *Skeptical Inquirer* 13 (fall 1988): 64.

42. Hilton, *Scientific Examination*, 129-30.

43. Osborn, *Questioned Documents*, 435-48.

44. Wilson R. Harrison, *Suspect Documents: Their Scientific Examination* (New York: Frederick A. Praeger, 1958), 518-19.

45. Kenneth L. Feder, "Piltdown, Paradigms, and the Paranormal," *Skeptical Inquirer* 24 (4): 397-402.

46. William Broad and Nicholas Wade, *Betrayers of the Truth: Fraud and Deceit in the Halls of Science* (New York: Simon & Shuster, 1982).

47. See, for example, Stuart Kind and Michael Overman, *Science against Crime* (Garden City, N.Y.: Doubleday, 1972).

48. John I. Thornton and Edward F. Rhodes, "Brief History of Questioned Document Examination," *Identification News* (Jan. 1986): 7.

49. Ibid., 7, 12.

50. Ibid.; Ordway Hilton, "History of Questioned Document Examination in the United States," *Journal of Forensic Sciences*, JFSCA, 24.4 (1979): 890-91.

51. Hilton, "History," 893.

52. *Ency. Brit.*, 1960, s.v. "expert."

53. Irving Goldstein, *Trial Technique* (Chicago: Callaghan, 1935), 383.

54. Ibid., 384.

55. Ibid., 404-6.

56. C.A. Mitchell, *The Expert Witness* (New York: D. Appleton, 1923), 2, 3-4.

57. Osborn, *Questioned Documents*, 633-34.

58. Hilton, *Scientific Examination*, 28.

59. Ibid., 166 (photo); see also Inbau, Moenssens, Vitullo, *Scientific Police Investigation*, (New York: Chilton, 1972), 54, photo.

60. See, for example, K. Rendell, *Forging History*, 76.

2. Handwriting Examination

1. "Identification of Handwriting" forensic instruction manual for course in Scientific Crime Detection (Chicago: Institute of Applied Science, 1962), lesson 1, p. 5.

2. Hilton, *Scientific Examination*, 15, 17; Inbau, Moenssens, and Vitullo, *Scientific Police Investigation*, 56.

3. See "Identification of Handwriting," lesson 1, p. 7-8.

4. Osborn, *Questioned Documents*, 219.

5. E. Patrick McGuire, *The Forgers* (Bernardsville, N.J.: Padric Publishing, 1969), 208.

6. Hilton, *Scientific Examination*, 209.

7. McGuire, *Forgers*, 209.

8. See Nickell, *Pen, Ink, and Evidence*, 115-46, 195.

9. Jonathan Goldberg, *Writing Matter: From the Hands of the English Renaissance* (Stanford, Calif.: Stanford Univ. Press, 1990), 247.

10. Ibid.

11. Herbert E. Klingelhofer, "Hidden Signatures," in *Autographs and Manuscripts*, ed. Berkeley, 106-10; Benjamin, *Autographs*, 166.

12. Gideon Epstein, "Examination of the Josef Mengele Handwriting," *Journal of Forensic Sciences*, JFSCA, 32.1 (Jan. 1987): 102. For Epstein's reference, see Von Ostermann, *The Manual of Foreign Languages*, 4th ed. (New York: New York Central Book Co., 1952).

13. "Identification of Handwriting," lesson 1, p. 3. For the use of "exemplar," see Charles E. O'Hara, *Fundamentals of Criminal Investigation*, 3d ed. (Springfield, Ill.: Charles C. Thomas, 1973), 787.

14. Hilton, *Scientific Examination*, 311.

15. Inbau, Moenssens, and Vitullo, *Scientific Police Investigation*, 46; 47-48 (photo).

16. Osborn, *Questioned Documents*, 34; cf. McGuire, *Forgers*, 204.

17. McGuire, *Forgers*, 203; Hilton, *Scientific Examination*, 310-13; Osborn, *Questioned Documents*, 32-33, 423.

18. O'Hara, *Fundamentals*, 794; Hilton, *Scientific Examination*, 299.

19. Inbau, Moenssens, and Vitullo, *Scientific Police Investigation*, 46-49.

20. *National Union Catalog of Manuscript Collections* (Washington, D.C.: Library of Congress, cumulative ed.); *American Library Directory*, current ed. (New Providence, N.J.: Bowker, 1994).

21. *Directory of Archives and Manuscript Repositories in the United States*, 2d ed. (Phoenix: Oryn Press, 1988).

22. *Biography and Genealogy Master Index*, current ed., in any sizeable library's reference section.

23. Osborn, *Questioned Documents*, 27-28.

24. Hilton, *Scientific Examination*, 309; 310 (photo).

25. K. Rendell, *Forging History*, 113-15.

26. Hilton, *Scientific Examination*, 310.

27. Osborn, *Questioned Documents*, 249.

28. I have condensed the four categories offered by O'Hara (*Fundamentals*, 786) into three and have rearranged the subcategories (e.g., to consider beginning and ending strokes as aspects of line quality rather than form), borrowing from "Identification of Handwriting," lessons 1-3, and Hilton, *Scientific Examination*, 154-60.

29. The term "eyelets" is defined in "Identification of Handwriting," lesson 1, pp. 8-9; "eyed" lowercase *o*'s are illustrated on p. 19.

30. "Identification of Handwriting," lesson 3, p. 25.

31. Ibid., 31-32.

32. Ibid., 12-13. For photographs illustrating the horizontal versus vertical shading and the attendant pen position in each case, see Osborn, *Questioned Documents*, 120.

33. "Identification of Handwriting," lesson 3, p. 29. See also Hamilton, *Great Forgers*, 2; K.Rendell, *Forging History*, 74.

34. Nickell with Fischer, "Crashed-Saucer Documents," in *Mysterious Realms*, 85, 88-89.

35. Paul L. Kirk, *Crime Investigation*, 2d. ed., ed. John I. Thornton (New York: John Wiley & Sons, 1974), 472.

36. "Identification of Handwriting," lesson 3, 30-31.

37. Joe Nickell, "Erasures and Corrections in Historic Documents: An Overview," *American Society of Questioned Document Examiners, Compilation of Papers*, Forty-ninth Annual Conference, Lake Buena Vista, Fla., Aug. 3-8, 1991.

38. Hilton, *Scientific Examination*, 108-17.

39. Nickell, "Erasures and Corrections," 6; for illustrations, see Herbert Cahoon, Thomas V. Lange, and Charles Ryskamp, *American Literary Autographs: From Washington Irving to Henry James* (New York: Dover, 1977).

40. O'Hara, *Fundamentals*, 786.

41. Ibid., 784.

42. The suggestion of notes is from Hilton, *Scientific Examination*, 353; the use of photocopies is my own recommendation, based on practices frequently followed by historical document specialists.

43. Gideon Epstein, testimony at Demjanjuk trial in Israel, May 5 and 11, 1987, transcript, 5720-21.

44. "Identification of Handwriting," lesson 4, p. 1.

45. O'Hara, *Fundamentals*, 785-86.

46. Inbau, Moenssens, and Vitullo, *Scientific Police Investigation*, 50.

47. "Identification of Handwriting," lesson 4, 1-8.
48. Epstein, *Scientific Examination*, 161.
49. Inbau, Moenssens, and Vitullo, *Scientific Police Investigation*, 52-54.
50. For more on this case, see K. Rendell, *Forging History*, 11-54.
51. Maureen Casey Owens, report to Kenneth W. Rendell, Aug. 30, 1993.
52. Chittenden, "Scrap Dealer."
53. This list is adapted from O'Hara, *Fundamentals*, 795-97, and is supplemented from Osborn, *Questioned Documents*, 410-11.
54. Osborn, *Questioned Documents*, 416-17.
55. Hilton, *Scientific Examination*, 169.
56. Ibid., 169.
57. Ibid., 171.
58. Jean F. Preston and Laetitia Yeandle, *English Handwriting, 1400–1650* (Binghamton, N.Y.: Medieval & Renaissance Texts & Studies, 1992), ix.
59. E.E. Thoyts, *How to Decipher and Study Old Documents* (1903; reprint, Chicago: Aries, 1974), 11.
60. Osborn, *Questioned Documents*, 365.
61. Mark Twain, *Roughing It*, quoted in Hamilton, *Great Forgers*, 242-44.
62. Osborn, *Questioned Documents*, 365.
63. *The Story of the Typewriter, 1873–1923* (Herkimer, N.Y.: Herkimer County Historical Society, 1923), 72-74.
64. "Identification of Typewriting" forensic instruction manual for course in Scientific Crime Detection, lesson 1, p. 3.
65. O'Hara, *Fundamentals*, 799.
66. Ibid., 801-2.
67. Inbau, Moenssens, and Vitullo, *Scientific Police Investigation*, 64-65.
68. Ibid., 65.
69. Hilton, *Scientific Examination*, 247.
70. Today's specialists rely on computer databases for type font identification and comparative identification. Hard copy files are no longer practical and are difficult to maintain, whereas computer files can be easily updated and searched.
71. Hilton, *Scientific Examination*, 334.
72. Ibid., 335.
73. Ibid., 232.
74. K. Rendell, *Forging History*, 67.
75. Richard Newnham, *The Guinness Book of Fakes, Frauds, and Forgeries* (Enfield, Middlesex, England: Guinness Publishing, 1991), 124-26.
76. Nicolas Barker, "The Forgery of Printed Documents," in *Forgery of Printed Documents: Proceedings of the 1989 Houston Conference* (New Castle, Del.: Oak Knoll Books, 1990), 7-9.
77. Nickell, *Pen, Ink, and Evidence*, 184 (photo).

3. FORGED WRITING

1. Hilton, *Scientific Examination*, 189.
2. Osborn, *Questioned Documents*, 329-31, 330, and 331 (photo).

3. K. Rendell, *Forging History*, 13.

4. Hamilton, *Great Forgers*, 48.

5. Ibid.

6. K. Rendell, *Forging History*, 14.

7. Hilton, *Scientific Examination*, 191.

8. Osborn, *Questioned Documents*, 115.

9. Osborn, Osborn, and Osborn, report to McGraw-Hill, quoted in Hamilton, *Great Forgers*, 171.

10. Hamilton, *Great Forgers*, 171.

11. Ibid., 92.

12. Ibid., 48.

13. Ibid., 179.

14. Ibid., 157.

15. Ibid., 157-65.

16. McGuire, *Forgers*, 173.

17. Ibid., 173-74.

18. Ibid., 174-75.

19. Ibid., 175.

20. Marian Pretzel, *Portrait of a Young Forger: An Incredible True Story of Triumph over the Third Reich* (New York: Knightsbridge, 1990).

21. Osborn, *Questioned Documents*, 167.

22. Hamilton, *Great Forgers*, 93 (photo) and 99.

23. Hilton, *Scientific Examination*, 187-89.

24. Osborn, *Questioned Documents*, 355.

25. Ibid., 111.

26. Hilton, *Scientific Examination*, 187.

27. Ibid., 185.

28. Osborn, *Questioned Documents*, 108.

29. Hilton, *Scientific Examination*, 185.

30. Osborn, *Questioned Documents*, 109, 283.

31. Ibid., 114-15.

32. Hilton, *Scientific Examination*, 20, 156, 185.

33. Osborn, *Questioned Documents*, 129.

34. K. Rendell, *Forging History*, 13.

35. Hamilton, *Great Forgers*, 264-65.

36. K. Rendell, *Forging History*, 13.

37. Hamilton, *Great Forgers*, 264-65.

38. Ibid., 48.

39. Ibid., 265.

40. Gideon Epstein, in testimony at the Israeli trial of the Nazi war criminal John Demjanjuk, May 5 and 11, 1987, transcript, 5814.

41. K. Rendell, *Forging History*, 9.

42. Hamilton, *Great Forgers*, 3, 57, 65.

43. Ibid., 116-17, 140-41.

44. Ibid., 30-31, 122, 128-29.

45. Ibid., 54-55.

46. Ibid., 210-11, 213.

47. Ibid., 69, 211.

48. K. Rendell, *Forging History*, 16.

49. Most faked books from Washington's library lack his bookplate, according to Hamilton, *Great Forgers*, 191.

50. Confidential client report.

51. Hamilton, *Great Forgers*, 38-43.

52. For a full illustration of the *carte*, see Nickell, *Pen, Ink, and Evidence*, 188.

53. Hamilton, *Great Forgers*, 31-34, 80, 224-26. K. Rendell, *Forging History*, 58.

54. Carlson Wade, *Great Hoaxes and Famous Imposters: Forgers, Swindlers, Robbers, and Con Artists throughout History* (Middle Village, N.Y.: Jonathan David, 1976), 236.

55. Ibid., 236-37.

56. Ibid., 232.

57. McGuire, *Forgers* 19.

58. Ibid., 57.

59. Benjamin, *Autographs*, 130-33.

60. Ibid., 133.

61. Ibid., 157-58.

62. Ibid., 115-17.

63. Ibid., 116.

64. See chapter 4 for a discussion.

65. For a discussion of the genuine order, drafts, and souvenir copies, see Joseph E. Fields, "Robert E. Lee's Farewell Order," in *Manuscripts: The First Twenty Years*, ed. Priscilla S. Taylor (Westport, Conn.: Greenwood Press, 1984), 260-65.

66. Steve H. Nolin, "Guide to Detecting Forgeries of Autographs," in *History Makers* (special issue, *How to Tell If It's Real: Detecting Forgeries*, 1991), 9.

67. Benjamin, *Autographs*, 112.

68. Hamilton, *Famous Forgers*, 29. For a full discussion of the Bixby letter, see chapter 7 of Joe Nickell, *Ambrose Bierce Is Missing* (Lexington: Univ. Press of Kentucky, 1992), 94-109.

69. Benjamin, *Autographs*, 113.

70. Ibid.

71. Ibid., 112-13.

72. Nolin, "Guide," 9.

73. K. Rendell, *Forging History*, 37.

74. Ibid., 38.

75. Adapted from ibid., 9-10; Benjamin, *Autographs*, 153, 158; K. Rendell, *Forging History*, 36-43; and Nickell, *Pen, Ink, and Evidence*, 65-66, 96, 192-93.

76. K. Rendell, *Forging History*, 105; Matthew Mrowicki, "How to Detect Autopens," *Autograph Times* (May/June 1994): 1.

77. K. Rendell, *Forging History*, 105.

78. Quoted in *Autograph Times* (Jan. 1995): 2.

79. K. Rendell, *Forging History*, 105.

80. Mrowicki, "Autopens," 22.

81. Ibid.

82. Ibid.

83. Nickell, *Pen, Ink, and Evidence*, 192-93.
84. Ibid., 193.
85. Benjamin, *Autographs*, 123.
86. *Autograph Times* (Jan 1995): 16.
87. Hilton, *Scientific Examination*, 74.
88. Nickell, *Pen, Ink, and Evidence*, 192-93.
89. K. Rendell, *Forging History*, 90-104.
90. Ibid., 102, 103.
91. *Autograph Times* (Jan. 1995): 16.
92. In addition to K. Rendell's *Forging History*, there is Charles Hamilton's two-volume *American Autographs* (Norman: Univ. of Oklahoma Press, 1993).
93. Joseph E. Fields, "Confused Identities," in Taylor, *Manuscripts*, 34-37.
94. Benjamin, *Autographs*, 198.
95. Ibid., 198-99, 206.
96. Fields, "Confused Identities," 35-37.

4. A MULTI-EVIDENTIAL APPROACH

1. Quintilian, *Institutio Oratoria*, ca. 88 A.D., quoted in Nickell, *Pen, Ink, and Evidence*, 169.
2. Hilton, *Scientific Examination*, xiv.
3. Linda Sillitoe and Allen Roberts, *Salamander: The Story of the Mormon Forgery Murders* (Salt Lake City: Signature Books, 1988), 299-318, 546. See also, "A Scandal in America," part 2, *Book Collector* 37 (spring 1988): 12-18.
4. S.L. Carson, "Has a Sixth Copy of the Gettysburg Address Been Found?" *The Manuscript Society News* 13.2 (spring 1992): 44.
5. David A. Warren, "Has Lincoln's Final Draft of Gettysburg Address Been Found? *The Lincoln Legacy* 4.3-4.4 (fall 1990-winter1991).
6. For further discussion, see Nickell with Fischer, "The Crashed-Saucer Documents," in *Mysterious Realms*, 83-108.
7. Stanton T. Friedman, "MJ-12: The Evidence So Far," *International UFO Reporter* (Sept./Oct. 1987): 16.
8. Osborn, *Questioned Documents*, 1.
9. Nickell, *Pen, Ink, and Evidence*, 190.
10. Carl David, *Collecting and Care of Fine Art* (New York: Crown, 1981), 67-68. See also Robert L. Volz, "Fair Copies and Working Copies," 129, and Franklyn Lenthal, "American Theater," 477, both in *Autographs and Manuscripts*, ed. Berkeley.
11. Benjamin, *Autographs*, 127.
12. See Nickell with Fischer, "The Legend of Beale's Treasure," in *Mysterious Realms*, 53-67.
13. "Caveat Emptor," editorial, *Civil War Times Illustrated* (Aug. 1977): 33-37.
14. Hamilton, *Hitler Diaries*, 1, 21.
15. For an account of the Vinland Map affair, see *Observer*, Jan. 27, 1974.
16. Hamilton, *Great Forgers*, 265.
17. Ibid.
18. Roy L. Davids, "English Literary Autographs," in *Autographs and Manuscripts*, ed. Berkeley, 281.

19. Nickell with Fischer, *Mysterious Realms*, 90-93.

20. Ibid., 93.

21. Ibid.

22. Hamilton, *Great Forgers*, 98-99.

23. Nickell, "D. Boone Riddles," in *Ambrose Bierce*, 78-80.

24. Ibid., 77-93.

25. Ibid.

26. Hamilton, *Hitler's Diaries*, seventh illustration following p. 116.

27. Ibid., 44.

28. Sir William Draigie and James Hurlbert, eds., *A Dictionary of American English on Historical Principles* (Chicago: University of Chicago Press, 1944); Mitford M. Mathews, ed., *Dictionary of Americanisms on Historical Principles* (Chicago: Univ. of Chicago, 1951); *The Compact Edition of the Oxford English Dictionary* (New York: Oxford Univ. Press, 1971).

29. Nickell with Fisher, "Unmasking a Nazi Monster," in *Ambrose Bierce*, 35-52.

30. A.Q. Morton, *Literary Detection: How to Prove Authorship and Fraud in Literature and Documents* (New York: Scribner's, 1978), 7.

31. Ibid., 38.

32. See D. Hayword Brock, "Jonson and Donne: Structural Fingerprinting and the Attribution of Elegies XXXVIII-XLI," *The Papers of the Bibliographical Society of America* 72 (1978): 519-27.

33. See Joe Nickell, "Discovered: The Secret of Beale's Treasure," *Virginia Magazine of History and Biography* 90.3 (July 1982): 321-22.

34. Ibid., 322.

35. Osborn, *Questioned Documents*, 574.

36. Nickell with Fisher, "Legend of Beale's Treasure," 57.

37. "Caveat Emptor," 33-37.

38. Nickell, *Ambrose Bierce*, 81-82 (photo).

39. Ibid., 81.

40. Samuel Taylor Coleridge, quoted in *Evidence for Authorship*, ed. David V. Erdman and Ephim G. Fogel (Ithaca: Cornell Univ. Press, 1966), 45.

41. Hamilton, *Great Forgers*, 261.

42. For more detailed information on all types of pens, see Nickell, *Pen, Ink, and Evidence*.

43. Ibid.

44. Hamilton, *Great Forgers*, 100.

45. Osborn, *Questioned Documents*, 153.

46. For more on writing fluids, see Nickell, *Pen, Ink, and Evidence*, 35-43, 198-99.

47. Ibid., 37. Punctuation added.

48. Ibid., 39-40, 199.

49. Ibid.; Hilton, *Scientific Examination*, 39.

50. Hamilton, *Great Forgers*, 181.

51. Ibid., 184.

52. Ibid., 267.

53. Sillitoe and Roberts, *Salamander*, 534, 539.

54. Ibid., 539.

55. Osborn, *Questioned Documents*, 449-50.

56. For more on papyrus, see Nickell, *Pen, Ink, and Evidence*, 71.

57. For additional information on parchment and parchment books, see ibid., 71-72, 121-22.

58. Benjamin, *Autographs*, 145.

59. For more on paper manufacture, see Nickell, *Pen, Ink, and Evidence*, 71-80; on watermarks, 81-87; on stationery, 88-111.

60. Quoted in Osborn, *Questioned Documents*, 496.

61. Quoted in ibid.

62. See nn 4 and 5.

63. Hamilton, *Great Forgers*, 134-36, 261.

64. Hamilton, *Hitler Diaries*, seventh illustration following p. 116.

65. Joe Nickell, *Ambrose Bierce*, 100.

66. Benjamin, *Autographs*, 93-94.

67. George J. Throckmorton, "A Forensic Analysis of Twenty-one Hofmann Documents," in Sillitoe and Roberts, *Salamander*, 544.

68. Hilton, *Scientific Examination*, 271-72.

69. *The Compact Edition of the Oxford English Dictionary*, 1971, s.v. "wafer." For more on paper fasteners and other writing materials, see Nickell, *Pen, Ink, and Evidence*, 88-111.

70. Throckmorton, "Hofmann Documents," 544.

71. Hamilton, *Great Forgers*, 33.

72. K.C. Owings, personal communication.

73. Ann Waldon, *True or False? Amazing Art Forgeries* (New York: Hastings House, 1983), 50-69; John FitzMaurice Mills, *Treasure Keepers* (New York: Doubleday, 1973), 76-77.

74. Ibid.

75. Sillitoe and Roberts, *Salamander*, 109.

76. Ibid., passim. See also "A Scandal in America"; Naifeh and Smith, *Mormon Murders*, especially 429-39.

77. Benjamin, *Autographs*, 143.

5. MACROSCOPIC AND MICROSCOPIC STUDY

1. *Ency. Brit.*, 1960, s.v., "Macroscopy."

2. Osborn, *Questioned Documents*, 454-55.

3. Ibid., 452.

4. Colin Haynes, *The Complete Collector's Guide to Fakes and Forgeries* (Greensboro, N.C.: Wallace-Homestead Book Co., 1988), 114; Benjamin, *Autographs*, 152.

5. Benjamin, *Autographs*, 151-52.

6. Naifeh and Smith, *Mormon Murders*, 430-31.

7. Osborn, *Questioned Documents*, 531, 535.

8. Nickell, *Ambrose Bierce*, 98.

9. Benjamin, *Autographs*, 152.

10. Osborn, *Questioned Documents*, 409.

11. Hamilton, *Great Forgers*, 49-50.

12. Ibid., 91.

13. Benjamin, *Autographs*, 98-99; Mark Jones, ed., *Fakes? The Art of Deception* (Berkeley: Univ. of California Press, 1990), 223.

14. Benjamin, *Autographs*, 98-99; Jones, *Fake?* 223.

15. Anthony Grafton, *Forgers and Critics: Creativity and Duplicity in Western Scholarship* (Princeton, N.J.: Princeton Univ. Press, 1990), 56.

16. Haynes, *Complete Collector's Guide*, 118-19.

17. Hamilton, *Great Forgers*, 195, 237, 255.

18. Ibid., 255.

19. Ibid., 264.

20. Nickell, *Pen, Ink, and Evidence*, 79, 201.

21. Hamilton, *Great Forgers*, 264.

22. Ibid., 102.

23. Hilton, *Scientific Examination*, 17; Osborn, *Questioned Documents*, 545.

24. Inbau, Moenssens, and Vitullo, *Scientific Police Investigation*, 57-58.

25. Osborn, *Questioned Documents*, 531, 565.

26. Hilton, *Scientific Examination*, 96-106.

27. See photographs in Nickell, *Pen, Ink, and Evidence*, 187.

28. O'Hara, *Fundamentals*, 819.

29. Hilton, *Scientific Examination*, 138-39.

30. Ibid., 189.

31. Sillitoe and Roberts, *Salamander*, 251, 540.

32. Osborn, *Questioned Documents*, 577, 580.

33. Ibid.

34. Hilton, *Scientific Examination*, 90-91.

35. Nickell, *Pen, Ink, and Evidence*, 80; an article cataloging two hundred such embossments (together with approximate dates), compiled by this author, is "Stationers' Crests," *Manuscripts: the Journal of the Manuscript Society*, 45.3 (summer 1993): 199-216.

36. Ibid.

37. Hilton, *Scientific Examination*, 133, 359.

38. Ibid., 18.

39. Nickell, *Pen, Ink, and Evidence*, 74-75.

40. Ibid., 75.

41. Ann Buchsbaum, *Practical Guide to Print Collecting* (New York: Van Nostrand Reinhold, 1975), 59.

42. Dard Hunter, *Papermaking: The History and Technique of an Ancient Craft*, 2d ed. (1947; reprint, New York: Dover, 1978), 225-26; Nickell, *Pen, Ink, and Evidence*, 75.

43. Nickell, *Pen, Ink, and Evidence*, 81-82.

44. Ibid., 78.

45. Ibid.

46. Ibid., 81-82.

47. Ibid. 83, 182.

48. Thomas L. Gravell and George Miller, *A Catalog of American Watermarks, 1690–1835* (New York: Garland, 1979), 178.

49. Hilton, *Scientific Examination*, 274-75.

50. Charles-Moise Briquet, *Les filigrantes. Dictionnaire historique des marques du papier*

des lur apparition vers 1282 jusqu'en 1600 (1907; Amsterdam: Paper Publications Society, 1968).

51. W.A. Churchill, *Watermarks in Paper in Holland, England, France, etc., in the XVII and XVIII Centuries* . . . (Amsterdam: M. Hertzberger, 1935).

52. Edward Heawood, *Watermarks, Mainly of the 17th and 18th Centuries* (Hilversum, Holland: Paper Publications Society, 1950).

53. Gravell and Miller, *Catalog of American Watermarks.*

54. Thomas L. Gravell and George Miller, *A Catalog of Foreign Watermarks Found on Paper Used in America 1700–1835* (New York: Garland, 1983).

55. *Lockwood Directory of Paper Manufacturers*, an annual publication; *The Paper Catalog* (Oradel: Walden Mott, n.d.).

56. Gravell and Miller, *Catalogue of American Watermarks*, xiii-xiv.

57. Nickell, *Pen, Ink, and Evidence*, 84.

58. Benjamin, *Autographs*, 147-49.

59. See "Facsimiles: A List of Items More Commonly Reproduced," in Kenneth W. Duckett, *Modern Manuscripts* (Nashville: American Association for State and Local History, 1975) 304-7.

60. Nickell, *Pen, Ink, and Evidence.*

61. Hunter, *Papermaking*, 416-25.

62. Ibid., 282-83.

63. For a photograph, see Nickell, *Pen, Ink, and Evidence*, 64.

64. Hilton, *Scientific Examination*, 119.

65. Osborn, *Questioned Documents*, 33-62.

66. Ibid., 339.

67. For a discussion, see Nickell with Fischer, *Mysterious Realms*, 93-95.

68. Hamilton, *Great Forgers*, 268.

69. Osborn, *Questioned Documents*, 340-41.

70. Carson, "Sixth Copy," 44.

71. Osborn, *Questioned Documents*, 348.

72. Ibid., 328-30, 349.

73. W. Thomas Taylor, *Texfake: An Account of the Theft and Forgery of Early Texas Printed Documents* (Austin: W. Thomas Taylor, 1991), 3-4.

74. Ibid., 46.

75. *Edmund Scientific 1992 Annual Reference Catalog* (Barrington, N.J.: Edmund Scientific Co.), 17.

76. Richard L. Brunelle, "Questioned Document Examination," in *Forensic Science Handbook*, ed. Richard Saferstein (Englewood Cliffs, N.J.: Prentice-Hall, 1982), 679.

77. Nickell, *Pen, Ink, and Evidence*, 206, and illustration on 180.

78. Ibid.

79. Ibid.

80. Ibid.

81. Keith W. Swape, "Determination of the Direction of Ball-Point Pen Motion from the Orientations of Burr Striations in Curved Pen Strokes," *Journal of Forensic Sciences*, JFSCA, 25.2 (April 1980), 386-89.

82. Jackson, *Story of Writing*, 168.

83. Brunelle, "Questioned Document Examination," 711-12.

84. For an illustration, see Hilton, *Scientific Examination*, 156.

85. Ibid., 20, 154-56; Osborn, *Questioned Documents*, 323-33.

86. Gideon Epstein, testimony at Demjanjuk's trial in Israel (criminal case no. 373/86), May 1987, Translators' Pool Ltd. transcript pp. 5840; see also Nickell, *Ambrose Bierce*, 50-51.

87. Osborn, *Questioned Documents*, 114-15, 331-32, 335.

88. Hilton, *Scientific Examination*, 21.

89. Nickell, *Pen, Ink, and Evidence*, 174, 189-90.

90. Carson, "Sixth Copy," 44.

91. Nickell, *Pen, Ink, and Evidence*, 208; Haynes, *Complete Collector's Guide*, 117.

92. See I. Isaenberg, *Pulp and Paper Microscoping* (Appleton, Wisc.: Institute of Paper Chemistry, 1967); *Tappi Standard Methods* (Atlanta: Technical Association of Pulp and Paper Industry, 1974); and B.L. Browning, *Analysis of Paper*, 2d ed. (New York: Marcel Dekker, 1977).

93. Brunelle, "Questioned Document Examination," 719.

94. Gaylord Johnson and Maurice Bleifeld, *Hunting with the Microscope*, rev. ed. (New York: Arco Publishing Co., 1978), 75-78, 86-89.

95. Brunelle, "Questioned Document Examination," 679; Hilton, *Scientific Examination*, 7; Osborn, *Questioned Documents*, 77-78.

96. Walter C. McCrone, et al., *The Particle Atlas*, 2d ed. (Ann Arbor, Mich.: Ann Arbor Science Publishers, 1979).

97. Brunelle, "Questioned Document Examination," 678.

98. This technique was used for an illustration in Nickell, "Stationers' Crests, 200.

99. Hilton, *Scientific Examination*, photo on 139; O'Hara, *Fundamentals*, 819; Osborn, *Questioned Documents*, 59.

100. Brunelle, "Questioned Document Examination," 679-80.

101. Hilton, *Scientific Examination*, 30.

102. Haynes, *Complete Collector's Guide*, 164.

103. Edmund Scientific catalog 1992, 41.

6. Spectral Techniques

1. Jones, *Fake?* 277, and photo on 279.

2. *Applied Infrared Photography* (Rochester, N.Y.: Eastman Kodak, 1972), 36-38, 52.

3. Ibid., 16-17.

4. John F. Fischer and Joe Nickell, "Laser Light: Space-age Forensics," *Law Enforcement Technology* (Sept. 1984): 26-27.

5. O'Hara, *Fundamentals*, 762.

6. Ibid.

7. Ibid., 763, 764.

8. Tom Teicholz, *The Trial of Ivan the Terrible* (New York: St. Martin's, 1990), 172; Hamilton, *Hitler Diaries*, 102.

9. Teicholz, *Trial*, 172.

10. Collection of Joe Nickell.

11. See Carson, "Sixth Copy," 44.

12. Throckmorton, "Hofmann Documents," 533.

13. Hilton, *Scientific Examination*, 126, 128-29.

14. Ibid., 44; O'Hara, *Fundamentals*, 764.

15. Nickell, *Pen, Ink, and Evidence*, 175.

16. Waldron, *True or False?* 22.

17. McGuire, *Forgers*, 183.

18. Ibid.

19. Hilton, *Scientific Examination*, 97, and photo on 99.

20. Inbau, Moenssens, and Vitullo, *Scientific Police Investigation*, 58-59, and photo on 62.

21. Hilton, *Scientific Examination*, 97.

22. Throckmorton, "Hofmann Documents," 534.

23. This effect is also revealed by argon laser light, as discussed later. See Nickell, *Pen, Ink, and Evidence*, photo on 193, and 194.

24. David A. Warren, "Has Lincoln's Final Draft of Gettysburg Address Been Found?" *Lincoln Legacy*, 4.3-4.4 (fall 1990-winter 1991), 1-18.

25. Hilton, *Scientific Examination*, 90.

26. Clarence Rainwater, *Light and Color* (New York: Western Publishing, 1971), 9-11.

27. *Edmund Scientific 1992 Annual Reference Catalog.*

28. *Applied Infrared Photography*, 12-17.

29. Waldron, *True or False?* photo on 26, and 27.

30. Joe Nickell and John F. Fischer, "The Image of Guadalupe: A Folkloristic and Iconographic Investigation," *Skeptical Inquirer* 8.4 (spring 1985): 243-55; reprinted as "Celestial Painting," chapter 8 of Joe Nickell with John F. Fischer, *Secrets of the Supernatural* (Buffalo: Prometheus Books, 1988), 103-17. See also Philip Serna Callahan, *The Tilma under Infra-red Radiation* (Washington, D.C.: Center for Applied Research in the Apostolate, 1981).

31. For an example, see the infrared photograph of a detail from Jan Van Eyck's *The Betrothal of the Arnolfini* in Waldron, *True or False?* 26.

32. The icon was coinvestigated by Joe Nickell and is mentioned (in reference to undersketching) in Nickell with Fischer, *Secrets of the Supernatural*, 111.

33. *Applied Infrared Photograph*, 57.

34. Ibid., photos on 56, and 57.

35. Samuel T. Williamson and Herman Z. Cummins, *Light and Color in Nature and Art* (New York: John Wiley and Sons, 1983), 298-99.

36. *Applied Infrared Photography*, 53.

37. Ibid., photo on 52.

38. O'Hara, *Fundamentals*, 816, and photo on 824.

39. *They Write Their Own Sentences: The FBI Handwriting Manual* (Boulder, Colo.: Paladin Press, 1987), 2-3.

40. O'Hara, *Fundamentals*, 816.

41. Hilton, *Scientific Examination*, 97-102.

42. Ibid., photo on 103.

43. Ibid., photo on 101.

44. M.G. Noblett, "The Use of a Scanning Monochromator as a Barrier Filter in Infrared Examinations of Documents," *Journal of Forensic Sciences*, JFSCA, 27.4 (Oct. 1982), 923-27.

45. Osborn, *Questioned Documents*, 451.

46. Nickell, *Pen, Ink, and Evidence*, 198.

47. O'Hara, *Fundamentals*, 767.

48. Joe Nickell, report to Jerome Meckier, Dec. 11, 1989; Jerome Meckier, "Dickens, *Great Expectations*, and the Dartmouth College Notes," *Papers on Language and Literature* 28 (1992): 111-32.

49. L. Bendikson, "Photechnical Problems: Some Results Obtained at the Huntington Library," *Library Journal* 57 (1932): 789-94, cited in *Applied Infrared Photography*, 52.

50. Ada Nisbet, *Dickens and Ellen Ternan* (Berkeley: Univ. of California Press, 1952).

51. *Applied Infrared Photography*, 52.

52. Inbau, Moenssens, and Vitullo, *Scientific Police Investigation*, 59.

53. Noblett, "Scanning Monochromator," 924. See also C.A. Sensi and A.A. Cantu, "Infrared Luminescence: Is It a Valid Method of Differentiating Among Inks?" *Journal of Forensic Sciences*, JFSCA, 27.1 (Jan. 1981), 196-99.

54. *Applied Infrared Photography*, 52.

55. O'Hara, *Fundamentals*, 767.

56. Ibid., 766.

57. Fischer and Nickell, "Laser Light," 26; Allen A. Boraiko, "LASERS: A Splendid Light," *National Geographic* 165.3 (March 1984), 335-62.

58. Boraiko, "LASERS," 335-62.

59. Fischer and Nickell, "Laser Light," 26-27.

60. O'Hara, *Fundamentals*, 660-70.

61. Fischer and Nickell, "Laser Light," 26. Although the laser can cause accidental burning of the sample, the risk is minimal in expert hands.

62. E. Roland Menzel, "A Guide to Laser Latent Fingerprint Development Procedures," *Identification News* (Sept. 1983): 7, 10-12.

63. D.W. Herod and R. Menzel, "Laser Detection of Latent Fingerprints: Ninhydrin Followed by Zinc Chloride," *Journal of Forensic Sciences*, JFSCA, 27.3 (July 1982), 513-18.

64. Brian E. Dalrymple, "Visible and Infrared Luminescence in Documents: Excitation by Laser," *Journal of Forensic Sciences*, JFSCA, 28.3 (July 1983), photo on 692-94.

65. Ibid., photo on 694.

66. Nickell, *Pen, Ink, and Evidence*, photo on 193, and 194.

67. Timothy W. Sinor, Jeffrey P. Wilde, Kathleen E. Everse, and E. Roland Menzel, "Lasers and Optical Spectroscopy in Questioned Document Examination," *Journal of Forensic Sciences*, JFSCA, 31.3 (July 1986), 825-39.

68. Ibid., 827.

69. Nickell, *Pen, Ink, and Evidence*, 176.

70. For an extended discussion of document reproduction, see Hilton, *Scientific Examination*, 361-88.

71. Ibid., 364.

72. A. Holloway, *The Handbook of Photographic Equipment* (New York: Knopf, 1981), 27, 203.

73. Elbridge Walter Stein, "Ultra-Violet Light and Forgery," *Scientific American* (Oct. 1932): 206.

74. Hilton, *Scientific Examination*, 126, and photo on 130.

75. Nickell, *Pen, Ink, and Evidence*, photo on 175.

76. McGuire, *Forgers*, photo on 183; Stein, "Ultra-Violet Light," 206.

77. For an extended discussion, see *Applied Infrared Photography*, 18-35, 51.

78. Ibid., 20-21.

79. Ibid., 51.

80. Hilton, *Scientific Examination*, photo on 118.

81. *Applied Infrared Photography*, 54.

82. Ibid., 57.

83. Hilton (citing Stein's files), *Scientific Examination*, 105.

84. Advertising brochure for "Laser Printfinder" (Orlando, Fla.: Laser Photonics, n.d.).

85. Dalrymple, "Visible and Infrared Luminescence," 694.

86. Ibid. See also other articles in the *Journal of Forensic Sciences*, such as B.E. Dalrymple, "Use of Narrow-Band-Pass Filters to Enhance Detail in Latent Fingerprint Photography by Laser," *Journal of Forensic Sciences*, JFSCA, 27.4 (Oct. 1982): 801-5.

87. Hilton, *Scientific Examination*, 102, and photo on 104.

88. *Applied Infrared Photography*, 36.

89. Ibid.

90. O'Hara, *Fundamentals*, 815.

91. Hilton, *Scientific Examination*, 365.

92. Ibid., photo on 100, and 101.

7. Chemical and Instrumental Tests

1. Osborn, *Questioned Documents*, 22.

2. Mentioned in Hilton, *Scientific Examination*, 357.

3. Ibid., photo on 358. Of course, professionals like Hilton decry such procedures.

4. William Wordsworth, "The Tables Turned," 1798.

5. George Martin Cunha and Dorothy Grant Cunha, *Conservation of Library Materials*, 2d ed., vol. 1 (Metuchen, N.J.: Scarecrow Press, 1971), 330. (Obviously, anyone today, using a papermaking kit to make his or her own paper from, say, junk mail, could well produce wood-pulp paper that was not machine made.)

6. Nickell, *Pen, Ink, and Evidence*, 201.

7. Cunha and Cunha, *Conservation*, 329-33.

8. Julius Grant, *Books and Documents: Dating, Permanence and Preservation* (New York: Chemical Publishing Co., 1937), 8-32.

9. "Forgeries Face New Arsenal of Anti-Hoax Techniques," *New York Times*, May 10, 1983, C3.

10. Purushottam H. Patel, "Age of a Document," *Identification News* (Aug. 1979): 5.

11. Brunelle, "Questioned Document Examination," 720.

12. Albert H. Lyter and Richard L. Brunelle "A Systematic Approach for the Comparison of PaperSamples," *Identification News* (May 1977): 3-6; Osborn, *Questioned Documents*, 479-98; Patel, "Age of a Document," 4-5.

13. Brunelle, "Questioned Document Examination," 717.

14. Osborn, *Questioned Documents*, 459-59.

15. Kenneth W. Rendell, "Detection of Forgeries," in *Autographs and Manuscripts*, ed. Berkeley, 79.

16. Cunha and Cunha, *Conservation*, 344.

17. Nickell, *Pen, Ink, and Evidence*, 207.

18. Ibid.

19. Osborn, *Questioned Documents*, 477-78.

20. Benjamin, *Autographs*, 158.

21. *Ency. Brit.*, 1960, s.v. "chromatography."

22. Brunelle, "Questioned Document Examination," 712-15.

23. Ibid.

24. Ibid., 716-17.

25. Throckmorton, "Hofmann Documents," 535.

26. Ibid.

27. Hilton, *Scientific Examination*, 101.

28. Ibid. For a formula see H.T.F. Rhodes, *Forensic Chemistry* (New York: Chemical Publishing Co., 1940), 135.

29. Hilton, *Scientific Examination*, 101-2.

30. O'Hara, *Fundamentals*, 820.

31. Ibid., 665-66, 820; Osborn, *Questioned Documents*, 535.

32. O'Hara, *Fundamentals*, 666; Hilton, *Scientific Examination*, 335-36.

33. Harry Edward Neal, *The Story of the Secret Service* (New York: Grosset & Dunlap, 1971), 96-100.

34. Osborn, *Questioned Documents*, 548.

35. Ibid.

36. Geoffrey Bibby, *The Testimony of the Spade* (New York: Knopf, 1956), 194-97; Gordon C. Baldwin, *The Riddle of the Past* (New York: Norton, 1965), 108ff; Nickell, *Ambrose Bierce*, 150.

37. For a fuller discussion, see Joe Nickell, *Inquest on the Shroud of Turin* (Buffalo: Prometheus Books, 1987), and Daniel C. Scavone, *The Shroud of Turin*, Great Mysteries series (San Diego, Calif.: Greenhaven Press, 1989).

38. Joe Nickell, "Les Preuves Scientifiques que le Linceul de Turin date du Moyen Age," *Science et Vie* (July 1991), 6-17.

39. Malcolm W. Browne, "Map May Be from Vikings After All," *New York Times*, May 10, 1987.

40. Brunelle, "Questioned Document Examination," 721.

41. O'Hara, *Fundamentals*, 719-23; John FitzMaurice Mills, *Treasure Keepers* (New York: Doubleday, 1973), 24, 29.

42. Mills, *Treasure Keepers*, 95.

43. Inbau, Moenssens, and Vitullo, *Scientific Police Investigation*, 130-31.

44. Mills, *Treasure Keepers*, 24, 32-33, 85, 87.

45. Ibid., 94.

46. Ibid., 29-31.

47. Browne, "Map."

48. Ibid.

49. Ibid.; Jones, *Fake?* 297; R.A. Skelton, Thomas E. Marston, and George D. Painter, *The Vinland Map and the Tartar Relation* (New Haven: Yale Univ. Press, 1965), passim.

50. W.C. McCrone, "Chemical Analytical Study of the Vinland Map," report to Yale University Library (New Haven: Yale Univ., 1974).

51. T.A. Cahill, et al., "The Vinland Map, Revisited: New Compositional Evidence on Its Inks and Parchment," *Analytical Chemistry* 59 (1987): 829-33.

52. Walter C. McCrone, editorial, *Microscope* (1986): iv. (He refers to *Time*, March 10, 1986, 75.)

53. Mills, *Treasure Keepers*, 42, 85.

54. David Sox, *Unmasking the Forger: The Dossena Deception* (London: Unwin Hyman, 1987), 74-90.

55. Roderick McNeil, "Scanning Auger Microscopy for Manuscript Ink Dating," *Literary Research* 13.2 (spring 1988) and13.3 (summer 1988): 135. See also Warren, "Lincoln's Final Draft," 16.

56. Walter C. McCrone, letter to David Warren, Jan. 17, 1992, quoted in Warren, "Lincoln's Final Draft," 15-16.

57. Throckmorton, "Hofmann Documents," 536.

58. See "A Scandal in America," 12-18.

59. McNeil, "Scanning Auger Microscopy," 147.

60. Throckmorton, "Hofmann Documents," 536.

61. Roderick McNeil, undated report to Lloyd Ostendorf, reprinted in Warren, "Lincoln's Final Draft," 14-15.

62. Maureen Casey Owens, opinion cited in Warren, "Lincoln's Final Draft," 16.

63. Roderick J. McNeil, telephone interview, quoted in Carson, "Sixth Copy," 44.

64. McNeil to Ostendorf, in Warren, "Lincoln's Final Draft," 15.

65. Kenneth W. Rendell. "Report on the Diary of Jack the Ripper," September 1993; reprinted in *The Diary of Jack the Ripper*, narrative by Shirley Harrison (New York: Hyperion, 1993), 305-12.

66. Maurice Chittenden and Christopher Lloyd. "Fake! The Detective Work that Revealed the Truth About Jack the Ripper's 'Diary.'" *The Sunday Times* (London), July 3, 1994.

67. James Gilreath, *The Judgment of Experts*, quoted in Warren, "Lincoln's Final Draft," 14.

68. James Gilreath, to Lloyd Ostendorf, quoted in Warren, "Lincoln's Final Draft," 14.

69. Mills, *Treasure Keepers*, 28-29.

70. Brunelle, "Questioned Document Examination," 700.

71. Sox, *Unmasking*, 140.

Recommended Works

AUTOGRAPHS AND FACSIMILES

Benjamin, Mary A. *Autographs: A Key to Collecting*. Rev. ed. 1963. Reprint, New York: Dover, 1986.

Cahoon, Herbert, Thomas V. Lange, and Charles Ryskamp. *American Literary Autographs: From Washington Irving to Henry James*. New York: Dover, 1977.

Greg, Walter Wilson. *English Literary Autographs, 1550–1650*. 3 vols. Oxford: Oxford Univ. Press, 1925–32. Reprint, Nendeln, Lichtenstein: Kraus Reprint, 1968.

Hamilton, Charles. *The Signature of America*. New York: Harper & Row, 1979. Comprehensive collection of facsimile signatures of American notables.

———. *The Book of Autographs*. New York: Simon and Schuster, 1978. Includes more than one thousand facsimile signatures of notable personages.

———. *American Autographs*. Norman: Univ. of Oklahoma Press, 1993.

———. *Big Name Hunting: A Beginner's Guide to Autograph Collecting*. New York: Simon and Schuster, 1973.

———. *Collecting Autographs and Manuscripts*. Norman: Univ. of Oklahoma Press, 1961.

Klinkenborg, Verlyn, Herbert Cahoon, and Charles Ryskamp. *British Literary Manuscripts, Series I from 800 to 1800*. New York: Dover, 1981.

Rawlins, Ray. *The Guinness Book of World Autographs*. Enfield, Middlesex, England: Guinness Superlatives, 1977. Alphabetically arranged facsimile signatures of world historic figures and notables.

Rendell, Kenneth W. *History Comes to Life: Collecting Historical Letters and Documents*. Norman: Univ. of Oklahoma Press, 1995. Comprehensive treatise with numerous facsimile autographs.

———. *The American Frontier, from the Atlantic to the Pacific*. 3 vols. Kenneth W. Rendell, 1980. Letters, documents, maps of the westward movement.

———. *Autograph Letters, Manuscripts, Drawings: French Artists and Authors*. Kenneth Rendell, 1977.

Taylor, John. *From the White House Inkwell: American Presidential Autographs*. Rutland, Vt.: Charles E. Tuttle, 1968.

FORGERS AND FORGERY

Bozeman, Pat, ed. *Forged Documents: Proceedings of the 1989 Houston Conference.* New Castle, Del.: Oak Knoll Books, 1990. Includes chapter on forged printed documents.

Fleming, Stuart. "Detecting Art Forgeries." *Physics Today* (April, 1980): 34–39. Overview of sophisticated analyses employed in uncovering forged paintings.

Hamilton, Charles. *The Hitler Diaries: Fakes That Fooled the World.* Lexington: Univ. Press of Kentucky, 1991. Definitive account of the famous forgery and hoax.

———. *Great Forgers and Famous Fakes: The Manuscript Forgers of America and How They Duped the Experts.* New York: Crown, 1980. Essential text for anyone interested in historic forgeries, providing an entertaining look at the lives of forgers; nicely illustrated.

Haynes, Colin. *The Complete Collector's Guide to Fakes and Forgeries.* Greensboro, N.C.: Wallace-Homestead Book Co., 1988. On detecting fake artworks, jewelry, manuscripts, ceramics.

McGuire, E. Patrick. *The Forgers.* Bernardsville, N.J.: Padric Publishing Co., 1969. Wide-ranging study of the crime of forgery, including modus operandi, case histories, personality profile, forgery prevention.

Mills, John FitzMaurice. *Treasure Keepers.* New York: Doubleday, 1973. Includes chapters on scientific testing, dating, detecting forgeries; intended for the layman.

Newnham, Richard. *The Guinness Book of Fakes, Frauds, and Forgeries.* Enfield, Middlesex, England: Guinness Publishing, 1991. Explores all types of frauds and swindles.

Nickell, Joe. *Camera Clues: A Handbook for Photographic Investigation.* Lexington: Univ. Press of Kentucky, 1994. Includes information on dating old photographs and detecting copies and fakes; chapter on trick photography.

Pretzel, Marian. *Portrait of a Young Forger: An Incredible True Story of Triumph over the Third Reich.* New York: Knightsbridge, 1990.

Rendell, Kenneth W. *Forging History: The Detection of Fake Letters and Documents.* Norman: Univ. of Oklahoma Press, 1994. Discusses major forgeries, including Hitler diaries, Mormon forgeries, and Jack the Ripper diary.

Rochette, Edward C. *Making Money: Rogues and Rascals Who Made Their Own.* Frederick, Colo.: Renaissance House, 1986. Stories about the counterfeiting of coins and currency.

Sillitoe, Linda, and Allen Roberts. *Salamander: The Story of The Mormon Forgery Murders.* Salt Lake City, Utah: Signature Books, 1988. Section on forensic analysis of the Mark Hofmann forgeries.

Taylor, W. Thomas. *Texfake: An Account of the Theft and Forgery of Early Texas Printed Documents.* Austin: W. Thomas Taylor, 1991.

Waldron, Ann. *True Or False? Amazing Art Forgeries.* New York: Hastings House, 1983. Discusses major forgers and forgeries, scientific detection; well illustrated.

PENMANSHIP

Backhouse, Janet. *The Illuminated Manuscript.* Oxford: Phaidon, 1979.

Berkeley, Edmund, Jr., ed. *Autographs and Manuscripts: A Collector's Manual.* New York: Scribner's, 1978.

Beyerstein, Barry L., and Dale F. Beyerstein. *The Write Stuff: Evaluations of Graphology.* Buffalo: Prometheus, 1992. Comprehensive.

Bickham, George. *The Universal Penman.* 1741. New York: Dover, 1954. Classic eighteenth-century penmanship book with engraved plates of alphabets and pen-flourished pictures.

Degering, Herman. *Lettering: Modes of Writing in Western Europe from Antiquity to the End of the 18th Century.* New York: Pentalic, 1965.

Hector, L. C. *The Handwriting of English Documents.* London: Arnold, 1958.

Jackson, Donald. *The Story of Writing.* New York: Taplinger, 1981. A nicely illustrated history of writing from its earliest forms to the present.

Johnston, Edward. *Writing and Illuminating and Lettering.* 1906. Reprint, London: Pitman, 1979.

Kirkham, E. Kay. *The Handwriting of American Records for a Period of 300 Years.* Logan, Utah: Everton, 1973. Guide to reading old writing.

Morgan, Marvin. "Handwriting Systems and Penmanship," *Identification News* (July 1985): 2–11.

Nash, Ray. *American Writing Masters and Copybooks: History and Bibliography through Colonial Times.* Boston: Colonial Society of Massachusetts, 1959.

———. *American Penmanship, 1800–1850.* Worchester, Mass.: American Antiquarian Society, 1969.

Nesbitt, Alexander. *The History of Technique of Lettering.* 1950. Reprint, New York: Dover, 1957.

Ogg, Oscar. *The 26 Letters.* New York: Crowell, 1948. A history of the origin and development of the alphabet.

Rendell, Diana J. "The Development of Writing." In *Autographs and Manuscripts: A Collector's Manual,* ed. "Edmund Berkeley Jr. New York: Scribner's, 1978, 3–27.

Tannenbaum, Samuel A. *The Handwriting of the Renaissance.* New York: Columbia Univ. Press, 1930. Standard treatise on the English secretary hand.

Thoyt, E.E. *How to Decipher and Study Old Documents.* 2d ed. 1903. Reprint, Detroit: Gale Research, 1974.

Whalley, Joyce Irene. *The Student's Guide to Western Calligraphy: An Illustrated Survey.* Boulder, Colo.: Shambhala, 1984.

———. *English Handwriting, 1540–1853.* London: HMSO, 1969.

QUESTIONED DOCUMENT EXAMINATION

Applied Infrared Photography. Rochester, N.Y.: Eastman Kodak, 1972. Includes information useful for document examiners.

Beardsley, Niel E. "The Photography of Altered and Faded Manuscripts." *Library Journal* 61 (1936): 96–99.

Epstein, Gideon. "Examination of the Joseph Mengele Handwriting," *Journal of Forensic Sciences,* JFSCA, 32.1 (Jan. 1987): 100–109. Example of handwriting comparison involving foreign handwriting.

Harrison, W.R. *Suspect Documents: Their Scientific Examination.* London: Grafton, 1937.

Hilton, Ordway. *Scientific Examination of Questioned Documents.* Rev. ed. Amsterdam: Elsevier, 1982. Excellent modern text on forensic document examination.

Inbau, Fred E., Andre A. Moenssens, and Louis E. Vitullo. *Scientific Police Investigation*. New York: Chilton Book Co., 1972. Chapter on questioned documents.

Isaenberg, I. *Pulp and Paper Microscoping*. Appleton, Wisc.: Institute of Paper Chemistry, 1967.

Kirk, Paul. *Crime Investigation*. 2d ed. Ed. John I. Thornton. New York: John Wiley & Sons, 1974. Chapter on documents.

Lyter, Albert H. and Richard L. Brunelle, "A Systematic Approach for the Comparison of Paper Samples." *Identification News* (May 1977): 3–6.

McGuire, E. Patrick. *The Forgers*. Bernardsville, N.J.: Padric Publishing Co., 1969. Broad study with chapter on scientific detection of forgeries.

Mitchell, C. Ainsworth. *Documents and Their Scientific Investigation*. London: C. Griffin, 1935.

Morton, A.Q. *Literary Detection: How to Prove Authorship and Fraud in Literature and Documents*. New York: Scribner's, 1978. Presentation of "stylometric analysis," a means of identifying authorship on the basis of certain stylistic elements.

Nickell, Joe. "Discovered: The Secret of Beale's Treasure." *Virginia Magazine of History and Biography* 90 (1982): 310–24. A case study in dating the text of a questioned manuscript the original of which had supposedly been destroyed accidentally.

O'Hara, Charles E. *Fundamentals of Criminal Investigation*. 3d ed. Springfield, Ill.: Charles C. Thomas, 1973. Includes chapters on "Invisible Radiation" and "Documentary Evidence."

Osborn, Albert S. *Questioned Documents*. 2d. ed. Montclair, N.J.: Patterson Smith, 1978. Classic text recommended as much for its treatment of the basics of document examination as for its technical information.

Rendell, Kenneth E. *Forging History: The Detection of Fake Letters and Documents*. Norman: Univ. of Oklahoma, 1994. Illustrates how to detect forged historical writings.

They Write Their Own Sentences: The FBI Handwriting Analysis Manual. Boulder, Colo: Paladin, 1987. Introduction to the work of the Document Section of the FBI Laboratory.

WRITING MATERIALS

Ball, Berenice. "Writing Tools and Treasures." Part 2. *National Antiques Review* (Sept. 1973). A brief look at quills and associated items.

Bishop, William. "Pens, Pencils, Brushes and Knives." In *The Calligrapher's Handbook*. 2d ed. Ed. C.M. Lamb. New York: Pentalic, 1968, 15–43. Historical background on pens, with instructions on cutting a quill.

Bodmer, Rudolph J., ed. *The Book of Wonders*. New York: Presbrey Syndicate, 1915, 15–17. Relates the history of the early steel pen; illustrates steps in the manufacture of nibs.

Bowyer, Mathew T. "Postmarks." *Antiques Journal* (April 1974): 45.

Briquet, Charles-Moise. *Les filigrantes. Dictionnaire historique des papier des leur apparition vers 1282 jusqu'en 1600*. 1907. Reprint, Amsterdam: Paper Pub. Soc., 1968.

Churchill, W.A. *Watermarks in Paper in Holland, England, France, etc., in the XVII and XVIII Centuries* . . . Amsterdam: M. Hertzberger, 1935.

"Envelope." In *Stories behind Everyday Things*, ed. Jane Polley. Pleasantville, N.Y.: Reader's Digest, 1980. Brief history of letter wrappers.

Fisher, M. Therese. "Ink." In *The Calligrapher's Handbook*. 2d ed. Ed. C.M. Lamb. New York: Pentalic, 1968, 65–74. History of ink, with recipes.

Gaskell, Philip. *A New Introduction to Bibliography*. New York: Oxford Univ. Press, 1972. Treats early handpress printing and bookbinding.

Grant, Julius. *Books and Documents: Dating, Permanence, and Preservation*. New York: Chem. Pub., 1937. Useful, if not error-free, text with data on dating manuscripts.

Gravell, Thomas L., and George Miller. *A Catalog of American Watermarks, 1690–1835*. New York: Garland, 1979.

The History of Ink, Including Its Etymology, Chemistry, and Bibliography. New York: Thaddeus Davids, ca. 1856–60.

Hodgson, Margaret L. "Skins, Paper, Pounces." *The Calligrapher's Handbook*. 2d. ed. Ed. C.M. Lamb. New York: Pentalic, 1968, 75–95. Information on manufacture, selection, and preparation of paper and parchment.

Hunter, Dard. *Papermaking: The History and Technique of an Ancient Craft*. 2d ed. 1947. Reprint, New York: Dover, 1978. Standard treatise on all aspects of paper and paper-making.

Jackson, Donald. *The Story of Writing*. New York: Taplinger, 1981. Chapter 9 discusses the evolution of the steel pen.

Maginnis, James P. *Reservoir, Stylographic, and Fountain Pens*. Cantor Lectures, Society for the encouragement of Arts, Manufactures and Commerce. London: William Trounce, 1905. Definitive text on the early history of reservoir pens.

Mitchell, C.A. "Section on Writing, Stamping, Typing, and Marking Inks." In Alfred Henry Allen, *Allen's Commercial Organic Analysis*. 1927. Rev. ed., Philadelphia: Blakiston, 1948, 5:205–44.

Nickell, Joe. *Pen, Ink, and Evidence: A Study of Writing and Writing Materials for the Penman, Collector, and Document Detective*. Lexington, Ky. University Press of Kentucky, 1990. Nuts-and-bolts approach to document study, in five parts: pens, ink, paper, writing, examining; profusely illustrated.

———. "Vintage Watermarks: Clues to the Origins of Paper on the Kentucky Frontier." *Journal of Kentucky Studies* 4 (Sept. 1987): 105–15.

Petroski, Henry. *The Pencil: A History of Design and Circumstance*. New York: Knopf, 1989.

Rhodes, Henry T.F. "The Oxidation of Ferrous Iron in Iron Gall Ink." *Chemistry and Industry* 59 (1940): 143–45.

Rivera, Betty, and Ted Rivera. *Inkstands and Inkwells: A Collector's Guide*. New York: Crown, 1973.

The Story of Paper-Making. Chicago: J.W. Butler Paper Co., 1901. Illustrated description of machine papermaking at the turn of the twentieth century.

The Story of the Typewriter, 1873–1923. Herkimer, N.Y.: Herkimer County Historical Society, 1923.

"A Trip through Inkland." In *The Story Your Ink Bottle Tells*. Boston: Carter Ink Co., 1919. Reprinted in *Pen Fancier's Magazine* (Feb. 1984): 26–27.

Whalley, Joyce Irene. *Writing Implements and Accessories: From the Roman Stylus to the Typewriter*. Detroit: Gale Research, 1975.

Wharton, Don. "Mighty Battle of the Pens." *Nation's Business*, Nov. 1946. Story of the origin of ballpoint pens.

Index

Note: Italicized page numbers indicate illustrations.

typography, anomalies in, 95, 96
Tyrrell, John F., 22

u, letter, 8
ultraviolet light, 155-59, *158,* 159; photography, 172-73. *See also* "ghost"
writing
uncials, 8, *9*
undersketching, 160-61
Utrillo, Maurice, 133
U.S. Secret Service, 182, 184

vanadium ink, 111
Van Buren, Martin, 89
van Meegeren, Han, 2-3, 122-24
vellum. *See* parchment
Vermeer, Jan, 2-3, 122-23
vertical writing, 12-13
Vicksburg Daily Citizen, 78
Vinland Map, 101, 186, 189-91
Virgin Mary, 160
vocabulary analysis. *See* linguistic analysis

w, letter, 8
Waldron, Ann, 160
Ward, James, 105
washable ink, 112, 156

Washington, George, 2, 60, 71, 74, 92,
102, 131, 140 (caption)
Waterman, Louis E., 109
watermarks, 115-16, *115,* 117, 137, 138,
139-42; fake, 84; recording of, 139-40
Watt, James, 17
wax seals. *See* seals
"white out." See correction fluid
Whitman, Walt, 42
Williams, William Carlos, 113
wirephoto system, 17
Wise, Thomas J., 56
wood-block prints, 16
Woodhouse, Henry, 73
Woodward, Joanne, 91
word processors, 16, 55
wove paper, 115, 137, 138, 151
writing materials, 108-22; implements,
108-10; inks, 110-13; paper, 113-18;
other, 118-22
writing systems, 8-15, *11, 13,* 25-29, *26, 27*

xerography, 17
x-ray analyses: diffraction, 194; photography, 187-88; other, 188-91. *See also*
radiography

Zaner-Bloser writing method, 14, 37